Marlowe, Tamburlaine, and Magic

MARLOWE, TAMBURLAINE, AND MAGIC

by
James Robinson Howe
University of Vermont

Ohio University Press: Athens, Ohio

Copyright © 1976 by James R. Howe
Library of Congress Catalog Number LC75-36978
ISBN 0-8214-0200-5
Printed in the United States of America by
Oberlin Printing Co.

To Carole, in whom wit, fortitude
and beauty gracefully reside.
                    and
To Richard Harrier, a teacher
whose questions about Tamburlaine
required thoughtful answers.

I should like to thank three members of the University of Vermont's English Department for their help: *mia sorella luna*, Susan Carol Morse, for her reading of the manuscript at an early stage, and for her crucial suggestions about it; Professor Littleton Long, who was kind enough to read the difficult opening chapters and to give them the benefit of his wide scholarship; and Professor Samuel Bogorad, who gave much-needed advice on the handling of the manuscript.

The patience of the staff of the Biblioteca Nazionale in Florence was of great aid; so also was the generosity of the University of Vermont in granting me a sabbatic leave to complete my researches in Italy, and of the University's Graduate College, whose additional grant made possible the completion of the manuscript.

CONTENTS

Marlowe, Tamburlaine, and Magic

INTRODUCTION

This book is an exploration of a narrow strand of the Hermetic philosophy as the Renaissance understood it, and as it applies to the plays of Christopher Marlowe. The "strand" is magic. The book is an exploration because it is hard to be sure about a current of ideas as diffuse and vague as Hermeticism often is, and still more difficult to be sure about the use of such ideas by an artist. This study is therefore an experiment, a trying-forth, to see if this approach can shed light on Marlowe.

No new information has been discovered. Rather, the complex of Hermetic ideas, by now well documented elsewhere, will be placed in new and suggestive combination with other ideas, also well-known, about the Renaissance. Those aspects of the "strand" which are useful for studying Christopher Marlowe, as well as people and other ideas suggesting his connection with it, will be reviewed and re-emphasized.

The topic suggested itself in part because of the limits of the brilliant and prestigious *Herculean Hero* by Eugene M. Waith. My problem with Waith's view of Tamburlaine is that although it makes him a legitimate hero to be admired, it denies him qualities of virtue (as opposed to virtù—a separation I see many renaissance writers ignoring, even in Reformation England); by contrast, my feeling for Tamburlaine is that he is admirable not only for his strength of arm and mind, but for his inner strength as well. There is something, some aura, about him which is more all-encompassing than Waith seems to allow.

3

It is this book's thesis that Christopher Marlowe was, during his dramatic career, exploring the ultimate nature and limits of the Renaissance ideal man. He expressed this idea most centrally through the metaphor of the warrior-king, but the system of ideas he tested is most fully discussed in the Renaissance with reference to the figure of the magus, and perhaps most pointedly discussed in Marlowe's time and place by Giordano Bruno.

Further, it is this book's thesis that a consideration of the concept of the magus leads directly to the aesthetic assumptions which underlie Elizabethan poetic drama generally. In this view, the metaphoric (i.e., "poetic") statement about life which the *Tamburlaine* plays make is best expressed by enclosing its action within the framework of the familiar Ptolemaic universe, where analogies and correspondences were already worked out and well-known. Marlowe's decision not to use the Copernican universe which Bruno, in modified form, espoused, is therefore nonetheless consistent with the magical inspiration of Bruno, and with the poetic usage which governs artists even as late as Milton.

An assessment of *Tamburlaine* in terms of magic will therefore force us to face the aesthetic principles of drama in the age, perhaps force us into a clear definition of them. It will assay one of the most difficult plays of the age on what may well be the age's most difficult ground for a modern man to work. And it will result in an assessment of Marlowe's achievement as a dramatist, for *Tamburlaine*, Part One was the first of his plays to be produced and, I believe, his most characteristic. It is the one in which his genius is most fully expressed, and is therefore his best play. Indeed, any full understanding of his other plays must be arrived at by viewing them in relation to *Tamburlaine*, and especially to *Tamburlaine*, Part One.

Scholars have always had a difficult time with this play. Guided by their own moral views, in which extreme ambition and cruelty are not virtues, and guided also by conventional Elizabethan tragedy which similarly condemns these characteristics, scholars generally have been unable to accept Tamburlaine in Part One for what he seems to be on the face

4

of it: a totally admirable man who not only believes himself to be in league with and then again equal to the gods, but indeed whose incredible successes suggest that he actually does possess this godlike stature.[1]

Thus, some find it difficult to take him seriously, and see him merely as an unusual extension of the Elizabethan penchant for hyperbole, for indulging in flights of poetic fancy[2]—a penchant which Marlowe rather obviously indulges in his incomplete *Hero and Leander*, itself a far more conventional poem on a far more conventional subject.

Those who do take him seriously, however, disagree strongly about how to understand him. F. P. Wilson, indeed, suggests two contradictory possibilities (to be discussed later), declares that he cannot decide between them, and brands the play ambiguous.[3] In general, one large group of scholars emphasizes Tamburlaine's lack of morality (the killing of virgins and the like), his proud challenges to the gods, his cruelty, his belief in naked power as the dominant value in the world. If Tamburlaine has a vision, he is a victim of bad idealism, the kind that neglects such primary virtues as charity, love, and humility.[4] Douglas Cole believes that he has little vision of the good;[5] Harry Levin, that his "virtues" are "vice" to conventional morality;[6] Robert Greene, Marlowe's contemporary, that Tamburlaine is an atheist;[7] Wilbur Sanders, that therefore Marlowe might not disagree with Machiavelli in separating the real from the ideal, power from virtue, ends from means.[8]

This view of Tamburlaine causes many critics, led by Roy W. Battenhouse, to see the two parts of *Tamburlaine* as one play, or at least as a unified vision of the character and of the curve of action which encompasses him.[9] Then it is possible to see Tamburlaine as a tragic figure, in keeping with what Elizabethan tragedy would generally have us expect for such a blasphemous and libertine major character. His fall, anticipated in Part One by the fall of Bajazeth, ethically and religiously a similar character, teaches us a moral or philosophical lesson. The precise nature of this lesson varies, of course, from scholar to scholar: the evil nature of excessive ambition,[10] whose recognition teaches us a fuller understanding of man's limits, as for example that we cause our own suffering by

5

aspiring too greatly.[11] This general approach makes it possible for Michel Poirier to state even about the early plays that Marlowe's dramatic conclusions are conformist ones for his age, not rebellious ones.[12]

So even within this admittedly large group of scholars who emphasize the negative characteristics of Tamburlaine, opinion runs from the belief that Marlowe was indulging his adolescent daydreams of Satanism,[13] or his ambivalence about what to believe,[14] or his skepticism,[15] or his Machiavellianism,[16] even to the belief that he was expressing ideas conformable to the conventional moral tenets of his day.[17]

However, the popularity of this play does not suggest that it is as difficult to penetrate as such disagreement seems to imply. Perhaps there is something so inherently wrong in a negative view of Tamburlaine that it leads inevitably to confusion.

There is another side to the controversy. There are also many who believe that Marlowe intended Tamburlaine to be seen in a positive light, particularly in Part One. Some, in fact, see him as an exaggerated type of the ideal Elizabethan.[18] Disagreeing directly with those who emphasize his negative qualities, they argue that in fact Tamburlaine does possess the Elizabethan virtues he is often accused of lacking: honor, morality, an appreciation of the beautiful,[19] even pity.[20] Although these critics might agree with Poirier that Marlowe's views are conformable to those of his age, they would disagree strongly over how this conformity is expressed, and particularly over the character of Tamburlaine.[21]

This view, however, while indulging the slow-dying fashion for detailed psychological character-analysis, largely ignores the main tone of the play, its vaunting, hyperbolic style in which a superman casts his mind along the heavens. At least by implication, by emphasizing normal human characteristics, this approach diminishes Tamburlaine to the level of other men.

A corrective view, though obvious, observes that Tamburlaine is the common man who, uncommonly, arises and controls his fate,[22] the superhuman man[23] who is admirable in spite of his cruelty,[24] perhaps the English Hercules, described in a grand style like that of the epic.[25]

But why create a superman? Is this play merely a dramatic version of a comic strip, a fantasy? Immediately we are hurled back into the maelstrom of critical controversy. Perhaps to show that even supermen who lack virtue must fall? That the gods rule above? Or to show Elizabethan virtues exaggerated to larger than life-size? Perhaps, as Eleanor Grace Clark suggests, to fan the flame of buoyant Elizabethan optimism and patriotism around the time of the Armada?[26]

To see Tamburlaine as admirable and superhuman is the first step, the obvious one, in understanding the play and the character. The next is to see that Marlowe is indeed offering us a giant to emulate, but of a kind so alien to modern sensibilities that it has not been noticed by scholars. He is telling us that man is ideally like this, like the gods, and that in this essential characteristic we men should all see our likeness to one another and to Tamburlaine. The hyperbolic verse is meant as an inspiration to us. The moral qualities are merely symptomatic of man's ideal state; they are secondary, and are created, as we shall see, out of his grandeur.

Una M. Ellis-Fermor begins to see this side of the play when she observes that Marlowe tried to get at "some profound truth of man's spirit, of some hitherto hidden source of his aspiration; the capturing of an ideal, shadowy vision, part sense and part intellect, part thought and part emotion; the revealing of some strange, inner significance beneath the outer event, an illumination irradiating the world with a sure intimation of immortality."[27] But she feels this "inner significance" to be inadequately expressed. She feels the character of Tamburlaine to be too simple, the playwright too naive, "too immature to know the meaning of civilization, too limited to perceive that the man civilized has many stains upon him, man uncivilized has all of these and more."[28] Ellis-Fermor sees the essential thrust of the play, but rejects this inspiration as "immature." She finally joins the ranks of those who see Tamburlaine as a negative figure.

However, Frank B. Fieler argues persuasively that "there is contained in *Tamburlaine*, Part One a comprehensive design of apotheosis which pervades every element in the play's structure."[29] The vision *can* be clearly seen. Benvenuto Cellini sees in Tamburlaine "a value of spiritual conquest, and he himself is the personification of an heroic ideal, which conception was perhaps not yet very clear in the mind of the poet."[30] And Nemi D'Agostino believes that there is "in *Tamburlaine* almost an incandescent Elizabethan version of the renaissance ideal of the prince. . . ."[31] Several readers, then, have seen the proportions of the hero, if not always their expression, as ideal.

A. D. Hope penetrates more deeply than the others into the nature of this ideality. Significantly, he is more poet than scholar. He argues that Tamburlaine is meant to be the perfect man in whom inner inspiration unites the various faculties, and whose inspiration and identity find outward expression in the exercise of power—in war, beauty, order: an absolute sovereignty which includes Zenocrate and love within it. It is a heroic view which, Hope sees, is hard to accept today because we cannot subscribe to a morality and world-order based on power. But Hope sees that the will to power, to dominate, is a form of the will for personal perfection. He who rules the highest creature, man, has proved his perfection; indeed, may be the only fully human person, the only person who has fully realized his human potential; such a man "subsumes all values into himself."[32]

If Hope is even approximately right, then all the qualms about the wisdom or morality of Tamburlaine and of Marlowe's vision in the play must seem irrelevant. For these qualms are based on a different view of the world than the one implied by the play *Tamburlaine*, Part One.

But this view is an imaginative intuition, an assertion of one man's vision of the play. It indicates the direction one must take in coming to terms with it. But for that direction to be clear, and for it to be convincing, we must define more precisely the nature of this inner inspiration. We must get beyond the symptoms: the will to power, and the like. If we can do that, the symptoms, the events of the plays, will be easily understood to fall into their proper pattern. And, indeed, so will the other plays in Marlowe's canon. A. D. Hope, though sensing as strongly as Waith, Ellis-Fermor, D'Agostino, and Cellini the importance of inner inspiration in Tamburlaine, and pursuing this intuition more single-mindedly than they, nevertheless writes a detailed analysis of only the externals of the play. We must ask still further, what inner inspiration allows power to be the sign of perfection in the Renaissance and in Marlowe's mind? Not belief in success in the world. Not Machiavelli. The answer is not so easy.

But this is the first essential question to pursue.

In a contentious vein, Marlowe's elder contemporary Robert Greene railed against "that Atheist *Tamburlan*" who was guilty of "daring God out of heaven"; in this context, he referred sneeringly too to "such mad and scoffing poets, that have propheticall spirits, as bred of *Merlins* race."[33] Greene did not look favorably on such modern magicians. Similarly, Ben Jonson's *Alchemist* and Marlowe's *Dr. Faustus* also condemn certain aspects of magic. However, this was not the only current attitude toward the subject in Elizabethan England. John Dee, Simon Forman, and the speculations of the Raleigh "school" are well-known examples of the Elizabethan fascination with it.

Therefore, one ought not to be defensive about magic. It ought to be viewed as historians can now view Ptolemaic, Copernican, Newtonian, even Einsteinian modes of patterning the universe. Given the right point of view—necessarily one limited by the era and also by the nature of the particular philosopher—each of these patterns is valid. It is now shopworn to observe that we still say the sun rises and sets, both of which are Ptolemaic observations. *All* human views are partial, and therefore in a strict sense wrong. The magical system of Bruno, or of anyone else, is a way of explaining how the many parts of the known universe fit together and interrelate. As such, any magical system is simply one more cosmology, partial and inaccurate like the others, representing an alternative perspective from which to view the same universe which the other cosmologists see.

Greene, then, may give us the crucial clue to the play; if Christopher Marlowe was a spiritual descendant of the famous wizard, it would seem a small step to believe that he in turn might create a sympathetic magician in a play.

Let us therefore consider the possibility that Tamburlaine represents the spirit of the magus, incorporated in a man of action. He is not the kind of magician who creeps into corners studying musty books, nor one who stands erect in some secret midnight glade, playing his lute and chanting to the stars. Rather, Marlowe has taken the grand idea of man which is implicit in the Renaissance view of the master magician and has embodied it in a man of action. To understand this hypothesis, we must review some Renaissance concepts of man and attitudes toward magicians.

It could then be assumed by many, as Agrippa showed, that man was not only able to reach, but was justified in reaching with his intellect for the stars and beyond:

> all things were created to be used by us; thus, not without foundation, the magicians believe that we are easily able to ascend these same steps again, to penetrate successively into each of these same worlds and to go as far as to the animating archetype of the world, the first cause on which all things depend and from which they proceed. . . .[34]

Thus, he argues, it is the magus who is the true philosopher, the man who sees most deeply and truly into the spiritual essence of things:

> Magic is the true science, the most elevated and perfect philosophy, in a word the perfection and the fulfillment of all the natural sciences, because all regular philosophy is divided into physics, mathematics, and theology.[35]

This thought is paralleled by Giovanni Pico della Mirandola when he states that non-demonic magic "is nothing else than the utter perfection of natural philosophy."[36]

The magus goes beyond the limitations placed on man by Plato. As the Renaissance understands such a man, he can see the ideal forms of created things, and their essential unity. One of Marlowe's contemporaries—a man four years younger than he, Tommaso Campanella—writes that the great mind operates

> by an intuition which functions under that light of God which knows and penetrates all the world of matter and of spirit, and which elevates the mind up to itself, in such a way that she does not see in the divine essence, but rather in the later ideal conception, the things which in a given moment are necessary to be known about all creation.[37]

Because his mind comprehends the nature of outward reality, the magus also has the power to transform that reality.

Ficino finds that this power is consistent with Christianity and its view of man in his Platonic Theology:

> not only does the human intelligence claim for itself as a divine right the ability to form and fashion matter through the medium of art, but also to transform the nature of existence by its own power.[38]

Such a man, according to Campanella, will work as nature does: "he will employ natural causes so that they work in astonishing ways."[39] The results may be amazing, but they are achieved by a superior understanding of nature's workings— by a kind of knowledge open to man, not forbidden, yet making him seem like a god in the power it confers. In transforming the world, then, the magus also transforms himself into the highest man, the closest to his ideal. Pico writes of man,

> We have made thee neither of heaven nor of earth, neither mortal nor immortal, so that with freedom of choice and with honor, as though the maker and molder of thyself, thou mayest fashion thyself in whatever shape thou shalt prefer. Thou shalt have the power to degenerate into the lower forms of life, which are brutish. Thou shalt have the power, out of thy soul's judgment, to be reborn into the higher forms, which are divine.

Of the man who chooses to remake himself in higher forms, Pico writes:

> And if, happy in the lot of no created thing, he withdraws into the center of his own unity, his spirit, made one with God, in the solitary darkness of God, who is set above all things, shall surpass them all. Who would not admire this our chameleon? Or who could more greatly admire aught else whatever?[40]

A modern scholar, Eugenio Garin, thus summarizes the stature of the magus in many Renaissance eyes:

> Among all human activities, magical work actually comes to assume a central position, so much so that in itself it expresses almost in the manner of an example that divine power of man which Campanella exalts in his justly famous verses. The man at the center of the cosmos is the man who, having grasped the secret rhythm of things, becomes a sublime poet but, like a God, does not limit himself to writing words of ink on perishable paper; on the contrary, he writes real things in the grand and living book of the universe.[41]

He is the man who closes the gap between thought and deed, contemplative and practical action. Garin further suggests that the infinite power of man is concentrated in the unity of the act. And here is the sage who rules the stars, the magician who shapes the elements; here is the unity of being and of thought, and the full span of reality. This, and no other, is the defense of magic which the Renaissance meant to include in its celebration of man.[42]

The magus is perhaps the bridge between old and new science and philosophy, as Frances Yates has suggested.[43] But he is also more than that. He is the embodiment of the ideal qualities of man, as the Renaissance saw them. He represents deep religion and philosophy tied to practical ability in this world.

His is the unifying mind which sees into the essence of things. Pico, studying Hebraism, says, "I saw in [it] . . . not so much the Mosaic as the Christian religion."[44] And Daniel P. Walker argues of Marlowe's contemporary, Campanella, that "by his religious writings he hoped to transform Catholicism, and to convert and unite all the religions and nations of the world. By his magic he hoped to gain the power to enforce this conversion. . . ."[45]

There are, of course, other images of greatness in the Renaissance mind. None are both so inclusive and so literally held, however. The artist, for example, combines thought with external form, "gives to airy nothing/ A local habitation and a name."[46] In Marlowe's view, however, at least so far as *Tamburlaine*, Part One is concerned, the poet cannot reach so high as the hero feels impelled to go: he asserts that if the combined inspiration and skill of all poets were to focus on the creation of one ideal poem,

> Yet should there hover in their restless heads
> One thought, one grace, one wonder, at the least,
> Which into words no virtue can digest.[47]

The poet is less than absolute perfection, less than ideal. Further, he is merely an analogue for essential human qualities. In himself as poet he does not necessarily possess unusual practical skills in this world. He may by analogy, as in Theseus' lines, suggest the union of thought and form, but only in the abstract, or in one kind of artistic endeavor.

In different ways, other conventional Renaissance figures of greatness also fall short of the ideal. The king and the

12

philosopher, for example, are partial figures of perfection. The king may represent power and worldly wisdom, but not necessarily spiritual intuition. The philosopher lacks the physical attributes of the king. And so on.

The magus, however, in his ideal form, is both all-inclusive and literal as an image of the ideal man. He has both understanding and power, is at home in both visible and invisible worlds, and in his every worldly act implies his spiritual guidance, since without inspired wisdom he would have no power.

Therefore, at least for the tradition of Renaissance philosophers who follow the neo-Platonic-Hermetic line of thought, from Pico della Mirandola and Marsilio Ficino, for the most part in or under the influence of the Florentine Academy, the ideal man is best exemplified by the figure of the magus.

Robert Greene obviously saw the lineaments of the magus in Tamburlaine's creator, even though he did not belong to that group which admired this type of man. But why would Marlowe, if he meant such an idea to be portrayed by Tamburlaine, use a warrior? He did, after all, write a later play, *Dr. Faustus*, whose major figure was a magician.

Perhaps he sensed that the grandeur of this conception could *not* be literally portrayed onstage—that, as Tamburlaine indicates, some things are beyond the power of the poet. Thus in a play designed to show the darker side of magic, where true grandeur is not intended, a black magician can be portrayed literally—as in *Dr. Faustus*. But for the positive view of those ideas about the ideal man which the magus embodies, a metaphoric figure had to be created. Since physical acts imply, in this conception of man, extraordinary intellectual and spiritual insight, what was needed onstage was a character capable of great and heroic deeds, and a poetry which could suggest that this insight behind the deeds was what made them possible.

Perhaps it should be emphasized that a man of large philosophical wisdom, efficient worldly powers, and a wide range of intellectual interests and physical abilities would not be sufficient for the purpose. He must show such insight into the workings of the world that it implies intuitive knowledge of God's purposes in that world. He must be able to do normally impossible things without any obvious physical effort, apparently as a result of this great intuitive understanding. He must be working toward these divine purposes in the world. He must therefore suggest a largeness of soul which is beyond most men's abilities, let alone achievement. In general, he must raise the qualities normally associated with the ideal Renaissance man to a new and higher dimension in order to embody those qualities of excellence which Ficino, Pico, and Bruno agree are conferred upon the magus. He must seem a semidivinity.

If Tamburlaine is such a figure, then an examination of ideas about the inspired nature of the magus-figure which were current in Marlowe's England, and about the world-view which encouraged belief in him, as well as a comparison of these ideas with those in *Tamburlaine*, will bear fruit. We will see the play more clearly, with new and, I believe, more admiring eyes. We will see in a new way how Marlowe is fascinated by man's power and its limits. We will see too how *Tamburlaine*, Part One indicates the direction of Marlowe's future development, both as artist and as thinker.

CHAPTER I

THE HERMETIC BACKGROUND

Until the work in English of Frances Yates on Giordano Bruno, published in 1964, it almost seemed that we knew the main outlines of the intellectual milieu of the English Renaissance.[1] Her new ingredient is summed up effectively by Wylie Sypher:

> . . . Over the years in a sequence of profoundly researched books she has been doing nothing less than reinterpreting the nature of Renaissance humanism. Indeed, she has gone far to prove that there were two different Renaissance humanisms: one originating in the fourteenth century with the revival of Latin texts by Petrarch, the other originating in the discovery of Hermetic texts in the fifteenth century.[2]

To the Renaissance, these Hermetic texts meant the wisdom of ancient religions. They showed not only that this world reflected the Divine Ideal, but also that it could be nearly a perfect reflection; that the human soul and even the physical forms of the universe were perfect, at least in potential, and therefore perfectable. In this universal harmony, all things were related to all others in their common reference to Divinity, their Creator and the Definer of their proper identities. Even different religious intuitions—Christian, Jewish, Egyptian, etc.— could be shown to be consistent with one another.

Hence existed the background for Hermetic magic. According to it, a man could become so spiritually pure that he could be informed by this Divinity common to all things—indeed, could learn to redirect its creative energy. The physical forms of the universe could be changed to more perfect reflections of this Ideal identity latent in all things. Hermeticism

15

asserted the potential unity of body and soul, world and spirit; Hermetic magic achieved this unity.

That the Renaissance mind, already immersed in Petrarch's humanist neo-Platonism, joined to it this new Hermeticism is clear from the example of the Florentine Academy in the 1460's. Cosimo de'Medici, its first patron, had in mind a major task of translation. It was typically humanist, this task of rendering Plato's works, and "other sources of Platonic thought," into Latin. Marsilio Ficino, the famed neo-Platonist who formulated lastingly influential ideas about Platonic love, completed Plato's works by 1468. But before completing the Plato or any of his other translation projects, Ficino began translating the Hermetic books, and these he finished first, in 1463.[3]

Ficino thus illustrates the idea that "one of the great virtues of Renaissance men was their tolerance of all philosophic opinions."[4] Perhaps the most breathtaking illustration of this catholicity of mind occurred only a little later, in 1486, when Giovanni Pico della Mirandola, another product of the Florentine Academy, journeyed to Rome to challenge the scholars of the world to a debate. He was to defend the proposition that his nine hundred theses, derived from all the known philosophical and religious traditions of which he was aware— including those of pagan Rome and Greece and even Egypt, as well as Hebraism and Christianity, himself being a good Roman Catholic—that these nine hundred theses were not contradictory, but consistent with one another. Indeed, the view that one should study the literature of classical antiquity to discover the universality of Christianity was not unusual. It was often assumed that religions had gradually evolved into an increasingly perfect form, Christianity being the natural completion of a chain of religions. The Egyptians (particularly, but not exclusively, the traditions attributed to Hermes Trismegistus), the Greeks and Romans (Pythagoras, Plato, Plotinus, to mention a few of the better known), and the Hebrews all anticipated in various ways the truths most fully revealed by Christ.[5]

The very idea of the universe which the Renaissance inherited encouraged this synthetic, essentially religious orientation. Its Aristotelian categories, Christianized by Thomas Aquinas, created a cosmological system whose various entities represented a system of values, unlike our modern sense of the universe. On the contrary, today we must impose our values (if any) on a universe which has concrete existence but which itself implies no value system.[6] Thus Copernicus, when proposing a rearrangement of that Ptolemaic universe, still thinks in terms of harmony and disharmony, good and bad, as appropriate scientific terms and even as concepts important enough to determine the legitimacy of a line of scientific inquiry. A good universe could not be found bad by mere scientific theory. He writes,

> . . . the universe is spherical; partly because this form, being a complete whole, needing no joints, is the most perfect of all; partly because it constitutes the most spacious form which is thus best suited to contain and retain all things; or also because all discrete parts of the world, I mean the sun, the moon and the planets, appear as spheres.[7]

Because all parts and aspects of this universe are bound up in the same value system, and are alike referrable to the higher power of their creator, they are seen to be closely related to one another. Each entity in the universe can be seen to represent an aspect of the same value system that every other entity of the universe represents. It is not a far step from this to the Renaissance habit, well-known, of seeing any two things in the universe as analogues for one another, no matter how far-fetched in visual terms the analogue seems to be. Kepler is credited, for instance, with having seen grass as an analogue for man's hair.[8]

This habit is given more specific philosophical validity by typical neo-Platonic assumptions, for example those of such diverse thinkers as Ficino and Agrippa. According to this view, there is a world-soul, or Idea, which is a spiritual expression of perfect forms. The outward expression of this Idea is our more familiar physical world which is, because material rather than spiritual, imperfect. Nonetheless, it is a reflection of the perfection of the spiritual Idea. There is, then, a close relationship between spirit and body, between soul and world. There is a spirit in all nature which our world reflects.[9] To this point, neo-Platonism is consistent in a general way with the Christianized Aristotelianism of the Ptolemaic universe. And, since all levels and kinds of physical existence are not only referrable to a similar Power, but indeed to that Power within themselves, it is reasonable to see all aspects of our universe as analogues for all other parts. It becomes a mark of a man's literary restraint that he uses only those analogues which have physical as well as spiritual resemblance.

In such a universe, it is natural to expect on earth a reflection of the Divine Harmony of God in Heaven, a reflection, however imperfect, of the Idea of perfection.[10] Just so does Copernicus finally judge his achievement in placing the sun at the center of our solar system: does this view of it enhance our sense of the system's harmony?

When one sees the universe in terms of its unity, it is natural to see resemblances and patterns. Thus occurs the further doctrine of signatures, in which it was held that each entity in the world somehow contained physical evidence of its identity, its reflection of its divine Idea. There is much disagreement about precisely what form such signatures take, however. As late as the seventeenth century, Sir Thomas Browne in England was arguing for the quincunx and the principle of five-ness, while Kepler saw it in mathematical and diagrammatic relationships: "Geometry is the archetype of the beauty of the world."[11] But he makes the close relationship between inner and outer, idea and expression, clear when he refers to this geometry of the cosmos as the "matching of external impressions with pre-existent inner images."[12] For him, the ellipse was a more appropriate form for planetary orbits than the circle, but his ultimate scientific criterion was, like that of Copernicus, the symbolic value attached to the particular geometrical form.

However, it is very difficult to see this natural and inner unity of the universe, as the general disagreement about the nature of signatures makes clear. Even the form or diagram of the cosmos takes on metaphysical significance. Thus Copernicus and Bruno, while agreeing about the central placement of the sun, disagree about the infinity of the universe, and at least partly for metaphysical reasons.[13] Bruno argues that it is limitless, with worlds yet undiscovered existing out in space. Later, of course, Galileo was to show that Bruno was probably right.

This belief in a universe of signed analogues led the Renaissance man to believe in a close relationship between the macrocosm (the universe, the heavens, all of creation), the geocosm (earth), and the microcosm (usually, but not necessarily, man). They could believe that the smallest act, therefore, had cosmic significance and at another moment, conversely, that astral influences could cause the smallest act. Plays of the period in England are full of unnatural and even supernatural events following inevitably upon the murder of a ruler. *Macbeth* is probably the most widely known example.

The Renaissance humanists were deeply religious.[14] To such men, the ideal man was he who could plumb the dimensions of the universe. For, as we have seen, inspired intuition was necessary to see into God's purposes, to understand the laws of the cosmos. And only the virtuous and humble man whose ends were pious could be expected to achieve such spiritual insight into the Idea of the creation.[15] So science was not pursued as an end in itself, but as another way of demonstrating the glory of God through demonstrating the inner and outer harmony of His work. It was the virtue that made the man ideal.

But, since the inner and outer man, the microcosm, should be harmonious, even as in the macrocosm, so the ideal and virtuous man would demonstrate his inner gifts by outward grace in the various skills valued by his age. And since, in the Renaissance, the world was full of analogues, the skills were diverse, including literary skill and musical, but also horsemanship and war skills. Thus the famous Renaissance man.[16]

This conception of man as reflecting his inner perfection in his outward graces gets us again to the influence of magic in the age's intellectual milieu. For in the neo-Platonic view, although in theory the spirit was reflected by the outer world, this reflection was imperfect.[17] Ficino writes of soul recognizing soul in this world in truest friendship and love, but this is rare. Such perfect inner virtue is seldom to be expected. And even when such an ideal relationship is formed, its basis is not physical, nor do the physical senses play a significant role in it.[18]

Hermeticism agreed with neo-Platonism that there was a correspondence between spirit and body, Idea and world, but did not encourage the philosophical contemplation or spiritual awareness of this correspondence as the major end of knowledge. It was more practical, its attitudes more self-assertive, dynamic, active. It emphasized the possibilities for closing the gap between this imperfect world and its perfect Idea by introducing into this world an understanding of what the Idea was, and how it worked. Thus Hermetic magic was not an attempt to manipulate the world for one's own selfish purposes, but rather to activate more fully the spiritual power which animates the world in an attempt to make it more perfect, to put it more fully in accord with the perfect Idea of a world in the Divine Mind.[19]

For example, it was believed that all metals were variants of one homogeneous basic mineral within a chain of minerals arranged in a hierarchy (in ascending order, according to Paracelsus, lead, mercury, copper, tin, iron, silver, gold).[20] The natural magician interprets nature and serves her by speeding natural processes—for example, like the alchemist who tries to find the principle for changing lead to gold, in which form metal is a more perfect reflection of the Ideal than it was before. Unfortunately, most alchemists were not natural magicians, but rather quacks or charlatans who were mainly out for their own gain.

But the great chemist-magician-pharmacist, Paracelsus, could say, "What the Saint is in the 'Realm of God', the magus is in the 'Realm of Nature'—the Saint working through God, the Magus through Nature."[21]

What for earlier neo-Platonism had been only philosophical theory became for the Hermeticists a practical possibility: that the world is, or could become, a reflection of Ideal existence. The positive side of neo-Platonism became for these men a fixed view. With Hermeticism, it seemed possible that this reflection could grow less and less imperfect. Outward manifestations of inward grace are suddenly significant. The measure of a man's wisdom and virtue is his power, his ability to perfect himself and the world. Paracelsus, Giordano Bruno, Cornelius Agrippa, and even Marsilio Ficino believe not only in signatures, but in signs. At the right astrological moment, when all the inner forces of the universe seem, by their outward signs, to be most propitious, they use talismans with carefully researched inscriptions. Thus they redirect or intensify the natural workings of the inner forces of the universe. It is an exacting labor requiring years of study. One must know what kind of energy comes from what star, what stone, what herb, etc., and what the effect of these combined energies on another specific stone, for example, will be, if all these powers together are trained upon it. The universe is indeed unified, as the magus sees it, but the unity is terribly complex. Only the spiritually awakened can see within it. Only the dedicated can master the details needed to use this vision.[22]

We may now return to the great scientists to observe that they were dedicated men. Copernicus and Kepler, to mention two, were great mathematicians. To mention one in another field, Paracelsus, the Swiss, father of modern pharmacy, master of botany and, for his age, of anatomy (Vesalius' careful diagrams came slightly later). They were highly skilled and learned men. To what do they owe their great insights? Paracelsus we have already quoted. He was a magus.

And Copernicus? Frances Yates argues that since Hermeticists saw the sun as the star whose energies were the source of life and, as a result, the sun was not only the dominant symbol of goodness and life, but also the symbol of divinity to be worshipped (the world being a physical reflection and symbol of the Ideal); that since Copernicus has been shown to believe in a universe which embodied a system of values and that its universal harmony was his main criterion for these values; that for such a man the natural and most perfect form of the solar system would be heliocentric. Copernicus a magus? Not certainly. But the inspiration for his great discovery may have come from a way of seeing the universe which also formed the philosophical basis for Hermetic magic.

And Kepler, who saw elliptical orbits? We have seen his view that "geometry is the archetype of the beauty of the world," and that scientific knowledge is the "matching of external impressions with pre-existent inner images." He believed that "the circle [is] the underlying principle of the harmonious proportions,"[24] but thought the sun imperfect (Galileo had seen sunspots recently). Therefore the universe was an imperfect reflection of the Ideal, God, who alone could be properly represented by a circle. Kepler too seems close to representing the magus' mental set, in which there is a direct equation between inner values and outward forms.[25]

We even learn that Harvey discovered the circulation of the blood and the cycles of aging only after "lifelong think[ing] on the mystery of circular phenomena."[26]

One of the most important contributions to the emergence of the new and still-held view of the cosmos—a world-view which is itself among the most dramatic achievements of the Renaissance—is the combining of neo-Platonic and Hermetic assumptions. Neo-Platonism allowed men to see their world as related to the Ideal. Hermeticism allowed men to believe that something near this Ideal could be achieved on earth, in the physical creation, as well as in inner virtues and within the soul. This combination of ideas formed the underpinnings of Hermetic magic.

At a time when men were increasingly restless, increasingly turning to the study of man and the amelioration of his physical and political condition, Hermeticism offered the Renaissance man his chance to hold the old faiths without giving up his growing interest in improving his world.[27] It may very well be that this central fact accounts for so many of the age's most brilliant and curious minds' being enthralled by the magician's view of his universe. Not alone did the great scientist sense the immanence of an animating soul, struggling to express itself more and more perfectly in this world, with scientists helping to interpret and, at least in theory, facilitate those efforts.

In art too. Michelangelo wrote,

The greatest artist has no single concept
Which a rough marble block does not contain
Already in its core: that can [be] attain[ed]
Only [by] the hand that serves the intellect.

And again,

. . . just as one already sees,
Concealed in the hard marble of the North,
The living figure one has to bring forth
(The less of stone remains, the more *that* grows);
So does the involucre of our flesh
Hide from the trembling soul,
With its burden of skin, unworked, rough, hard,
Deeds of both light and worth.[28]

This is a parallel idea to that uttered casually, as an aside, by John Donne in "The Crosse":

As perchance, Carvers do not faces make,
But that away, which hid them there, do take.[29]

An artist must be inspired in order to create a fine sculpture. The inspiration, however, is not of some never-before-conceived image or pose or creature. Rather, the inspiration is the ability to intuit the nature of the dumb stone or wood, to intuit the Ideal identity of that material as dictated by the spiritual forces within it. The great statue, then, is the perfect physical realization of the inherent spiritual qualities in the statue's material: it is the Ideal made physical. It is as close as the physical universe can ever come to an accurate reflection of spiritual perfection. The artist is like a magus, and his work is, like the quite different work of the scientist, a religious work.[30] Donne makes this view clear a century later when he sees the cross as the most perfect form for a piece of wood and, in the Christian context, who would argue? In the Gallery of the Academy in Florence, indeed, the statues are arranged almost as if to suggest this view of art. One approaches that work of incredible beauty, the "David", by passing a series of half-finished sculptures. In these, it is almost as if half-shaped forms just dimly recognizable are struggling with the very rock itself to assert their proper form. In the "David" at the end of the Gallery, the hand of the in-

23

spired artist has lifted the veil of stone and shown the full statue.

As the passage from Donne suggests, the probability is fairly high that Hermeticism was as fully assimilated into English neo-Platonism as it was into Italian. There was a sizeable group of educated Italians in London before and after 1600,[31] many of whom supported themselves by tutoring the English aristocracy in the Italian language and, generally, in things Italian. John Florio began his career in England in 1576 (curiously, the year of The Theatre), though his father had tutored in Italian earlier: among others, for Henry Herbert, Earl of Pembroke, and Lady Jane Grey. His son John is credited with teaching four earls, three lords of state (including Fulke Greville), and James' Queen Anne, and also as being influential in a London philosophical club which included Bruno, Sidney, Greville, Harvey, Bacon, Raleigh, Marlowe, and others.[32] Obviously, Italian language and ideas were popular. Indeed, Inigo Jones went to Italy to study scene design and theatrical machines as well as architecture; the ideas he brought back became sufficiently influential to change the course of English drama—one is tempted to say, forever. Certainly Shakespeare's alleged satire against Florio in *Love's Labour's Lost*,[33] and Jonson's against things Italian in *Every Man In* (Captain Bobadil, chiefly, in the second, English, version) indicate how serious a threat Italian fashions generally were thought to be for English culture—at least by two men in a position to know.

Further, it is clear that in England in the 1590's and before, Hermeticism was an important part of this intellectual inheritance from Italy. Frances Yates asserts that "the core of the" Renaissance neo-Platonic—specifically Ficino's—"movement was Hermetic, involving a view of the cosmos as a network of magical forces with which man can operate."[34] In addition, Keith Thomas has shown that the belief in and practice of magic was pervasive at every level of Renaissance society, from the use of home medicines by peasants to the "holy quest; the search for knowledge . . . by revelation."[35]

There was John Dee, who became Elizabeth's astrologer and who, like Agrippa, believed in a threefold magic: natural for work on earth, mathematical for the middle celestial world, and numerical conjurings for the super-celestial.[36] His library contained Ficino, the Hermetic books, the works of Paracelsus and Agrippa, as well as Vitruvius (of whom more later) and other classical writers. To him, "all is science, all is important, and this mysterious world [is one] of magic and science. . . ."[37] There is strong reason to believe that he popularized such science, in England, for the artisan and middle class, and also for an inner circle of lords and intellectuals centering around Sir Philip Sidney, and including Leicester, Edward Dyer, Spenser, and Greville.[38]

In *John Florio*, Frances Yates details another group nearby, at Syon House:

> The existence of a semi-secret association of daring thinkers a few years after Bruno had left England [in 1585] is . . . no myth. 'Sir Walter Rawley's School of Atheism,' as enemies termed it, has attracted a good deal of attention of late. . . . its main features[:] Raleigh seems to have been the centre of a coterie interested in philosophical and scientific speculation. Marlowe was the most notorious of these so-called 'atheists'. Others interested were Raleigh's brother Carew, Thomas Harriott, the mathematician, Matthew Royden and possibly Chapman the dramatist.
> . . . This society . . . seems to have been interested in astronomical speculation.[39]

Indeed, "Ralegh cites Hermes, who was translated by Ficino, and therefore probably known to Chapman also."[40] Henry Percy, 'the wizard earl,' "was an Italian scholar," and also a member of the group.[41] French would also include John Donne.[42]

Another leading influence, one connected to both these groups, was Giordano Bruno, the Italian magus who traveled from university to university throughout Europe in the late sixteenth century.[43] A Copernican who could see Christianity and magic as complementary, and could believe in an infinite universe containing many worlds,[44] Bruno was in England from 1583 to 1585. He engaged in a famous debate at Oxford in which he espoused his views against more traditional and scholastic ones about Aristotle and cosmology generally. He lived a full intellectual life in London, writing six books there and generally spreading his intellectual influence throughout the city.[45] He was a distinguished and outspoken visitor; one can imagine how he must have been noticed in a city already caught up in the fashion for things Italian.[46]

Indeed, these influences of neo-Platonism and Hermeticism were both strong enough to last beyond the immediate fashion for Italianate things. The existence of the Cambridge Platonists in the 1630's and '40's by itself suggests as much. There was as well the group of Hermeticists which surrounded Thomas Vaughan, twin brother to the poet Henry, in the 1640's and after.[47]

These Hermetic ideas also influenced the English theatre in various ways. There has, for example, been some recent work on Giordano Bruno's influence on Chapman. Presumably one of the "school of night" and therefore heavily influenced by that "school's" philosophical questioning, Chapman offers himself most obviously to this context.[48]

In a more general vein, Frances Yates' *Theatre of the World* has suggested that the very theatre itself is constructed to suggest the magical relationships among the various parts and levels of the universe. At times, it may be that her comments on specific elements in the theatre are not fully convincing; however, it is the general world-view which these theatres represent, after all, and therefore the way a professional might look at the idea of a theatre and of making plays for it, that is of concern here. From this larger view, her book must be seriously considered.

In one sense, of course, all art—or at least its creation—is magical. The artist has an idea, a creature of the mind, which he gives outward expression, form and substance. The analogy between creating a substantial artwork from an insubstantial idea and the Divine creation of a universe from the Divine Idea of that universe is an obvious one, and has been observed by generations of artists, whether neo-Platonists or not. For the Renaissance, Shakespeare's Prospero in *The Tempest* gives perhaps the best-known example, although this is by no means his only comment on the issue.

More precisely, in the drama, a theorist as early as Aristotle observes that a serious (i.e., tragic) play does not try to be realistic, to reflect the common details of everyday life, or even to portray everyday kinds of people. He says, rather, that such plays represent ideal patterns of life. They enact philosophical ideas of the way life would be without its unaccountable accidents, and when one's view of these large patterns is not obscured by the needless minutiae with which every life in the mundane world is filled. These plays try to give outward expression to that ideal conception of life which is normally obscured.

The Elizabethan presentation of plays in the public theatres further suggests this philosophical orientation. Dumb shows; plays within plays; prologues; epilogues; occasionally a chorus to introduce individual acts; the generally declamatory acting style with exaggerated gestures and facial expressions; the use of unlocalized stages and emblematic properties and costumes; the use of formal, even ritualized action, and of dance and music; all in a large theatre which may have seated as many as three thousand in the audience from all classes of society: all these characteristics suggest that plays of the time sought to express universal ideas in their plots, situations, and characters. The formal acting style suggests that more emphasis was put on representing human types and qualities than in representing individuals. The use of dumb shows, chorus, and the like suggests that the audience was often carefully guided to see the significance of the action of the play. The use of dance and music suggests another way of reinforcing an audience's perceptions by formal patterns of action in which the pattern, not the individual, is of prime importance.[49]

This view is consistent with, and enriched by, another aspect of this theatre—an aspect represented by its open-roofed structure, and combined with the presentation of plays in daylight; its apron stage; and its stable acting company whose tendency was to type-cast its actors, or at least to put them in similar parts as often as possible. These other characteristics work in another direction, toward the audience's identifying individual characters and responding to them directly, instead of recognizing only some more general and philosophical idea. The stability of the troupe and its casting encouraged the audience to recognize the actors and, we must imagine—since similar phenomena occur in the Restoration—

identify them with their accustomed roles, and thus respond to them as individuals. The human dimensions of otherwise "thin" characters are enlarged in this way. In addition, the apron stage put the actors in greater proximity to the spectators than is possible on a stage more remote from the audience, whether it be the circle in the center of a huge amphitheater, as in classical Greece, or the picture-frame stage still familiar today. Proximity also encourages spontaneous reaction to the individual actor-character. And the fact that natural lighting was used, that no artificial visual barriers like modern footlights separated actors from audience, in conjunction with the stability of the company and its proximity onstage to the audience, all must have encouraged direct reactions to particular individuals. The English public theatre, or what little we know of it, seems conducive to displaying the individual as well as the general, the details of life as well as broad ideas about it, realism as well as Idealism. A remarkable theatre indeed.

Thomas B. Stroup suggests the significance of this theatre-concept for the magical world-view which we have been developing. He observes that the Elizabethan stage was a world in little, reflecting the Elizabethan's sense of the importance of religion in life. Life is seen as a cosmic drama in which every man is tested by Christian principles; the audience sees a play's characters in the larger context of the cosmos, from a Christian point of view.[50] Surely, without so emphasizing the Christian elements (though they often exist and are almost always at least implicit), we can see immediately that the stage and many of the plays do encourage us to see particular characters and events for themselves, but also in larger perspective: to see, perhaps, the relationship between the microcosm and the macrocosm, and the interdependence of all things in the play's world. The Elizabethan practice of using a double plot must surely derive importantly from this point of view, in which we are often invited to see analogues between two quite independent chains of events. Further, the multiple acting levels, with the heavens decorated underneath by painted zodiacal symbols, and with a third level above from which the gods occasionally descended, suggest that the theatre itself was not only meant to facilitate plays which showed the relationship of the microcosm to the macrocosm, but was itself a larger emblem of the world in all its complex interrelationships.[51] From this point of view, a play is an emblem—a physical representation of an idea—within an emblem. Add plays within plays and the like, and the complexity with which Elizabethan artists were capable of commenting on the universe and on the analogy between God's and the artist's creation seem nearly inexhaustible.

Frances Yates' *Theatre of the World* adds to the suggestive probability that neo-Platonic and, more particularly, Hermetic influences were important in the theatre itself. Despite much uncertainty about several specific ideas, much of what she says seems solid. These points are, for my purposes, enough. Although her speculations about Robert Fludd, and about John Dee's relationship with James Burbage, are only circumstantially documented, however, they should not be dismissed entirely. Much other circumstantial evidence is suggestive in a parallel direction.

What seems certain is that the classical Roman architect, Vitruvius, gave England most of its ideas about the classical stage—which, of course, to the Renaissance mind was an important model. Several years ago, with no polemical axe to grind, Lily B. Campbell asserted that both the Swan and the Theatre were built almost certainly from Vitruvius, without doubt after Roman theatre ideas.[52] The acting area is before the scenery, and the apron stage is a rough parallel to the Roman proscenium in this regard. Vitruvius' ideas were of course available: not only was he "the 'authority' on architectural theory and practice" to Renaissance Italy,[53] but Italians were all over London, and Englishmen traveling to Italy; in 1563 John Shute published a book on architecture based on his study of these ideas while in Italy.

And Vitruvius took as a matter of course the relationship between his theatre and the cosmos at large. The zodiac which is painted under the heavens, where the actor will be constantly reminded of it as he looks up, is central to the Vitruvian system: the ground plan is "based on cosmology as then understood, on the circle of the zodiac with its twelve signs, within which astrologers inscribe four equilateral triangles, the *trigona* which join related signs."[54] Thus we have the universal analogues which join the many parts of the world, all under the unifying inspiration of the zodiac and interpreted with the aid of geometry in the manner of astrologers.[55] In addition, the geometrical principle of the four triangles also "establishes the relationship of the theatre with the *musica convenientia astrorum*"—the music of the spheres—Yates argues as a climax of her discussion on music and harmony.[56] Neo-Platonism also takes its place in the theatre in this way.[57]

This is not only a conception of a theatre which encourages playwrights to create universal dramas, nor alone a theatre which is itself an emblem of the universe. It is also a theatre whose very plan mirrors the complex interrelationships of the varied parts of the universe. It asserts the neo-Platonic system of correspondences in its own design. It also represents the astrological principles which are central to the manipulations of an Hermetic magician. It is clearly a theatre easily exploited by writers with an Hermetic-magical cast of mind who wish to assert onstage that this world (or stage) can be an ideal physical reflection of the universal harmony, and that the religiously inspired and deeply knowledgeable man is the one who can achieve such perfection on earth. The probability that the Elizabethan theatre encouraged plays not only of universal and philosophical dimensions, nor only of religious significance, but also on ideas and subjects which were consistent with Hermetic magic, is very strong.

This belief immediately throws several well-known plays into new perspective. For example, the play *The Jew of Malta* was printed as a tragedy. However, the moral problems posed by Machiavellianism are apparently not to the taste of our age. Surprisingly, it was a moralist, T. S. Eliot, who led the view earlier in this century that the play might be considered a farce rather than a tragedy.[58] The case of Helena in *All's Well That Ends Well* was, until recently, similar. Her play was often called a problem comedy, chiefly because the apparent heroine pursues Bertram with more regard for her own desires than for either morality or the feelings of Bertram himself.[59] Only recently has this view changed.[60] In a more limited way, there is also Shylock. On the one hand he is seen as pitiable, in which case he sets the amoral tone of the play because the unmerciful Christians triumph.[61] Alternatively, we have a romance, but in this case the Elizabethan willingness to make a Jew into a comic stereotype with no redeeming features is invoked.[62]

All of these ways of viewing Shylock and *The Merchant of Venice*, though, oversimplify the moral issue which surrounds an unrighteous revenger. The fact that "revenge" is admittedly an issue at all suggests that the avenger is at least wronged, and that the prospective victim, at the very least, has sometime been less than virtuous. It is also hard to believe that Shylock is not somewhat more human than the stereotype he is often made to seem. Elizabethan audiences were no doubt ready to accept comic stereotypes of various kinds, including Jewish usurers, but it may be that they also could tell when they were *not* being offered such a character, and therefore when they should not respond to him as if he were. It seems likely that Shakespeare was writing this play within the formula of the romance, in which Bassanio would be a hero and Portia a hero-ine, in which the merchant Antonio is ultimately admirable; but also it is a play in which the villain of the formula is partly human and, even, partly admirable too. Must hero and heroine have *only* admirable qualities? Did the pagan gods? Is it pos-sible that Shakespeare, in *Merchant*, is posing difficult ques-tions about the nature of romantic comedy, and about the re-demptive qualities of neo-Platonic and Hermetic Ideas? About how one comes to recognize the inner Idea as more significant than appearance (the caskets), and then about how to actualize these Ideas in life through religious ritual and liturgy (the ring problem and its resolution in marriage in Act V), set up in V, i by a series of speeches which refer to the harmony of the spheres, and to the fact that Belmont now is the closest ap-proach to realizing this harmony on earth that can be made?[63] Can Plato and Hermes be joined and sanctified by Christian love?

Indeed, Hermetic as well as Christian assumptions about the joining together of body and soul, of two into one, etc., in mar-riage may very well be at the bottom of the great marriages which solve all problems in this world, now idealized, at the end of all the subsequent romantic comedies Shakespeare wrote. These endings are more than conventional. They are deliberately infused with the kind of philosophical significance which the Christian magus might offer.[64]

Thus Helena in *All's Well* may be the ideal neo-Platonic heroine who, through self-assertion (Hermetic influence), makes the Ideal real. If she is viewed as perfectly virtuous (and several passages suggest this orientation), as having God on her side, as being in pursuit of still greater virtue; and if one adopts the Hermetic (more than strictly Christian) view that Ideal ends justify self-assertive action, and that only the magus among men knows both what such Ideal ends are and how to achieve them; then Helena becomes explicable, and so does the play. Helena wins her man because the Heavens are allied with her. Bertram, inexperienced and easily misled, has much to learn from her. Helena, in converting Bertram by teaching him to appreciate virtue's beauty, helps to perfect the world while at the same time completing her own ideal identity by yoking it with her beloved. In this view, the play is no longer either cynical or a problem.

And so *The Jew of Malta*. Appealing as Eliot's suggestion is, that the play is consistently entertaining if the ending is read as farce, it is impossible to avoid the feeling that this view is merely a brilliant cop-out. Lacking any standards of probability or even consistency except that exaggeration be extreme enough to be absurd, farce becomes a label which encourages the scholar to evade the moral and philosophical problems raised by the play when seen as seriously intended. Our age finds Machiavellianism so totally evil that its immorality is too obvious to be intellectually interesting. It is by no means clear that the *avant garde* intellectuals of the Renaissance so regarded this cast of mind, despite their moral and religious beliefs, and despite the distorted view of Machiavelli so often perpetrated on England.[65]

In this set of problems, too, Tamburlaine can be seen to fit. He is merciless and ambitious much of the time, even as Helena is often charged with lacking virtue and being selfishly motivated, and even as Bassanio is accused—he goes to Belmont more for the dowry than for the girl. But Bassanio would not win the girl if he were not worthy of her love; nor would he get the money (which the girl gives freely, knowing what she is about). Nor would Helena win. Nor would Tamburlaine. In a world under the gods, and each of these plays clearly places its world in the larger context of the cosmos, including the greater heavens and the supernatural, one wins because one somehow conforms to the standards of the supernatural forces ruling the universe. It is a cosmos full of such forces, and men are subject to them.

Surely, Shakespeare's dramatic universe is more conventionally Christian than Marlowe's. In *Julius Caesar*, when Caesar compares his steadfastness to that of the heavens, when a man considers himself near the gods in stature, he must be and is cast down. And in *Richard III*, even a man who successfully does God's will, scourging England of evil, must fall and then die, for he did it in a self-seeking way, with deceit and evil. Shakespeare, though not so bourgeois as he is sometimes thought[66] —his approval of Helena makes this clear—is nonetheless far more conventional in his beliefs in the 1590's than is Marlowe. Marlowe takes a man, Tamburlaine, who challenges the gods themselves at times, at others represents himself as their scourge, and who makes his boasts good, and survives, and is happy.

Even Dryden, writing an heroic play, *The Conquest of Grenada*, and creating a character very much like Tamburlaine, will not go so far. Almanzor refers all value judgments to his own character and inner motives as if they formed the moral standards of the universe, just as Tamburlaine does. The neo-Platonic influence is obvious in various ways, even to the "lethargy of love" frequently caused by love at first sight as two equal souls glimpse one another—paralleled in *Tamburlaine*, Part One by Tamburlaine's enthralment of Theridamas. But Dryden is more fully a rationalist, not an Hermeticist, and he writes at the time when the Enlightenment was getting its glimmering start. So even a character like Almanzor must not be permitted full triumph, and must submit himself at the end to a more conventional morality.

Still, Harry Levin's suggestion that *Tamburlaine*, Part One, is possibly an heroic play indicates the similarity. Each is a study of the grand hero. And in each the plot is treated casually. It often seems in *Conquest* that it is made up as it goes along, and in *Tamburlaine* it is merely so simple that it causes no distraction from the main point: the nature of the hero. In each there is a man whose sense of divinity gives him power and makes him, himself, a measure of what is right in the world. Awe and wonder are appropriate responses, as we learn from Dryden's dramatic theory.[67] The same is true for Ned Alleyn as Tamburlaine.

Indeed, it may be that Marlowe, in his willingness to so glorify an unconventional hero, is merely reflecting the spirit of his times. They were momentous ones for England: the year he left Cambridge, 1587, Mary Queen of Scots protected Elizabeth's throne by losing her head, and in the next year the Armada was blown awry. Spain conquered Portugal, and England had to find its own routes for spices. Drake had only recently returned from his great voyage. The greatness of England, and its challenges, were inspiring. What a hub was London for a single young man!

And the theatre, too, only eleven years old in 1587, yet already filled with writers and actors of talent.

To be young then was to be of an age with Shakespeare: twenty-three. Essex and the future King James were twenty. Robert Cecil, son of the prime minister, and himself prime minister-to-be, was also twenty-three. The elder statesman of this youthful generation, Raleigh, was only thirty-three.

This then is an exciting, toughly competitive age in which a talented and footloose Marlowe emerges to prominence in the drama, while working in dimly mysterious ways behind the scenes in the momentous historical events of the day. That he should be intellectually venturesome should therefore not surprise us when exploration and opportunity offered so many new directions. Marlowe was not one to drink deeply of one vocation, but rather to taste the excitement of several. And this too was his way intellectually.[68]

These intellectual connections show themselves in his plays, and make it all the more likely that he was influenced by Hermeticism as well as neo-Platonism. Everyone was so influenced to some extent, of course; as we have seen, even a less self-conscious intellectual like Shakespeare would probably have been touched by both strains of thought. But my belief is that Marlowe was in *Tamburlaine* quite consciously trying on the idea of man as it was reflected in the concept of the magus. He would have to have studied Hermeticism, at least, more consciously in order to be able to draw a valid portrait.

As is usually the case in this age, we have only circumstantial evidence to suggest Marlowe's connection with believers in magic, but it is enough to justify looking at the plays anew to see what kind of fruit these supposed connections may have yielded.

There is in the first place at least one informed opinion to the effect that Marlowe may have read Henry Cornelius Agrippa, the great magus of Europe in the sixteenth century. Francis R. Johnson, in surveying Marlowe's astronomical beliefs and considering where he might have gotten them, suggests that he probably got his information on such theories from "the full review of the diversities and inconsistencies in astronomical theories given in Chapter 30 of Henry Cornelius Agrippa's *Of the Vanitie and Uncertaintie of Artes and Sciences.*"[69] There had been two English translations of that work from Latin by 1580, when Marlowe went up to Cambridge.

The contemporary influence, though, would most likely have been Raleigh's "School of Night," and perhaps most particularly the Italian magus who sometimes seems to have joined it for philosophical discussions, Giordano Bruno. We have already seen that Marlowe was probably within this famous "school." It speculated on philosophical and scientific problems of the day. Theology, astronomy, geography, and chemistry were among the interrelated subjects which interested the group—subjects whose interest not only to Raleigh the explorer and navigator, but also to the "Wizard Earl" of Northumberland, dabbler in magic and astrology and alchemy, is clear. Thomas Harriot, another member and a noted mathematician, with Raleigh, was "generally suspected of atheism," even as Marlowe was.[70] Muriel C. Bradbrook insists that "the school must have dabbled in the occult."[71] Indeed, enemies termed this gathering "Sir Walter Rawley's School of Atheism."[72]

Two different sources have commented on Marlowe's themes

and images, noticing how similar they are to the imaginations of others in this "school." John Bakeless speculates that his celestial imagery might well have come from his association with Thomas Harriot, and his war imagery from a similar connection with Raleigh.[73] Eleanor Clark suggests that he participates in the school's cult of Diana, in which the moon is likened to a perfect Eldorado. This theme often occurs within the group—for example, in Drayton and Chapman as a way of praising the Virgin Queen.[74] It is true, of course, that other writers, not of the "school," often praised Elizabeth hyperbolically, and often in terms of the moon. Lyly and his play *Endymion* is an obvious example. But there is a special quality to Bruno's references which sets him apart from such conventional compliments. Particularly in the *Cena de le ceneri*, he seems to set her up as Queen of some "vast, mystical universal empire."[75] This idea suggests more than a common heritage of Petrarchism; it suggests also a particular offshoot of it: the school of night. It is in this context that Bruno's Filoteo must be read in *On Cause, Principle and Unity*: "This Divine Elizabeth who reigns in England. She is so highly endowed, exalted, favoured, protected, and sustained by the heavens, in vain the words or forces of others will strain to overthrow her."[76] Such a view of Elizabeth, together with the moon imagery which suggests a feminine ideal, make a Bruno-Marlowe connection in this School seem likely. The fact that Bruno, arriving in England in 1583 speaking Italian and Latin, but no English, probably could not have read the poems written by these "schoolmembers," suggests that they may have conversed about their poetic ideas in one of Bruno's own tongues, or through the good offices of a translator like Florio.

Such a connection as Bruno seems to have made with the leading intellectuals of the day in London would be the main way of accounting for his influence on Marlowe.[77] Marlowe was at Cambridge while Bruno was in London and, for at least one famous debate, in Oxford. But there is some evidence that Marlowe's attendance at his university was spotty in the extreme.[78] He could have spent a lot of time in London and, as Secretary Walsingham's agent during this period, almost certainly did.

And so, aside from the "school of night" association, it would hardly be surprising to see him turn up at the French Embassy, where Mauvissière had given Bruno a refuge.[79] Bruno himself claims in his *Cena* that he often discussed "philosophical and scientific questions . . . [with] Sidney, Greville, Harvey, Temple, Bacon, Raleigh. . . . But there is no evidence outside Bruno's own writings."[80]

However, during this period, John Florio was still living at the French Embassy (and continued until at least 1606, apparently). We have his testimony in his *Second Fruits*, published in 1591, that Bruno had been there.[81] We also know that Florio was used as a go-between from Raleigh to Mauvissière, the French ambassador, and back. This knowledge "considerably strengthens the possibility that Raleigh met Bruno."[82] It also increases Bruno's credibility about his other activities, now that the probability of one of them is established. Marlowe seems likely to have been associated with Raleigh in the "school," and through that association to have heard, at least, Bruno's views at some length.

Indeed, one biographer has gone so far as to suggest that Marlowe could scarcely have avoided connecting his own sense of identity with Bruno's. Marlowe's "atheistic" opinions were not unlike those for which Bruno burned; and Bruno was "arrested by the Holy Office in Venice just a year before the Privy Council sent for Marlowe. . . . The parallel with Marlowe's case is so close that it is clear where many of his opinions came from."[83] The certainty of the evidence here is exaggerated. However, this extreme view emphasizes that it is not unusual to see in Marlowe a strong resemblance to Bruno.

We should therefore recognize at the outset that this influence is a likely possibility, while at the same time awaiting the evidence of *Tamburlaine* to determine the question more fully. We have here, after all, a volatile, footloose, talented young man in an age of intellectual and political ferment. The old order was still in the process of breaking up. The schizophrenia of the civil war had not yet quite arrived, but Elizabeth was aging, Mary of Scotland had been executed, and in 1549 peasants had actually taken over the country's second city, Norwich, for a while; there was inflation, and the budget was so unbalanced by military expenditures that Elizabeth had to depend on funds from the capture of Spanish treasure ships.[84]

How does one, in such circumstances, hang on to the prevalent optimism? If you're not an intellectual, and not starving, it's easy: don't think about these problems. But if you are an intellectual, it's not so easy. You have to fit what you can still believe of your old faith into what you know of new discoveries and ideas, and try to transmute all that into a set of beliefs of your own, probably not like anyone else's, that makes the universe coherent, that unites the various planes of existence so you can know where you are in it again.

It may be that many of us today have suspended our belief in religious systems for so long that we can no longer sense the urgency of a man used to faith. But Marlowe would feel this urgent need. And Bruno represented a strain of thought that seemed, to some, to offer a way to keep it.

CHAPTER II

TAMBURLAINE, MAGIC, AND BRUNO

In order to see how Marlowe's ideas are related to Bruno's style of Hermeticism, we must first review the specific ideas which Bruno held. For him, the universe is both infinite and diverse.

> Naught standeth still, but all things swirl and whirl
> As far as in heaven and beneath is seen
> All things move, now up, now down,
> Whether on a long or short course,
> Whether heavy or light.[1]

In the world there is "mutation, variety, and vicissitude."[2]

But within, there is unity. Even the greatest differences, as between matter and spirit, are merely the expression of "different aspects of a unitary substance."[3] Indeed, matter contains "a potency of being and [acts] as the universal subject of substratum from which all things and beings arise and into which they return."[4]

> Let a thing be as small and diminutive as you like, it still possesses in itself a part of spiritual substance which, if it finds a suitable subject becomes plant, becomes animal, and receives the members of one or other of the bodies that are commonly called animate; for spirit is found in all things and there is not the least corpuscle that doesn't contain internally some portion that may become alive.[5]

There is, then, a world-soul which animates, gives both life and form to the infinite and diverse things of the universe, while maintaining its essential unity. Thus, it should not be disturbing to observe that this is a world in flux. "Spiritual substance is no less real than material. So, . . . outer forms change and are even destroyed, since they are not things, but of things; they are not substances, but accidents and circumstances of substances."[6] There is even the possibility of transmigration of souls, therefore.[7] Yet within all this, Bruno cries out that "It is Unity that doth enchant me."[8]

Further, Bruno affirms with Plato that man can know this inner spirit of the world. In a passage of dialogue in *Cause, Principle and Unity*, Eliotropio is clearly indebted to Plato's cave in Book VII of the *Republic* when he describes man's situation:

> It's as convicts grown used to the gloom: when they are freed from the dungeon of some dark tower and go out into the daylight. In the same way, many men who've been trained in vulgar philosophy, and others as well, become scared and bewildered: unable to sustain the new sunlight of your clear concepts, they are thoroughly disturbed.
> . . . You want to bring us up out of the blind abyss and lead us into the open, tranquil, and serene aspect of the stars, which we see scattered about in such lovely variety on the cerulean mantle of the heavens.[9]

However, Bruno also believes that some *things* (not just souls or intellects) in this world of change are capable of developing until they achieve perfection. Perhaps he even believes in "the total possibility of the universe's development [in its] ceaseless struggle to realize the full possibility of the existence of things."[10] Or as Arelio Dicson argues in the second dialogue of *Cause, Principle and Unity*, "The aim, and the final cause which the efficient [cause] sets before itself, is the perfection of the universe."[11] Within this universe which reflects a value system of higher and lower spiritual awareness, Sophia argues in *The Expulsion of the Triumphant Beast* that "every pleasure consists only in a definite transit, journey, and motion. Just as troublesome and sad is the state of hunger; so, displeasing and grave is the state of satiety; but that which does delight us is the motion from the one [state] to the other."[12] Not only is man and his universe perfectible, but development and change toward perfection is the basic law of its creation. Only the most enlightened know this, however. Most are seduced by the outward appearances of this universe.

Enlightened man, however, thus becomes an image in microcosm of the macrocosm, the universe, and in several ways. He is like the larger universe in being the meeting ground of the four elements in harmonious combination, and in providing the common ground for body and soul, thus uniting in himself the most basic qualities of the universe. Indeed, "the human species in its individuals reveals the variety of all other species put together. Each individual comprises the whole lot more expressly than do the individuals of the other species."[13] Equally important, his natural impulse toward perfecting himself also obeys the same law that moves the larger universe in the same direction. This is neither a Christian nor a Platonic concept, since Christianity believes perfection is to be achieved only in the next world, and Platonism, only by the soul.

This enlightened man's mind is also a microcosm of the tendencies and forces within the universe. In *The Expulsion*, an allegory of the world, when Jove describes himself he is also describing man: he refers to "the heaven which intellectually is within us, and then [to] this sensible one which corporeally presents itself before our eyes."[14] The mind is to be compared to the world, and both are compared to the heavens and to divinity.

Man is not merely a microcosm of the larger universe, however. He transcends it. In his best moments he penetrates its deepest mysteries and knows the power of spirit to create life from matter. He is capable of "a certain divine rapture which makes some become superior to ordinary men."[15] It is

> a rational force following the intellectual perception of the good and the beautiful comprehensible to man to whom they give pleasure when he conforms himself to them, so that he is enkindled by their dignity and light, and is invested with the quality and condition which make him illustrious and worthy. By intellectual contact with that godlike object he becomes a god.[16]

"In every man, in each individual, are contemplated a world and a universe where, for governing Jove, is signified Intellectual Light."[17] The Hermetic books which helped form Bruno's thinking on this subject make this point about the divinity of man's intellect just as clearly. "If then you do not make yourself equal to God, you cannot apprehend God; for like is known by like."[18] Or again in the *Asclepius*: "Man is a marvel then, Asclepius; honour and reverence to such a being! Man takes on him the attributes of a god, as though he were himself a god."[19]

The mind, then, is not merely exalted. It is active, powerful. Great men "embrace in their own mind all things that are, the things on earth and the things in heaven, and even what is above heaven, if there is aught above heaven."[20] The memory system Bruno created, based partly on the work of Ramon Lull, clearly indicates his belief in this comprehensive power of the mind. "The Hermetic principle of reflection of the universe in the mind as a religious experience is organized through the art of memory into a magico-religious technique for grasping and unifying the world of appearances through arrangements of significant images."[21] The creation of a cosmology, as we have seen in the case of Copernicus, is an act of creation in which a great mind gives pattern to the universe.

The philosopher who sees into the hidden nature of things is indeed not only in harmony with nature and its soul, he is like a god himself.

Obviously, then, this great man depends not on the grandeur of his birth, but on his own intellectual and spiritual power— qualities which have been seen in common as well as in noble families. Indeed, in *Cause, Principle and Unity*, Eliotropio says, "We usually find the rarer and choicer wits turning up where the commonfolk are very ignorant and bumble-headed, and where in general people are less urbane and courteous."[22] Shortly after, he makes a specific example: a Scythian, like Tamburlaine.[23] Harry Levin's observation that Marlowe's hero is the common man who controls his fate is very much to the point here.[24] Indeed, Bruno himself came from Nola, a rustic village then, several miles outside of Naples.

Thus one is wholly dependent on his "divine rapture" if he is ambitious to know the True and the Good. Bruno concedes that this is a dangerous belief, for it can let loose all sorts of maniacs intent on imposing their own private visions on the countryside. In *The Heroic Frenzies*, Tansillo says that there are, to simplify his views, two basic kinds of frenzy, one tending "to bestial folly," but "the second consists in a certain divine rapture. . . ."[25] And in *Cause, Principle and Unity*, Eliotropio observes to Filoteo that "your philosophy . . . lays down that contraries coincide both in the principles and in the related subjects. Thus the same wits, which are most apt for lofty, virtuous, and noble enterprises, are liable, if they turn perverse, to throw themselves into extreme vices."[26]

In this diversity even within the heroic frenzies, Man of course in yet another way parallels the diversity of the universe itself. He remains the microcosm. But this frenzy is at the same time a sign that man is trying to control the macrocosm, or at least see it to its depths. Bruno does not oversimplify the problem of heeding irrational impulses, but he also does not take the line which some rationalists have, that because it is difficult to know true voices from misleading ones, neither should be pursued. To Bruno, the rewards are worth the risk:

> Though deeply rooted you are held by earth,
> Mount, lift your summit to the stars in strength.
> A kindred force from the height of things is calling,
> Mind, making you the bound twixt hell and heaven.
> Maintain your rights, lest, sinking to the depths,
> Assailed, you drown in Acheron's black waters.
> Rather go soaring, probing nature's lairs;
> For, at God's touch, you'll be a blaze of fire.[27]

It is part of our best nature so to aspire. Indeed, it is in this way that we can hope to make the universe a perfect reflection of soul. Dicson says in *Cause, Principle and Unity* that "we should hence speak rather of matter containing forms and implicating them than think of it as void and excluding them. And matter which unfolds what it holds folded-up should be called a thing divine, the best parent, generator, and mother of natural things—indeed, nature entire in substance."[28]

It is not only the goals of aspiration, however, which are rewarding. Striving itself is sufficient justification for exalted ambition. In *The Expulsion*, Sophia reminds us that "that which does delight us is the motion from the one [state] to the other. The state of venereal ardor torments us, the state of requited lust saddens us; but that which satisfies us is the transit from one state to the other. . . . Labor does not please except in the beginning, after rest; and unless in the beginning, after labor, there is no pleasure in rest."[29] Not only is it a law of being to be in flux, like the macrocosm which we parallel, but our pleasures are mental, in anticipation and novelty. So by movement we heed our deepest impulses, rather than by rest and stability.

Thus even for the great man, worldly ambition is not to be demeaned as unworthy (an argument often made to demean Tamburlaine). In *The Heroic Frenzies*, this becomes clear:

> To men who are well disposed the love of material beauty not only does not at all delay them from the greater enterprises, but rather gives them wings to accomplish them; for love's constraint is transformed into a virtuous zeal which forces the lover to progress to the point of becoming worthy of the thing loved, and perhaps worthy of some greater and still more beautiful object; so that either he begins to feel content that he has gained his desire, or he is gratified that the particular beauty of his object gives him just reason to scorn any other as a beauty that he has conquered and surpassed; consequently, either he rests in tranquility, or bestirs himself to aspire to more excellent and more magnificent objects. For this reason the heroic spirit constantly renews its efforts, as long as it does not see itself uplifted toward the desire of the divine beauty in itself.[30]

Even the worldly desires of a conqueror are stages in the ascension of the aspiring mind. They are to be honored in themselves, and also for their part in the ascending dialectic of the human soul.

Indeed, this journey is necessary for all who would fulfill the impulses of the soul. In *The Heroic Frenzies*, Tansillo teaches that "it is enough that all attempt the journey. It is enough that each one do whatever he can; for a heroic mind will prefer falling or missing the mark nobly in a lofty enterprise, whereby he manifests the dignity of his mind, to obtaining perfection in things less noble, if not base."[31]

Both for the value of movement itself, which is built into the flux of our physical and even mental nature, and also for the fulfillment of the soul, which requires an appropriate vision for its satisfaction, ambition and a restless mind are necessary for the great man. Even in failure, the noble nature will at least partly fulfill itself by having tried. The parallel with judgments on Tamburlaine is obvious. He too can be interpreted as a dynamic hero struggling to realize his full human potential.

Another example of this attitude toward even worldly ambition can be taken from the sonnets of *The Heroic Frenzies*, all of which "are written in the inflated hyperbolic style of the later Petrarchists, with great exuberance of imagery and conceit."[32] It is clear in these sonnets, as in Dante and Petrarch, that the poet is being inspired by love of a woman (or an idea of a woman, or of love) to sense higher and higher kinds of love, finally spiritual. But unlike the others, for Bruno "the death of the beloved is not necessary to aid the lover's progress toward the *summum bonum*."[33] Bruno can see in the actual woman a reflection of what is divine, can in fact see divinity within her. He can use her, then, "as a symbol for the ultimate object of aspiration"; she has taken on "primarily a metaphysical connotation."[34] In his exuberant sonnet-opening, Bruno suggests this higher concern in the midst of his ardor for a woman:

> I who carry the lofty banner of love, have frozen hopes and burning desires: at one and the same time I tremble, freeze, burn and sparkle, I am dumb and I fill the sky with ardent shrieks.
> My heart throws off sparks, while my eyes distil water; and I live and die, laugh and lament; the waters remain living, and the fire does not die, because I have Thetis in my eyes and Vulcan in my heart.

These are emotions which may begin with desire for the love of a woman, but are clearly directed at the heavens as well. A second sonnet may make this point even more clearly:

> She who kindled my mind to the higher love, she who rendered every other goddess base and vain to me; she in whom beauty and sovereign goodness are uniquely displayed . . .
> And he to me:—Oh fortunate lover! Oh spouse favored by your destiny! She who alone among so many
> has within her bosom life and death, and adorns the world with holy graces, her you have achieved by labor and by fortune.[35]

In the context of *The Heroic Frenzies*, this is clearly more than conventional Petrarchism, though several of the images are drawn from this convention. The exuberance and the philosophical context indicate instead Bruno's ability to see the spirit pulsing just under the outer skin of physical existence, to bring into his perspective body and soul at the same time, to see, in other words, a person whole even as his philosophy suggests he should. From his mode of perception worldly interests are not incompatible with spiritual, nor demeaning. We must remember this too with Tamburlaine.

45

To such minds, soul dictates physical forms, and that spiritual giver of forms is implicit—indeed, sensed—in every worldly entity. "I say then that the table as table is not animated, nor the clothes, nor the leather as leather, nor the glass as glass; but as natural things and composites they have within themselves matter and form."[36] And the magus is one who sees this fact, who sees the universe wholly, not just the surface of things but into its causes and soul. "Magic is that by which reason grasps, in the changing world of time, the constancy of its appearances."[37] He sees the point where intention (soul) and act (physical form) meet and are one. Indeed, for those individuals whose consciousness is so spiritually attuned, and who therefore can conform their bodies to their souls, there is an "absolute substance in which potency is one with act."[38] To such natures, as with God, will and act are one, just as men with such vision see as simultaneous the spiritual design within the world and its expression, the outward world itself. In this way too, there is power in the penetrating, comprehensive mind.[39]

That Marlowe was trying to inspire his audience, to persuade it to suspend its conventional moral judgments and be swept up, through Tamburlaine, in this high vision of the divinity of man, is suggested not only by the hyperbolic sweep of his verse, but also by his use of sources. In none of the known sources for the play's materials is there any indication that Tamburlaine is in any way divine, or even connected in some way to divinity. And although some sources indicate his cruelty,[40] none see him as self-consciously ruthless. Marlowe has added both the sense of divinity and the intensified ruthlessness which, together, many have seen as blasphemous.[41]

We need not to see their combination in this light. Partly the moral view is simply anomalous. Despite many contemporary sermons teaching the contrary, Renaissance Europe generally tolerated acts which we in the twentieth century could only characterize as barbarous. Indeed, somewhat earlier, the Crusades graphically demonstrate the distance between moral teaching and the lengths to which inspiration could send a man. Or consider this description of the French actions after having taken the fortress of Monte San-Giovanni, near Naples, in 1494:

46

What occurred then was merely a commonplace in transalpine war-
fare. . . . Up and down through the narrow passages of the fortress,
human quarry were hunted, were dragged screaming to the walls, and
tossed down to be crushed by the fall or caught on pikes; or they were
butchered in every corner. The gutters ran blood. Nine hundred men
were slaughtered without mercy, and the town with its castle was
pillaged from roof to cellar. It was a comparatively humane operation
inasmuch as the women and children were spared. In the North such
proceedings would have been taken for granted, when a town, which
had refused surrender, allowed itself to be captured by storm. It was a
recognized privilege of the troops, and thus besides were other stiff-
necked garrisons induced more readily to capitulate.[42]

And all of this could be done in the name of a higher principle
like honor. Whatever its limitations, "it gave dignity and splen-
dor to human striving, a standard and pilot star."[43]

The good Aeneas, favored of the gods, carrying out their
destiny for him, a man of great wisdom, virtue, honor, etc.,.
does the same kind of thing. So, having given Lucagus his
death-wound with his spear so that, "Pitched from the chariot
he rolled in his dying agony / Over the earth and good Aeneas
mocked him." Then, when Ligus, the brother, begs for mercy,
"Aeneas cut him short. / 'Just now you spoke a different tune.
Now die!—/It is not brotherly to forsake a brother!' "—presumably by not dying with him.[44] What would seem to be cruelty
to us seems not to have disturbed many in the Renaissance,
nor the classical authors they so much admired.

But one need not go so far afield. Bruno offers ideas which
may justify in more contemporary philosophical terms this general attitude toward others. Some men are "nightowls, [who]
will have no sooner glimpsed the rosy messenger of the sun
come up in the shining East than immediately screwing up
their weak eyes they'll feel themselves drawn back slinking to
their dim retreats."[45] These men have lower natures than that
of the magus. Indeed, Bruno's attitude toward Calvinists is not
unlike Tamburlaine's toward those he conquers.

If after they are warned, revealing themselves incorrigible, they stand
firm on their feet of Obstinacy, Judgment should . . . dissipate, scat-
ter, and annihilate them; and that she, by the use of any kind of force,
power, and industry, should extinguish the very memory of the name
of such a pestiferous germ.[46]

For fortune does not attempt justice in this world. All men are
put into an urn as if equal, and without judging them Fortune

47

pulls out some to be wealthy, some to be poor.[47] It is for each man to obey the law of his nature. The magus, godlike,

> has thoughts of nothing but things divine and shows himself insensible and impassible to those things which ordinary men feel the most and by which they are most tormented. . . . He becomes gold proven and pure, acquires the feeling of divine and internal harmony, and conforms his thoughts and acts to the common measure of the law innate in all things. . . . Without disturbing his balance he conquers and overcomes the terrible monsters.[48]

Cruelty can be explained on two levels, therefore. In the first place, it was not unusual, and could even be justified in the name of some principle like honor or patriotism or religion. And more importantly, to the aspiring mind, the stimulae which most affect a mind of a lower order are no longer effective. The magus finds it difficult to react as less gifted and disciplined men do, and so finds it difficult to be sensitive to the feelings of these others.

And generally, in *Tamburlaine*, Part One, it is Tamburlaine's thoughts which determine not only the value system of the play, but the physical fate of men and nations. Ideas must be referred to his thinking for approval; he never bends to the will of another. Indeed, it is rare that we are given an affecting portrait of how other characters feel—least of all Zenocrate, even at first, when her will opposes Tamburlaine's.

This consciousness of great worth, however, leads to another characteristic which many readers of the play have felt unappealing: his egoism. It is a characteristic which Bruno shared. He wrote to Michel de Castelnau in the prefatory epistle to *Cause, Principle, and Unity*, referring to his dialogues there enclosed, "accept then with a grateful mind."[49] In the body of this book Filoteo, when asked how he thinks that he is a philosopher if he is unaccepted by the people, answers that he believes because of "the divinities who have set me here, I who find myself here, and those who have eyes and see me here,"[50] the great mass of men being blind "like dazzled moles."[51] Again and again he states his belief in his own divine inspiration, in its superiority to that of other men.[52] For the magus whose great comprehension of the universe so far exceeds the common understanding, and whose aspirations therefore also outstrip those of other men, such egotism may be necessary. If one cannot judge by the world, but instead judges the world by the standard of oneself, clearly strong faith in oneself—of the kind that unsympathetic men might call egoism—is required. So with Bruno. So with Tamburlaine.

The magus Paracelsus, whose history of persecution and startling achievement is in many ways a preview of Bruno's, makes one of the clearest statements of this absolute belief in oneself:

> From the middle of this age the Monarchy of all the Arts has been at length derived and conferred on me, Theophrastus Paracelsus, Prince of Philosophy and of Medicine. For this purpose I have been chosen by God to extinguish and blot out all the fantasies of elaborate and false works, of delusive and presumptuous words, be they the words of Aristotle, Galen, Avicenna, Mesva, or the dogmas of any among their followers.[53]

Neither the personal sense of divinity, or at least connection with it, nor the cruelty, the unwillingness to respond to lesser forms of perception and inspiration, are necessarily to be condemned by the Renaissance. Both these qualities, indeed, are consistent with those ideas about man implied by the existence of the magus, and forcefully represented to England at about the time of Marlowe by Giordano Bruno.

It is true, of course, that there were other Renaissance views of man's relation to destiny which might explain Tamburlaine's worldly success if arrogant self-righteousness and cruelty were his only important personality traits. For example, Don Cameron Allen demonstrated several years ago that the Renaissance believed there were men who were fortune's darlings. He quoted from Giovanni Pontano's *De Fortuna* to show that such a man "does not need a code of conduct; he has only to follow his impulses and be carried to the highest goals." However, such a man was not intellectual, for "the *fortunati* often lose their occult powers when they begin to study or try to work out a course of action."[54] But Tamburlaine does undergo considerable intellectual strain, and does seem to go against the kinds of impulses he has been having earlier when he shows mercy to the Soldan of Egypt in Act V. I will try to show later that this and other acts clearly suggest Tamburlaine's

mental effort and discipline. Although Pontano believed that
fortune "is governed by the stars," his portrait is of an intellectually passive hero who is entirely the victim of his impulses,
which in turn the stars direct.[55]

What we have seen with Bruno is that the deepest impulse of
man is to understand the universe, and from this understanding
to achieve, among other things, power. He is quite the reverse
of intellectually passive; nor is the idea of a unifying inspiration, or "impulse," inconsistent with the idea of intellectual
aspirations, nor inconsistent with the desire for worldly power.
While Pontano sees the importance of astrology, he does not
see the importance of magic, of the man himself turned into a
positive force to help control his fortune. Bruno does. Still, that
the Renaissance believed in the remarkable man is clear. What
remains is to demonstrate the nature of that remarkable man as
seen by Marlowe. The step from Pontano to Bruno or Agrippa
is small, consisting largely in the way one conceives of astrological power.

Tamburlaine clearly takes this step. In three well-known
passages, one from each of the first three acts, he demonstrates
his general beliefs about himself and his universe. On the assumption that we are meant to believe him right—and this assumption is principally to be judged on the basis of the action
of the final two acts, with Bejazeth, the virgins of Damascus,
and the Soldan of Egypt—his general resemblance to the beliefs
of magi in general is clear in these earlier speeches. Many of
the ideas he utters, however, were in the air at the time, and not
held only by magi. Therefore, when this resemblance is seen,
we cannot say definitively that Marlowe had magic in mind
while writing *Tamburlaine*. We can say, however, that the ideas
about men which are implied most fully in the Renaissance
concept of the natural magus, are also the ideas about man
which Marlowe is trying to express here.

In Act One, scene ii, Zenocrate has just been captured. It is
a scene which she ends by lamenting her capture: "Wretched
Zenocrate" (I, ii, 258). Yet in her second speech she is already
calling Tamburlaine "my lord—for so you do import" (I, ii, 33).
It is Tamburlaine's physical appearance and his manner, his
natural nobility, to which she responds—responds in spite of

50

herself. This is objective testimony to his grandeur. It also suggests that inner ability is, in this play's universe, reflected in outward beauty and grace. It is a neo-Platonic universe, and potentially magical. Tamburlaine answers:

> I am a lord, for so my deeds shall prove:
> And yet a shepherd by my parentage.
> But, lady, this fair face and heavenly hue
> Must grace his bed that conquers Asia,
> And means to be a terror to the world.
> Measuring the limits of her empery
> By east and west, as Phoebus doth his course.
> Lie here, ye weeds that I disdain to wear!
> This complete armour and this curtle-axe
> Are adjuncts more beseeming Tamburlaine.
>
> (I, ii, 34-43)

We have here a metamorphosis from the ultimate pastoral shepherd to the ultimate warrior. Zenocrate's opening speech, also in this scene, had been a typical distressed maiden's appeal to an idealized shepherd in a conventional pastoral: "Ah, shepherd, pity my distressèd plight" (I, ii, 7). But, as we have seen, Marlowe immediately takes the pastoral idea as far as it can go: he makes the hero literally a shepherd, and literally an ideally powerful and gracious and beautiful man. It cannot be argued that Marlow ignores the non-magical traditions of his age, but he does carry them into the realm of magic. This pastoral shepherd is not, like the shepherds of conventional pastoral verse, a well-known metaphor for perfection; he is *literally* a perfect man. In this early scene, he has captured his maiden, but although she is unhappy at her capture, she is stunned by her captor's magnetism. Her will is no longer fully her own.

What kind of man, according to his own testimony in the speech quoted above, has such power? He is a man whose inner nobility will find outward expression in deeds (line 1), for whom increasingly perfect expressions of his inward qualities will be found. So war and power and kingdoms seem not to be ends in themselves, but worldly expressions of inner qualities—of virtues.[56] It is the quality of the magus' mind to believe that the Ideal will be more and more perfectly reflected in the material world, perhaps even fully realized. So the shep-

51

herd's "weeds" must be thrown off for the fuller expression of "armour and . . . curtle-axe." But this transformation is clearly here because the new appearance is "more beseeming Tamburlaine," who himself does not change. In this respect, of course, Tamburlaine becomes the perfect microcosm, for his inner virtues and spirit remain unchanged within the transient outward appearances he makes, just as the world remains at base stable, though physically always in flux (Tamburlaine makes this clear, as we shall see, in the next act).

Indeed, Tamburlaine invites us to see him not so much as a microcosm, but as a rival to the world itself. His empery will be the world; he will be titled ruler of the world; he compares himself in greatness to the sun, Phoebus.

However, this is not only boasting. There is a standard of excellence implicit in this claim which, from the Brunonian point of view, justifies it. Zenocrate possesses "this fair face and heavenly hue." She is a standard for beauty in color and in proportion, like the perfectly circular movement and godlike aspect of Phoebus (Cosroe, in the play's second speech, describes the sun as "Jove"—I, i, 14). By conquering the world, Tamburlaine will impose his own order on it and realize his godlike potentiality; at that point he will deserve Zenocrate as wife (finally, with the last lines of the play, after the Soldan has satisfied himself that Tamburlaine has not "kept the fair Zenocrate so long / As concubine . . . to feed his lust,"—IV, iii, 47-48—they plan to marry). So, even this early in the play, it is implicit that the ideal of perfect beauty is the image which pushes Tamburlaine forward.[57] Restlessness is endemic in such an inspired soul, as it moves to fulfill its natural ambition of perfect self-realization.

It is in this context that we must read the prologue. In this context, Tamburlaine is justified in "scourging kingdoms" because these kingdoms exist on the same plane as does Zenocrate's physical beauty: as physical rewards for the achievement of an inner ideal. What is to be emphasized also is the prologue's "high astounding terms." Tamburlaine is elevated by language to a godlike plane on which ambition is fully justified. Indeed, the hero's higher inspiration is very clear a little later in I, ii, when he states the relative value of gold and nations in his scale of values:

Disdains Zenocrate to live with me?
Or you, my lords, to be my followers?
Think you I weigh this treasure more than you?
Not all the gold in India's wealthy arms
Shall buy the meanest soldier in my train.
Zenocrate, lovelier than the love of Jove . . .

(I, ii, 82-87)

Friendship, beauty, the meeting of great and equal souls, all are worth more. But they must, in this world, have physical expression to exist perfectly.

In Act II, scene vii, Tamburlaine makes a much fuller description of his view of the cosmos (not long after he has echoed Meander's "And ride in triumph through Persepolis!"):

The thirst of reign and sweetness of a crown
That caused the eldest son of heavenly Ops
To thrust his doting father from his chair,
And place himself in the empyreal Heaven,
Move me to manage arms against thy state.
What better precedent than mighty Jove?
Nature that framed us of four elements
Warring within our breasts for regiment,
Doth teach us all to have aspiring minds.
Our souls, whose faculties can comprehend
The wondrous architecture of the world
And measure every wandering planet's course,
Still climbing after knowledge infinite,
And always moving as the restless spheres,
Wills us to wear ourselves and never rest,
Until we reach the ripest fruit of all,
That perfect bliss and sole felicity,
The sweet fruition of an earthly crown.

(II, vii, 12-29)

It is a test for the hero. He is consciously justifying worldly ambition to Cosroe, whom he has turned against even though Cosroe has treated him honorably. Tamburlaine meets this challenge to morality and honor well. His justification is not greed, nor even worldly ambition itself. There is in this speech much about the "sweetness of a crown," but nothing about specific kingdoms, even Cosroe's, which our hero has just won. The speech is, rather, an explanation of what constitutes "the sweet fruition of an earthly crown." As explanation, over half of it is about "aspiring minds" and "our souls, whose faculties can comprehend / The wondrous architecture of the world." So the crown is the "fruition" of mental and spiritual ambition, it would seem. In other words, the ultimate physical expression on earth (to paraphrase the last line of the speech) of mental and spiritual aspiration. Thus does the shepherd justify changing to warrior. It is, perhaps, "perfect bliss and sole felicity" because this crown is the most perfect physical embodiment, the fullest realization, of ideal virtue, of fidelity to one's natural aspirations, to one's potential divinity.

It also seems clear from this passage that knowledge—not power for its own sake, but as the outward measure of the fulfillment of his soul—is the primary object of Tamburlaine.[58] And this high-mindedness, in turn, would seem to offer one Hermetic explanation for his alleged cruelty (though we will observe some others later). Such a man, "strong in the assurance of that in him which is divine, . . . scorns the merely human part of his nature."[59] It suggests, further, an active, searching intellect, not at all the mentally passive recipient of divine impulses which he must simply obey, as Pontano describes in writing of the Fortunati. This man, rather, "comprehend[s] / The wondrous architecture of the world / And measure[s] every wandering planet's course, / Still climbing after knowledge infinite." He is rather like the description in the *Hermetica* of men who "embrace in their own mind all things that are, the things on earth and the things in heaven. . . ."[60]

In this he resembles the magus very strongly, the secret of whose power is precisely that he sees into the pattern of the cosmos and understands not only how it works, but why it works as it does; hence he can harness its ruling forces in order to perfect their expression in the physical universe. He "assumes *secret powers* of nature which do not satisfy our notions of *cause and effect*."[61] Teofilo says, in *Cause, Principle and Unity*, "In ascending to perfect cognition, we proceed by bringing together multiplicity [into one]."[62] And so Tamburlaine, who with eternal restlessness pursues "knowledge infinite," seeks its unified and perfect expression in a crown, the union of physical symbol with the Ideal of the soul; ultimately, he plans to unify the whole world (as the sun has) under one dominion; and at last, he will marry (unite body and soul; merge two people into one entity; combine his power and knowledge with the principle of beauty and love, Zenocrate).

54

The parallel between this generalized portrait of the ideal man as the *Hermetica* and Bruno define him, and Tamburlaine, seems to fit. However, we must establish that it continues to fit throughout the play, while at the same time exploring the source of these ideas, and the degree of relationship which Marlowe seems to have had with Bruno.

To be complete, however, this general portrait must first be filled out by another characteristic, whose most explicit treatment occurs in III, iii:

> . . . 'will' and 'shall' best fitteth Tamburlaine,
> Whose smiling stars give him assurèd hope
> Of martial triumph, ere he meet his foes.
> I that am termed the scourge and wrath of God,
> The only fear and terror of the world. . .
>
> (III, iii, 41-45)

Clearly, the qualities described earlier are implicit here. For such an aspiring mind, only the future tense is adequate. His eyes are always in that direction. This clarifies the problem of ruthlessness and cruelty in new terms. To the inspired mind, the present is merely a road to the future. The qualities of the present are not in themselves significant. Therefore to judge Tamburlaine on the basis of his cruelty is rather like judging Falstaff on the basis of his cowardice: in the total identity of the man, it is an irrelevance.

But what is more important in this passage is the almost *instantaneous* embodiment of the aspirations of his mind into physical form, in nations and power. It is this union of physical and spiritual perfection, of course, which is preeminently the aspiration of the magus. But further, since Tamburlaine wins victory after victory almost immediately upon declaring his intentions, and since battles occur offstage so that we are usually presented with a *fait accompli* seconds after it is begun, it seems onstage that the future almost immediately becomes the present, and that *will* and *is* are also nearly joined. His victories, as they pile up, begin also to seem inevitable. The pattern is established and repeated unvaryingly. His talk of being "scourge and wrath of God, / The only fear and terror of the world," therefore seems by Act III almost the proper expression of his grandeur. With Tamburlaine, as with God, will and power, idea and act are one, joined. God images the Creation in His mind, and it is formed; similarly, Tamburlaine images a nation as his, and it is. Ultimately, the world. This divinity of man is of course also part of the belief of the true magus. And the necessary self-confident egoism, which has been discussed above, is also obvious here.

It is true that Tamburlaine is not consistent about the source of his power and vision. At several points he attributes his success to "smiling stars" (III, iii, 42), "our long-expected fate" (II, iii, 44), or "gracious stars" (I, ii, 92), as if he were one of Pontano's Fortunati. But shortly afterward he claims that

> I hold the Fates bound fast in iron chains,
> And with my hand turn Fortune's wheel about,
> And sooner shall the sun fall from his sphere
> Then Tamburlaine be slain or overcome.
>
> (I, ii, 173-176)

as if he were a magus who had found the secret to controlling even the gods. At other times, however, he claims a special relationship with the king of heaven. He is at one time under Jove's special protection (I, ii, 179-180), and shortly thereafter sees himself as very like Jove himself, able to "become immortal like the gods" (I, ii, 198-200). Even here, though, there is a close resemblance to the Hermetic view of man: "Think that for you too nothing is impossible; deem that you too are immortal, and that you are able to grasp all things in your thought."[63]

At other times, it is the inner perfection of his soul which perfectly reflects the harmonious outer universe, and which is "a heaven of heavenly bodies, . . . / That guides his steps and actions to the throne" (II, i, 16-17). In this vision he bears the universe within him; his desire to possess the world is analogous to his desire to possess himself, to govern himself fully, to be perfect outwardly as he is inwardly. His power and impetus come from his own inward perfection. At last he can join the idea of his own perfection to the power of the stars:

> Smile stars that reigned at my nativity,
> And dim the brightness of their neighbour lamps;
> Disdain to borrow light of Cynthia,
> For I, the chiefest lamp of all the earth,
> First rising in the East with mild aspect,

But fixèd now in the meridian line,
Will send up fire to your turning spheres,
And cause the sun to borrow light of you.

(IV, ii, 33-40)

Tamburlaine progresses, grows physically, becomes more perfect, until finally he is greater than the stars.

Thus Tamburlaine, though at various times crediting various
sources with his remarkable successes, in general refers to a
unity among himself, the gods, and the stars or fates. In some
passages it is Jove, in some the stars, in some himself who has
greatest power. But if one considers the idea of universal harmony and power as reflected materially in one man; and if one
considers the Renaissance allegorical habit in which the classical gods may represent the divine in man and the world, and
in which the stars often reflect the divine recognition of this
same high human quality; then one can entertain the possibility that these various sources are expressions of the same essential spiritual power which underlies the physical universe
and all physical action. Tamburlaine, taking this basic unity
for granted, perhaps not even conscious of the philosophical
implications of all that he says, expresses now one, now another
aspect of this underlying unity, depending on the turn of his
mind and the kind of emphasis he wants at any given moment.
The Elizabethan audience, or at least the educated and elite part
of it, used to the Hermetic ideas current in the age's intellectual milieu, would also have accepted the premise that unites
Tamburlaine's varied attributions of power, and would have
seen no contradictions among them.

And so Marlowe, who constantly emphasizes Tamburlaine's
divine nature—his connection to this spiritual basis of the world.
There is, for example, the objective testimony of Theridamas
who, in his first look at his enemy, says,

A Scythian shepherd so embellishèd
With nature's pride and richest furniture!
His looks do menace Heaven and dare the gods.
His fiery eyes are fixed upon the earth. . . .

(I, ii, 154-157)

Theridamas, of course, is transformed into an ally by this appearance. "What strong enchantments tice my yielding soul"

(I, ii, 223)! and he describes himself as "conquered with thy looks" (I, ii, 227). It may be well to emphasize that it is *nature's* furniture which "menaces Heaven." This is not an unnatural man, but simply the best earth can make. And earth's best is, of course, a best reflection of the Ideal, the soul, which she can make. "Menace" may then be read "challenge"; a man has reached divine proportions. It is no longer clear whether human or divine identity is more perfect; indeed, they may be the same. As the magus would wish, soul and body are one.

Another potential enemy, Cosroe, gives still more objective testimony at the start of the second act. Tamburlaine is

> The man that in the forehead of his fortune
> Bears figures of renown and miracle.
>
> (II, i, 3-4)

Menaphon, Cosroe's advisor, adds:

> His lofty brows in folds do figure death,
> And in their smoothness amity and life.
>
> (II, i, 21-22)

Here we have not only an imposing figure, but one who literally reflects his inner intentions and destiny and divine identity in his physical features, even in the changes of his expression. A frown brings death. The doctrine of signatures has been made manifest in Tamburlaine. Each entity of the earth was thought to contain the secret mark of its identity in its physical being; only the enlightened could find it; it was the special business of the magus to recognize it so that he could manipulate outward identity to better conform to the inner one. As the ideal man in whom outward appearance and inner virtues are one, the signature of Tamburlaine's identity is obvious, out front for all to see. He is as transparent as it is possible for physical existence to be. One sees his inner will through his outer existence. He embodies the goal of the art of the magus. He is as nearly able to "menace Heaven and dare the gods" as is possible for a man.

However, his spirituality is not absolute; indeed, in the opening of the play, it is merely relative to other men. There is always a greater perfection to aspire to. The journey never ends; the awakened soul is forever in a state of becoming. Indeed, as Bruno suggests, it may be this very restlessness that maintains the soul's wakefulness and consequent high-mindedness, that keeps it from sinking to the baser levels of other men.[64] And so, near the beginning of the play, Tamburlaine vows friendship to Theridamas:

> Theridamas, my friend, take here my hand,
> Which is as much as if I swore by Heaven
> And called the gods to witness of my vow.
> Thus shall my heart be still combined with thine,
> Until our bodies turn to elements,
> And both our souls aspire celestial thrones.
>
> (I, ii, 231-236)

There is still the further purity of another mode of being, beyond physical existence, to which Tamburlaine turns his restless mind.

However, because Tamburlaine exists in this mundane world, he must express his spirituality in this world's terms. Thus even on the level of physical strife, this need to aspire, to test his mettle against greater and greater objectives, also rules. When Tamburlaine is given Mycetes' crown, he says,

> Here, take it for a while; I lend it thee
> Till I may see thee hemmed with armèd men.
> Then shalt thou see me pull it from thy head;
> Thou art no match for mighty Tamburlaine.
>
> (II, iv, 37-40)

It is not the crown, but the proof of his mettle which a battle will give him, that Tamburlaine needs. The crown and the battle are merely the media of expression for his soul. And they are his tests to prove his ability, his charm, his divinity; he seeks through them to find if there are limits to his identity, knowing of none.

In this regard, it is often asserted that Tamburlaine is motivated primarily by earthly ambition, perhaps even by acquisitiveness, and that Tamburlaine's echo of Menaphon, and then comment on that echo, are vivid proofs of this view:

> And ride in triumph through Persepolis!
> Is it not brave to be a king, Techelles?
>
> (II, v, 50-51)

Indeed, there is a speech a few lines later that adds greater substance to this idea:

> A god is not so glorious as a king.
> I think the pleasure they enjoy in heaven
> Cannot compare with kingly joys in earth:
> To wear a crown enchased with pearl and gold,
> Whose virtues carry with it life and death;
> To ask and have, command and be obeyed;
>
> (II, v, 57-62)

However, this speech is by Theridamas, who in his next speech says that "though I praise it, I can live without [kingship]" (II, v, 66). Then the following dialogue:

> Tamburlaine: What say my other friends? Will you be kings?
> Techelles: Ay, if I could, with all my heart, my lord.
> Tamburlaine: Why, that's well said, Techelles; so would I.
>
> (II, v, 67-69)

So that Theridamas seems almost set up by Marlowe to say the conventional things about kingship: the delights of power, but the stoic or moral ability to do without it.

Tamburlaine specifically opposes these views. To him kingship is necessary, but not because of the delights of power it brings. Tamburlaine has all the power he needs, king or not. He merely needs to exert himself:

> . . . I am strongly moved,
> That if I should desire the Persian crown,
> I could attain it with a wondrous ease.
>
> (II, v, 75-77)

He needs to exert himself to *prove* his power, not to achieve it. Exertion in battle and in dominion keeps his sense of identity and inner strength awake, and also his sense that his inner will is easily translated into outward power. Thus it is not surprising that he again eschews the judgment of Theridamas when his new general fears the battle against Cosroe because he expects great losses. Tamburlaine says, "Judge by thyself, Theridamas, not me" (II, v, 93).

Tamburlaine again shows his need for self-expression in battle by dealing with Cosroe honorably, giving him fair warning of impending war:

> . . . Bid him turn him back to war with us,
> That only made him king to make us sport.
> We will not steal upon him cowardly,
> But give him warning. . . .

(II, v, 100-103)

The *process* of winning is important; the contest, the proof of identity; the reward itself is incidental, merely a symbol of the inner virtue and strength which makes victory possible. It is therefore not surprising that Tamburlaine thinks it "brave to be a king," and still does not hold the more conventional view of kingship which Theridamas expresses.

This restlessness continues as the play goes on. By the start of Act Three, Tamburlaine has "the sweet fruition of an earthly crown," and needs new tests. The geography of the play expands to accommodate him. Bajazeth, "Dread Lord of Afric, Europe, and Asia" (III, i, 23), becomes his adversary, and Tamburlaine can now boast that

> . . . from the East unto the furthest West
> Shall Tamburlaine extend his puissant arm.
> . . . .
> . . . I'll win the world at last.

(III, iii, 246-247, 260)

This man who has demonstrated that he is the best microcosm possible because he mirrors clearly not only the physical nature of the macrocosm, but its spiritual design as well, is now extending himself. His dominions are to include all the world! In title, he will in fact *be* the macrocosm. As other kings are called England, France, Morocco, and the like, he will be called World! What are the limits of such a man? How far does his identity spread? His power is a sign of virtue, of alliance with God, and its extent indicates the greatness of this virtue:

> The chiefest God, first mover of that sphere,
> Enchased with thousands ever-shining lamps,
> Will sooner burn the glorious frame of Heaven,
> Than it should so conspire my overthrow.

(IV, ii, 8-11)

61

A little later, Tamburlaine makes it clear that his approach to conquering the world is appropriate for demonstrating his inner ability:

> I will confute those blind geographers
> That make a triple region in the world,
> Excluding regions which I mean to trace,
> And with this pen reduce them to a map,
> Calling the provinces, cities, and towns,
> After my name and thine, Zenocrate.

(IV, iv, 73-78)

So here is the prospective king of the world having the world's regions named after him and his spouse-to-be, his love. The aspiring mind in its progressive becomings can be nothing more that requires physical power. And for him, since will and power, idea and act, are one, the world *is* his once it is so imagined. In his mind, the deed is done. The imperfection of this physical world requires some elapsed time in which to do the deeds, but we have no doubt, based on Tamburlaine's past performances, that he will conquer all if he sets out to do it.

So he must seek new tests, beyond the world. He does this, as we shall see, but first he makes it clear that conquering the world and remaking its geography is a worthy thing for the ideal man to do.

In the speech quoted above, he makes two things clear beyond the obvious fact that he plans to conquer the world. He implies that he understands the principle underlying the operations of the world, that he and Zenocrate embody them, and that therefore a proper world should be renamed as he suggests. This is clearly the thinking of the magus who recognizes the perfection of the spiritual Ideal, but feels that for its outward expression his aid may be needed. Tamburlaine shows that he understands the geography—that is, the physical organization—of the world better than anybody else ever has. The geographers are all wrong. His "pen" is his sword, of course, and visually, onstage, this use of "pen" with its implications of knowledge and wisdom, will be obviously merged with ideas of power, battle, and violence. The symbolism of war, representing knowledge which is dependent on inner virtue, is in this passage clear, at least onstage. Tamburlaine is not merely a conqueror, though by necessity he is that too; nor can he be thought intellectually passive. But he shows that his expansion to embody the physical macrocosm is, from an intellectual and spiritual point of view, not a shallow ambition (the advantages of aspiration in any form—though they too are considerable, as we have seen—for the moment set aside).[65]

For all these reasons, then, and since worldly ambition is justified, we should see it as expected of Tamburlaine to be ruthless. His own identity is allied to divinity and is the determiner of what is virtuous and right. His aspirations are necessary to keep his spiritual sense awake and lively. He is so inspired that he is insensitive to the concerns of less inspired individuals. When we condemn him for cruelty, we condemn him for being superhuman. Why not instead, as an earlier age could perhaps do, be inspired by the possibility within us which Marlowe portrays—the possibility of being divine? It is for other souls to take solace in the meek humanity which will be given mercy by God and Christ at Judgment Day. For Marlowe, it must be remembered that Christ, born of a divine Father, lived on earth in earthly form. Tamburlaine is hardly the Christ. But he is the divine man who realizes his divinity in other forms. Indeed, one need only remember John Milton's avenging Christ, expelling the rebellious angels from Heaven in *Paradise Lost*, to know that men's view of Jesus Christ himself has not always been of one of a gentle nature.

But beyond all of this there is something demonstrated by the cruelty—something about the whole point of view and idea behind the play. Indeed, the supposed cruelty goes to the heart of the play and its intentions. Marlowe does not condemn Tamburlaine for his cruelty. Why not, aside from the reasons already suggested? What positive idea might it embody?

The answer is suggested briefly near the beginning of the play, in I, ii. Tamburlaine turns to Zenocrate and her defenders after Theridamas has changed sides, and says to them,

> And now, fair madam and my noble lords,
> If you will willingly remain with me,
> You shall have honours as your merits be,
> Or else you shall be forced with slavery.

> (I, ii, 252-255)

To one convinced, as Tamburlaine is, that he possesses absolute inner virtue and that others must recognize it, as Theridamas just has, it is a fair choice. These people must recognize virtue and serve it, or else they deserve nothing. Virtue is the highest aspiration of men; it brings with it knowledge, understanding, power, and the like. A man either wants to be as perfect as he can be, or he is spiritually dead, a slave, a clod, a physical thing only, fit to serve perhaps in a servile, unthinking way, with the body only, but not fit to rule, to converse, to make decisions, or to pretend to think. Tamburlaine offers them their choice: be true to yourselves and follow me, or be physically what in fact you are mentally: nothing, dung, clods from the earth which by accident were given animation. It is a harsh view, but a just one.

We must also see the progressive white, then red, then black colors which he shows to a besieged town, from this point of view.[66] He first gives them a chance to choose the right allegiance:

> The first day when he pitcheth down his tents,
> White is their hue, and on his silver crest
> A snowy feather spangled-white he bears,
> To signify the mildness of his mind.
>
> (IV, i, 50-53)

Then, if they refuse to follow him voluntarily, from the recognition of superior power and all that it implies, he gives them an object lesson, killing all those who fight against him. And if they resist still,

> Black are his colours, black pavilion;
> His spear, his shield, his horse, his armor, plumes,
> And jetty feathers menace death and hell;
> Without respect of sex, degree, or age,
> He razeth all his foes with fire and sword.
>
> (IV, i, 60-64)

It is true that the white, red, and black colors are in Fortescue's *The Foreste*, and are not Marlowe's invention. But he emphasizes where he could have omitted. Why?

Clearly, in Act Four the emphasis of the play is changing away from its earlier stress on how much power Tamburlaine has. His power by now is established. More and more Marlowe begins to emphasize the *manner* of Tamburlaine's conquests: how he operates and why he does things as he does. Here in IV, the absolute nature of Tamburlaine's demands, and the dramatic color symbolism which underlines it, put his absoluteness, his lack of mercy for his enemies, his self-righteousness, at the front of our attention. If those whom he approaches are so inert, so unable to feel the divine spark within themselves that they would be led by an inferior prince, then they are spiritually as good as dead. How better to represent this idea than by demonstrating it literally? Tamburlaine kills them.[67] He is the "all or nothing" man but, unlike Ibsen with his Brand, Marlowe seems to admire the hero. The Renaissance did not oppose elitist views either of society or of salvation.

In Act IV, though, Tamburlaine also faces an inner conflict. Zenocrate repeatedly begs for her father's safety (IV, ii, 123-124; IV, iv, 63-70). At first, Tamburlaine refuses. His aspiration is absolute, a necessity to him, part of his identity: "Not for the world, Zenocrate, if I have sworn" (IV, ii, 125), as if Tamburlaine's swearing is as binding as God's, as if his will is absolutely inflexible and perfect.

This refusal is followed by a scene of absolute inhumanity. He gives the imprisoned Bajazeth a dagger so that he may kill his wife:

> . . . Dispatch her while she is fat, for if she live but a while longer, she will fall into a consumption with fretting, and then she will not be worth the eating. (IV, iv, 48-50)

Bajazeth may stay alive if he will eat his wife.

And then, almost immediately afterward, Tamburlaine agrees to keep Zenocrate's father safe. This is not a complete change, for earlier it had been the kingdom, not just the man, which Tamburlaine had threatened; and here, Zenocrate is careful not to push the point too hard, but rather to leave this merciful decision up to her love:

> Honour still wait on happy Tamburlaine;
> Yet give me leave to plead for him, my lord.
>
> (IV, iv, 83-84)

She submits her will to his power, but makes her desire clear. She wins, and he asserts his will in granting mercy.

But still, at a glance this mercy, small though it is, seems the first time that Tamburlaine has made his ambition less than absolute. It seems for the first time relative, able to be changed, less than divine.

We have seen already that Tamburlaine's actions are embodiments of his thoughts; will and act are united in him. We have further seen that he is growing, becoming a progressively greater figure, as the play goes on. And that worldly dominion implies something about the grandeur of his soul. Now, his dominion over the world will not be lessened, yet his absolute cold-heartedness is. Can it be that here his inner and outer lives are separate? That his great outer power is not paralleled by absolute inner virtue? Perhaps even that at this point we are meant to see most clearly that Tamburlaine's conquests are not related to virtue—indeed, that he is mistaken about how fine he is, just as most of his enemies are mistaken about how fine they are—for they all think very well of themselves indeed. It is possible to see the increasing cruelty of the play, with Bajazeth and the virgins, in particular, as strong evidence to this effect.

What makes this view possible is that between the change toward mercy, itself sudden and unexpected, and the explanation of how it could occur without inner contradiction, Tamburlaine exercises still more cruelty toward Bajazeth, and also kills the virgins. Mercy does not seem to be Tamburlaine's middle name. Nor, to this point, has the change toward mercy been explained. It seems to be more a lover's reassurance than a substantial decision. During this part of the play, late IV and early V, Tamburlaine is less comprehensible than elsewhere. It can be asked if in fact he has really changed. Perhaps all would be better if his great speech in V, i, were to occur in IV, iv. But it does not.

The thing to keep in mind, and which V, i, will make clear, is that Marlowe is *not* making Tamburlaine less absolute. Rather, he is continuing Tamburlaine's expansion. His dominions will not be lessened by his mercy to the Soldan, but his spiritual qualities will be enlarged. His process of becoming continues. Marlowe is, I believe, trying to demonstrate that mercy and absolute power are compatible. That Tamburlaine can add a new element to his spiritual make-up without subtracting anything that was already there. His soul is becoming increasingly comprehensive. We have already seen that it is susceptible to beauty and to love as embodied in Zenocrate. We are now being shown that absolute power which is great enough to coexist with beauty and love is also great enough to include mercy within itself.

This is close to being a mystical idea, since in rational or allegorical terms mercy and cruelty seem to be opposed. Only the highest spiritual natures, those whose ultimate inspiration is beyond any single quality, no matter how absolute, can contain within themselves qualities which seem contradictory to less awakened minds.

I believe that after Tamburlaine's willingness to save the Soldan, Marlowe includes the cruelty to Bajazeth and the implacability in killing the virgins in order to demonstrate that this new mercy for the Soldan has not made Tamburlaine different in the greatness of his power, nor in his cruelty, nor in his sense of personal righteousness. The demonstration is so devastating that it has misled some readers into construing the play in moral terms. However, Marlowe, I believe, allows the virgins to speak on at some length precisely to demonstrate how pitiable they would be to the average person —to ourselves, who do not see from Tamburlaine's exalted height. The more pitiable they seem, the more absolutely can Tamburlaine once again assert his sense of self-righteousness and power. These virgins, this governor, are pleading not out of wisdom, but out of terror. Their abjectness before Tamburlaine is emblematic of their willingness to change faiths, to value physical existence before all. They waited until the battle was almost lost. They did not recognize superior power until it demonstrated itself in battle. Soulless, they have no true life. Their murder is simply a demonstration of what was already true: that they lacked life.[68] Tamburlaine is here consistent with himself, and Marlowe effectively shows that his hero has not lost will or power or vision when he bestows mercy at the request of his love. He asks,

> . . . could they not as well
> Have sent ye out, when first my milk-white flags,
> Through which sweet Mercy threw her gentle beams, . . . [?]
>
> (V, ii, 4-6)

67

It is not a thoughtless slaughter, but one committed out of principle and conviction:

> . . . my customs are as peremptory
> As wrathful planets, death, or destiny.
>
> (V, ii, 64-65)

He associates himself with the spirit of the universe, as if his will were a kind of universal law.

This absoluteness established, he returns to his inner conflict, and for the first time states it clearly. Looking into his beloved Zenocrate's eyes, he sees angels in armour fighting "for Egypt's freedom and the Soldan's life" (V, ii, 90) against his own "tempted thoughts" (V, ii, 89). Earlier, we saw Tamburlaine's features referred to as reflections of a perfect universe within him;[69] now the reference is to Zenocrate. It is as if she were also his mirror, showing his need to resolve his ambition with Zenocrate's own wish for mercy. And this image, in turn, is really a metaphor for his own inner struggle about how to resolve the demands of absolute ambition with a mercy that could conceivably threaten that absoluteness.

Looking at Zenocrate, musing at the power her attraction has for him, he abstracts her into the idea of beauty, then asks,

> What is beauty, saith my sufferings, then?
> If all the pens that ever poets held
> Had fed the feeling of their masters' thoughts,
> And every sweetness that inspired their hearts,
> Their minds, and muses on admirèd themes;
> If all the heavenly quintessence they still
> From their immortal flowers of poesy,
> Wherein, as in a mirror, we perceive
> The highest reaches of a human wit;
> If these had made one poem's period,
> And all combined in beauty's worthiness,
> Yet should there hover in their restless heads
> One thought, one grace, one wonder, at the least,
> Which into words no virtue can digest.
>
> (V, ii, 97-110)

Beauty, then, is beyond tangible expression in words. It is beyond what man can reproduce. It is beyond rational distinction or definition or the power of words. It exists in the mind, the "restless heads" of men, as an ideal. And this ideal is called up to consciousness by Zenocrate, who alone in the world seems to Tamburlaine to embody, to make tangible, this ideal. Thus it is that she is worthy to have the world's places named for her, when it is perfected by Tamburlaine's dominion over it. Thus it is that the absolute ambition of the perfect warrior is neither bounded nor demeaned by his being touched by beauty, for in this view beauty is another name for ambition. It is the infinite, unreachable beyond which the dreams of absolute ambition finally encounter. Tamburlaine's ambition had to grow before he could fully appreciate Zenocrate. He praises her more and more fulsomely as the play progresses. And as his ambition grows, his soul expands, for his ambition finally is only outwardly for empire; the empire, as we have seen, represents knowledge and virtue, inner qualities. So does Zenocrate. The love of beauty and the love of knowledge merge in their common desire for the dream of the Ideal.

Again: as we have seen that mercy for the individual, the Soldan, is not inconsistent with the desire for empire, the outward expression of inner striving; so now we see that the inner impulse itself, the love of beauty, is also consistent with the quest for knowledge.

Tamburlaine is aware of the *seeming* contradiction, and he resolves it quickly:

> But how unseemly is it for my sex,
> My discipline of arms and chivalry,
> My nature, and the terror of my name,
> To harbour thoughts effeminate and faint!
> Save only that in beauty's just applause,
> With whose instinct the soul of man is touched;
> And every warrior that is wrapt with love
> Of fame, of valour, and of victory,
> Must needs have beauty beat on his conceits.

(V, ii, 111-119)

He sees that it is conventional to think the love of beauty effeminate, or at least unworthy for a warrior, but he quickly sees that beauty is the crown of achievement and of ambition and reputation, that it touches the soul of man, that it inspires him. It is, in short, another side of the same quenchless mind which aspires constantly beyond itself. He ends this famous speech by suggesting

> That virtue solely is the sum of glory,
> And fashions men with true nobility.

(V, ii, 126-127)

In the context of this discussion about the nature and uses of beauty, it is clear that beauty and virtue are closely related, perhaps even the same.[70] It is also clear that this sense of virtue-beauty consists in recognizing the ideal behind physical events—and this vision it is which crowns earthly events, gives them significance and luster. A man's virtue, his vision, is composed of all his talents and qualities. It is the summation of the whole man.[71] It is made up of many characteristics, is many-sided, the inspiration for many kinds of achievement. Thus Tamburlaine, to be supreme in virtue, must be the perfect conqueror-warrior, but also the perfect lover, the perfect appreciator of the perfect beauty. This, he says, is "true nobility," subject not to social rank at birth, but to the inner qualities of the man.

This is Tamburlaine's eloquent, though belated, explanation of how mercy can be consistent with absolute cruelty and ambition.

It is obvious that what follows, the results of cruelty on Bajazeth and Zabina, and the lamentations of Zenocrate in fearing for her father, are meant to arouse tension in the audience about what Tamburlaine will decide: mercy or absolute destruction? humility, or pride? These events, however, are also intended to show us once again that Tamburlaine, though now seeking "beauty's just applause" and having turned philosopher, is nonetheless still Tamburlaine, the ruthlessly ambitious warrior. Not only Bajazeth, but also Zenocrate is convinced, and so are we. He remains absolute in ambition and conviction about what to do with soulless creatures like his captives.

Indeed, he seems so absolute that Zenocrate is allowed some rather conventional moralizing:[72]

> Those that are proud of fickle empery
> And place their chiefest good in earthly pomp,
> Behold the Turk and his great Emperess!
> Ah, Tamburlaine my love, sweet Tamburlaine,
> That fights for scepters and for slippery crowns,
> Behold the Turk and his great Emperess!

Thou, that in conduct of thy happy stars,
Sleep'st every night with conquest on thy brows,
And yet wouldst shun the wavering turns of war,
In fear and feeling of the like distress,
Behold the Turk and his great Emperess!
Ah, mighty Jove and holy Mahomet,
Pardon my love! Oh, pardon his contempt
Of earthly fortune and respect of pity,
And let not conquest, ruthlessly pursued,
Be equally against his life incensed
In this great Turk and hapless Emperess!
And pardon me that was not moved with ruth
To see them live so long in misery.

(V, ii, 289-307)

The end of this speech indicates that as Tamburlaine, without the pleadings of Zenocrate, would not spare the Soldan, so Zenocrate, without the striving inspiration of Tamburlaine, would spare anyone pain and suffering. The lovers represent opposed principles in the physical world of deeds, even though, as we have seen, they are inspired by the same ideal vision. It is this spiritual vision which unites them in ideal love; this vision they hold in common also is what expands Tamburlaine's soul to include mercy, and may be thought to expand Zenocrate's to include righteousness. Zenocrate's growth is not emphasized in the play, but is consistent with the fact that when she is under the influence of Tamburlaine, she does not urge mercy for Bajazeth. Their relationship seems to be reciprocal; it represents a merging of different aspects of the perfect human existence and aspiration. Besides emphasizing Tamburlaine's absolute righteousness and cruelty, then, Zenocrate's lamentation emphasizes her difference from Tamburlaine, and therefore the degree of his expansion when merged with her; it also emphasizes once again, and in a new key, the need for virtue in the perfect man.

There is a fourth, and more dramatically compelling, reason for this lamentation speech. We as audience do not yet know if we can trust Tamburlaine's promise of mercy for the Soldan. Zenocrate's uncertainty is also ours. Because his explanation of the unity of beauty and war, mercy and cruelty, is delayed until V, ii, well after his promise and separated from it by his cruelty to Bajazeth and Zabina, we cannot know how seriously he takes this promise. When made, it seemed done too quickly,

71

perhaps too lightly, for our full belief. And so there is suspense. We are not encouraged to see the whole man yet; rather, we still believe in the potential contradiction within. We wonder if he can resolve the inner conflict.

And, shortly after this speech, the lamentations end. Tamburlaine demonstrates the expansive nature of his soul, the breadth of his virtue, by arriving back in camp with the Soldan alive.

He does more than that. For a man whose power is so great that he can conquer any kingdom at will—and almost instantaneously, as it seems in the play—more and more territory is not necessary to extend power. The power exists prior to the conquests. The battles merely continue to affirm its existence. A crown is a symbol of inner virtue which can be translated into power at will, and thence to deeds. When Tamburlaine realizes this fact about himself, he will no longer need to have such worldly ambitions. He will be able to allow himself more mercy and kindness and generosity, even to old enemies. This will be a measure of his self-confidence and self-knowledge. He will then be like a god. His aspirations can turn beyond the world, perhaps to the intangible, to beauty.

The movement toward this still more comprehensive soul seems to begin as Tamburlaine leads the Soldan in and, to the applause of Zenocrate, proclaims that

> 'Twas I, my lord, that gat the victory,
> And therefore grieve not at your overthrow,
> Since I shall render all into your hands,
> And add more strength to your dominions
> Than ever yet confirmed th'Egyptian crown.
> The god of war resigns his room to me,
> Meaning to make me general of the world.

> (V, ii, 382-388)

He has won; the mercy and generosity are on his terms; his will remains absolute. So is his self-confidence. But now, at last, in giving the Soldan back his kingdom and more, he shows that the earthly pomp against which Zenocrate just finished moralizing is no longer Tamburlaine's main concern. He has now such virtue that he recognizes a symbol as a symbol, nothing more substantial, and that his inner virtue, including power, is in itself sufficient. Thus it is that in the closing passages of the play he can turn with love to devote himself to Zenocrate. He does *not* receive the fate of Bajazeth, as Zenocrate had feared, because he is not fundamentally like the Turk. His worldly ambition is but a reflection of the higher aspirations of his mind, while Bajazeth is concerned only for worldly power.

We have now seen in detail how the aspiring mind expresses its virtue and knowledge in terms of earthly power; and how, throughout the play, Marlowe creates a dramatic context in which we are encouraged to see his conquests in this way. However, we have noticed the importance of Zenocrate and beauty only at the end. In observing Marlowe's treatment of her from the beginning onward, we will be able to see her thematic significance more precisely, and see also that Marlowe consistently creates a dramatic context for her which encourages us, by Act V, to see this significance clearly. She therefore adds much to the meaning of the play, and to our understanding of Tamburlaine himself.

Her physical beauty is described very early as a mirror of divine beauty: Tamburlaine refers to "this fair face and heavenly hue," and makes her the crown, the reward, for him "that conquers Asia" (I, ii, 36-37). So she has at the outset the greatest physical beauty, and therefore is the proper reward for the man with the greatest physical accomplishment. The gods can do no better.

However, she is valued not for the conquests she represents, but in herself. "Think you I weigh this treasure more than you" (I, ii, 84) ? "Thy person is more worth to Tamburlaine / Than the possession of the Persian crown" (I, ii, 90-91). Indeed, she is "lovelier than the love of Jove" (I, ii, 87), a seeming hyperbole which may be more literal than conventional. Hyperbole in this play is often more than a young writer's enthusiasm; it is his characteristic way of expressing a vision beyond normal reality. Zenocrate's ideality, the vision she represents beyond even that of conventional divinity, is this early, in I, ii, beginning to take form.

Zenocrate is not merely a figure to reflect Tamburlaine's sentiments, however. She also emerges as an aspiring character who, though she is with Tamburlaine and adored by him and has long since stopped disdaining him, nonetheless has "a farther passion" which, given the character of her beloved, seems a very great ambition: to "live and die with Tamburlaine" (III, ii, 13, 24)—to be his wife.

Much of the play repeats this ideal view of Zenocrate in essentially consistent terms. Her "looks canst clear the darkened sky / And calm the rage of thundering Jupiter" (III, iii, 122-123), so that she seems to have the same degree of power that Tamburlaine has over the physical world, but working in the opposite direction, toward calm. Throughout, she is individualized with respect to Tamburlaine, as well as idealized. Thus she rivals the gods in power, like her beloved; she is "divine" (IV, iv, 28), worthy of the whole world as a symbol of her value:

> We mean to travel to th'antarctic pole,
> Conquering the people underneath our feet,
> And be renowned as never emperors were.
> Zenocrate, I will not crown thee yet,
> Until with greater honours I be graced.
>
> (IV, iv, 133-137)

It is not, then, that worldly empery is the main thing to Tamburlaine, and Zenocrate just a beautiful woman, a bauble to the emperor. Rather, she represents a principle larger than the world. The world is symbol of *her* worth, not the reverse. She in herself embodies the greatest values in existence. In her eyes, those reflectors of inner identity, of soul, sit militant angels, deciding the fate of nations, forwarding the cause of mercy and love (V, ii, 88-90).

Such a power is able to calm even Tamburlaine (though, such is his equal but different inspiration, it does so without diminishing his violence); he finds pity an appealing trait in her

> That in thy passion for thy country's love,
> And fear to see thy kingly father's harm,
> With hair dishevelled wip'st thy watery cheeks;
> And, like to Flora in her morning's pride,
> Shaking her silver tresses in the air,
> Rain'st on the earth resolvèd pearl in showers,
> And sprinklest sapphires on thy shining face,
> Where Beauty, mother to the Muses, sits,

And comments volumes with her ivory pen,
Taking instructions from thy flowing eyes.

(V, ii, 74-83)

She is like a force of nature whose inspiration is divine, beyond even personified Beauty, closer, presumably, to the inner vision and virtue which outward beauty represents physically. The description in earthly terms, particularly the rain and gems, makes her seem in the lover's view like the natural earth itself, having therefore the power to change the earth at her every changing mood, now raining, but perhaps sometime shining like the sun. Tamburlaine too has often compared himself to the sun, or to Jove who himself is often compared to the sun, or again to Phoebus; it seems therefore natural for him to desire mercy now. It is no accident that his great speech on beauty which, as we have seen, rationalizes the giving of mercy to the Soldan, directly follows these perceptions of his beloved. It seems clear that Zenocrate is not only beautiful, but also that she represents the principle of beauty and, further, that she embodies the inner vision of divinity whose perfect outward reflection this beauty is.[73] She is the perfect reflection of her identity, her soul. Neo-Platonism has been extended by an author who has taken Hermetic ideas seriously, whether by reading them directly or merely by hearing of them and finding them much to his taste. Not only does her physical beauty reflect her soul, but it does so perfectly. She is both herself and the physical embodiment of the ideal, just as Tamburlaine is the perfect shepherd of the pastoral convention now taken literally. That is what we are compelled to believe when he changes from shepherd to warrior and demonstrates his ability to express in physical terms that virtue which every other pastoral shepherd possesses only inwardly.[74]

This is true also for Zenocrate. The great summation of this view is Tamburlaine's hymn to beauty, which we have already seen. In it, she comes to represent the idea of beauty which is beyond tangible expression, which is the forever beyond that the aspiring mind cannot yet formulate but must always pursue. Indeed, the moment he stops to formulate, to enjoy, to be content, he ceases aspiring. The only match for Tamburlaine must be with the ever-expanding frontier of the mind, of the

75

ideal. Zenocrate represents all this for him, as he says in his great speech. She is so divinely beautiful that the inner vision beyond formulation shines through her physical being; indeed, he sees angels in her eyes (V, ii, 88); in her perfection, her divinity is not only immanent, but obviously so. She is the union of the ideal and the physically real; the miracle; the god made flesh; the mystery of the universe, and its beauty. Under this inspiration, conquest reflects the restless spirit. Worldly ambition signifies spiritual aspiration. Mercy and cruelty are inspired by a common vision and exaltation.

It is in this context that the play's ending, referring to the marriage of Tamburlaine and Zenocrate, must be viewed. This is not merely a conventional happy ending, although of course it is that—enough in itself, one might think, to persuade everyone that Marlowe intends us to approve Tamburlaine. Nor does it represent for Tamburlaine a conventional kind of "rest" (V, ii, 441). The marriage is between two people who each embody the perfect physical reflection of the inner ideal identity, the soul. Neither, therefore, is more than seemingly finite. Each extends infinitely, stands for ceaseless aspiration. Tamburlaine will never be able to loll back on a couch, taken up with sensuality, as Shakespeare's Antony can do. For Zenocrate is not Cleopatra. She is the forever beyond, as the beauty hymn makes clear. Tamburlaine will aspire even at "rest" when with her, for to be worthy of her he must always be becoming, always seeking the further boundaries of his vision. The play must end because the warrior's world has become too small adequately to mirror his aspiration. For the further aspirations of the spirit, a different kind of play, a different kind of symbol, is needed. And so we end with the equilibrium of two different people of equal power and soul, two equal forces moving in opposite ways under the same inspiration in the same ultimate direction. The ending is not a conventional period, but a launching forth into another voyage, in which physical symbols have been all but exhausted. Perhaps we have returned to the geometry of the circle.

The ending, then, first records Zenocrate's perfection:

> Her state and person want no pomp, you see,
> And for all blot of foul inchastity,
> I record Heaven, her heavenly self is clear.
>
> (V, ii, 422-424)

She is physically and morally perfect, chaste, and with such inner value so obviously embodied in her beauty that "no pomp" is necessary. Thus the proper solemnity and respect which she deserves is automatically accorded her.

The marriage reference is the final symbol of the play. It is a union of two people into one living unity, a union of their souls and bodies. As Zenocrate and Tamburlaine individually represent the union of soul and body, the perfect physical expression of the ideal of identity within; and as they each represent the union of idea and act, will and power (analogues to the union of spirit and body); so their marriage represents a further extension of that physical-ideal unity. It is the most obvious Christian expression of magic, of the wish to achieve a perfect outward form for the perfect aspirations of the soul, the Ideal.[75]

This largeness of significance is prepared throughout the play. The power of the spirit to effect physical occurrences is evoked in various ways, always under the control of Tamburlaine or his co-equal Zenocrate. As a result, the sense of magic-like powers is often present, though without the formal trappings of ritual incantations and the like. The crucial fact in this regard is that although Tamburlaine often thinks of himself as being the scourge of God, or at least as having his goals smiled upon by the gods, one feels throughout that it is his will which decides what is to be done, and which then gets it done. It is, indeed, this universally held feeling that Tamburlaine is captain of his fate, which allows many to condemn him for choosing the wrong things to do. We must, then, if we grant him spiritual or miraculous powers, grant that he controls these powers to earthly ends, and is therefore a type—perhaps a metaphor for—that type of man of divine potential and inspiration which the Renaissance most fully defines in terms of the magus.

Thus Tamburlaine can say,

> Legions of spirits, fleeting in the air,
> Direct our bullets and our weapons' points,
> And make our strokes to wound the senseless air.
>
> (III, iii, 156-158)

When he wins the battle, are we to contradict him? If success is not a measure of his assessment of his power in battle, what is? It is conventional, and too easy, to read such lines as the thoughtless hyperbole of an over-imaginative and careless young writer. Hyperbole, once again, is precisely the appropriate language in which to describe remarkable events. Indeed, what seems hyperbole from the mundane point of view, is perhaps merely literal from the spiritual. Thus too, as we have seen, Zenocrate is credited with eyes whose "angels in their crystal armours fight" (V, ii, 88) against Tamburlaine's thoughts. She too has harnessed a kind of spiritual power, and it can be used in argument on the combative level of mental life.

And when we remember that world-conquest implies for Tamburlaine remapping that world, which in its turn implies deeper understanding of the pattern of the world than others have had, the following passage takes on a fuller meaning:

> We mean to travel to th'antarctic pole,
> Conquering the people underneath our feet,
>
> (IV, iv, 133-134)

Tied as this expectation is to the marriage of Tamburlaine and Zenocrate, it embodies the way in which physical accomplishment is dependent on the spiritual insight and superior knowledge which these very accomplishments express. To ask whether the insight or the power comes first is like asking about the relative origins of chickens and eggs. They are indissoluble, the spirit giving the body life, the body giving the spirit its only outward expression. So with the magus, whose knowledge implies spiritual insight into the nature of the world, and whose worldly power implies both that knowledge and spiritual insight. Here, Tamburlaine's new-mapped world embodies knowledge, spirit, power, the unity whose most appropriate symbol will be, as we have seen, marriage.

Curious parallels, at least in idea, to *Paradise Lost* begin to show up in this unlikely source, from this point of view.[76] If we take Tamburlaine to be the good man, then his wreaking terror on the world is not unlike Christ's dramatic purification of Heaven by routing the rebellious angels (those whose wills were turned from spiritual aspiration, from God, the source of their identity). And in IV, iv, Tamburlaine shows another similarity when he says,

78

. . . let them see, divine Zenocrate,
I glory in the curses of my foes,
Having the power from the imperial heaven
To turn them all upon their proper heads.

(IV, iv, 28-31)

Here we have the grand perception that the empty egoism of
his enemies—empty because, separated from Tamburlaine
who is the measure of right in the world, these enemies have
neither knowledge, spirituality, nor power comparable to his
—is ultimately self-defeating. It will be turned against them.
One is reminded of the perception in *Paradise Lost* of the ultimate irony of Satan's predicament: that even in his most wil-
ful, rebellious moments he is not only acting as he is because
God allows him to, but also because that wilfulness and re-
belliousness will ultimately contribute to God's greater glory
and to Satan's own greater ignominy.[77] So the lady in Marlowe's play is seen to be "divine" not only as a conventional
courtly hyperbole. For only one with a spiritual orientation,
tuned in as it were to the divine wave length, can see this
profound truth. Egoism is always blindly self-defeating. And
this perception in turn is tied to Tamburlaine's magus-like
powers: his ability to use "power from the imperial Heaven,"
seat of God.[78]

There is also a further perception: about the implications of
the existence of free will. With the virgins of Damascus (V,
ii), Tamburlaine makes it clear that they made the wrong
choice and, now, their "submissions comes too late" (V, ii,
10). Tamburlaine is described in the stage directions at the
beginning of this scene as being "melancholy"; he is reluctant
to kill the virgins, but feels the righteous necessity of that
decision nonetheless. The point at issue in this situation is
analogous to the fact of moral choice in *Paradise Lost*, with
the consequence of Hell or Heaven depending on that choice.
Man after Eden is responsible; that is the unavoidable implication of the existence of free will, and also its justification.
Tamburlaine is equally stern in his postlapsarian world with
the virgins, who are the most extreme demonstration of this
idea. Their city has chosen allegiances badly, and they must
be responsible for their choice. Tamburlaine and Christ are
both agencies through which the spiritual force of the universe

is acted out in the arena of the world. Both are divine men; both are magi. It is no accident that the three magi, the wise men from the East, were able to follow their star so well. They came to honor the greatest of their own kind. Nor is it surprising that we should find in the Christian view of marriage one which makes the same assumptions about the relation of body to soul and of the one to the many which Renaissance magic makes.[79]

Thus that idea and act, will and deed are united is also not surprising in such a man. When Tamburlaine says, "This is my mind, and I will have it so" (IV, ii, 91), it literally will be. The idea is law if it comes from Tamburlaine. This indissoluble mixture of thought and act may be most clearly expressed in the following:

> So shall our swords, our lances, and our shot
> Fill all the air with fiery meteors.
> Then, when the sky shall wax as red as blood,
> It shall be said I made it red myself,
> To make me think of naught but blood and war.
>
> (IV, ii, 51-55)

Obviously, Tamburlaine is already thinking of blood and war. It is this thought which causes him to plan the swords, lances, and shot, and to visualize them as meteor-like. But the deed will fuel his thoughts which, presumably, will fuel his deeds once again, and so on. Thought therefore becomes a reflection of action, but action is also a reflection of thought. Mind and body are indissolubly intertwined in this man. He is a new form of the magus, the man whose mind so fully harmonizes with and penetrates the recesses of the universe that it is natural for that mind to express itself completely and effortlessly, like a divinity, in action.

We begin to see, then, this alternative cosmology; this alternative way of seeing the universe and making sense of it which gives dignity and power to man. It is a world in which knowledge and wisdom are reflections of spiritual insight, of virtue, and imply power. Thus one's image of the universe matters very much; thus Agrippa's concern with various contemporary theories,[80] and Bruno's emotional espousal of Copernicus' vision, though with revisions allowing for infinite worlds. Here is a universe in which we can tell by a man's face what his station should be in life, if we are properly informed. Tamburlaine foretells Theridamas' greatness:

> Art thou but captain of a thousand horse,
> That by characters graven in thy brows,
> . . . .
> Deserv'st to have the leading of a host!
>
> (I, ii, 167-168; 170)

We know from later events that this is not mere flattery in a difficult situation. Theridamas will lead a great host under Tamburlaine.

It is a universe in which the knowledgeable man knows his precise place because he makes that place, but also because he understands the pattern of the universe so that he can place himself effectively.

> Now clear the triple region of the air,
> And let the majesty of heaven behold
> Their scourge and terror tread on emperors.
> Smile stars that reigned at my nativity,
> And dim the brightness of their neighbour lamps;
> Disdain to borrow light of Cynthia,
> For I, the chiefest lamp of all the earth,
> First rising in the East with mild aspect,
> But fixèd now in the meridian line,
> Will send up fire to your turning spheres
> And cause the sun to borrow light of you.
> My sword struck fire . . .
>
> (IV, ii, 30-41)

For such a man, a man who harnesses spiritual power to knowledge so perfectly that mind and body, idea and act are unified; whose motive is perfection in his soul, his love, his world, in all; such a man is like the noblest magus and, like him, represents the noblest blending of spiritual insight with worldly activities. He is the metaphoric expression of human perfection. The key to judging him lies not in his morality, nor in his psychological consistency, nor even in his psychological interest, but rather in the growing comprehensiveness of his soul.

In order to describe such a man dramatically, Marlowe had to build on the contemporary genre of romance. The happy ending, the hero defined by his inner virtue, the neo-Platonic assumptions about the world and man, the emphasis on spiritual love, all stem from that genre as practiced, for example, by Lyly. Marlowe changes the mode, however, and makes it into something very like the heroic plays which had their vogue in the Restoration, particularly in its interest in evoking awe and wonder as audience responses to Tamburlaine, rather than the tears of sympathy which the romance (and, indeed, in its different context, the heroic play) often managed during the distress scenes in the middle acts. And to get that fully heroic effect, Marlowe had to create a more fully linear plot line than, perhaps, any other playwright in English had ever done, or has done since. Tamburlaine just keeps on conquering bigger and bigger opponents. He always wins, always with the same ease, always against a slightly more powerful enemy. By the end of Act Three there is no suspense about the exterior action of the play. Only the interior dynamism of the hero maintains interest in any phase of the action, except for the occasionally sensational scenes, as when Bajazeth dashes out his brains. The characters are few, and the action obvious, straightforward, relentless, unchanging. The plot has been tailored to fit the hero, who may never falter, may never be near defeat, and never does, or is.

It is full of the glitter of jewels, of the brilliant colors of cloth and the heavens and metals. It is a bright but essentially lifeless, inert world, depending on the hero to endow it with significance. It is obviously imaginary, not at all like our mundane earth, and it must be, for in this play the impossible must be done, the visionary beyond reached. The illusion of such a far-away world as exists more in dream or fancy than in our everyday vision is essential. Tamburlaine must transport us.

It is a huge, panoramic arena. Not only are continents fought for by two men on a bare stage, but the constant references to the gods and the heavens make it a cosmic arena as well. Indeed, it often seems that the whole universe is involved in the action. It is partly the glitter and partly the hyperbole of the imagery which achieve this effect, but from a philosophical point of view it is crucial. From the Brunonian point of view, indeed, universes *are* at stake when one considers the vastness of the human soul. Cosmology is the expression of one soul's point of view toward the universe: toward existence.

It is, then, preeminently a poetic play. It is almost as if Marlowe, wanting most of all to concentrate on his poetry, sensing that it was the crucial element of the play in creating not only the great hero, but also his philosophical significance, needed to simplify the plot so that he *could* devote himself totally to the verse. And his greatest play results. This is Marlowe's truest line of genius: a simple idea, more the product of inspiration and generalized thought than careful calculation, directly expressed in imagery that goes to the heart of the matter in bold, visionary symbols. He imagines the world's correspondences on a universal scale. It may be not only Marlowe's most characteristic and best play but, in its concentration on the power of poetry, the essence of Elizabethan playwriting; as a result of this poetic nature, *Tamburlaine*, Part One, may also be the purest statement of that view of the world and of man which received general, although sometimes vague, emphasis from every playwright of the age. The thought of men like Bruno, whether profound or not, managed at least to crystallize some of the major tendencies of the age, and to do it around a concept of magic which could also inspire other writers to crystallize their ideas of their age and of man.

A. D. Hope would go further in suggesting the importance of poetry in this first part of *Tamburlaine*. He points out that Tamburlaine's power is like the power of poetry. Both exalt one major effect, and use facts or arms or whatever weapons are necessary to achieve it. Indeed, they use these weapons ruthlessly, for the one major effect is in each case the sole controlling consideration. More, poetry is like the law of arms in that each keeps only the very best for itself. The rest is ruthlessly expunged.[81] One might observe in this regard that the weakest and least worthy of Tamburlaine's enemies, Mycetes, is the only one who is condescending to poetry, counting it but "a pretty toy" (II, ii, 54). Nevertheless, it is probably too much to say that this play is at bottom about poetry. Indeed, Tamburlaine, in his famous hymn to beauty (V, ii), indicates that poets cannot ever quite reach it, although Tamburlaine the man, merged at the end with Zenocrate, seems to. But the play is obviously by a playwright whose main technical concern is here with his poetry, and poetry, like other worthy deeds, finds its truest inspiration in the same place that Tamburlaine finds his, in the restless spiritual aspiration for beauty, for the impossible beyond. If not a statement about poetry, this play is certainly a demonstration of poetry's power.

It may also be in one way, at least, a key to the Renaissance's inheritance of medieval religious drama, just as in another way *Tamburlaine*, Part One, is the essential Elizabethan poetic play. In the medieval resurrection play, for example, which tried for verisimilitude while dramatizing a mythic subject in ritual form, there are recognizable human figures. Their mode is representational. But the form of action is pre-ordained, meant to demonstrate the religious mysteries which are already well-known in the well-known symbolic form of ritual. There is a union of real and symbolic forms, of mundane and spiritual meaning.[82] The simple linear plot of *Tamburlaine*, Part One, the recognizable characters, but the essential divinity of two of them, and the profound philosophical meaning of their existence and their acts, suggests this same fusion in a new form.[83] A simple linear plot no more dominates the mind of the auditor than does a ritualistic one, assuming the ritual is familiar. It too is finally predictable. Instead, it suggests significance and pattern, and leaves the auditor's mind free to concentrate on the depth and power of the portrayal of characters and ideas within that pattern. Marlowe is writing another religious play, under the influence of the religious and magical philosophy he shared with Bruno, in which real and symbolic forms, and mundane and spiritual meaning, are united.[84]

Indeed, it is precisely when Marlowe leaves his religious inspiration, and turns to more complex ideas and plots, that his dramatic powers seem to decline. He is reduced to inconsistency, to farce, to episodes, to plays of petty wills which lack direction.

Although it may be possible to interpret this loss of direction as an early example of seventeenth-century disillusionment, this is an extremely dangerous course to follow. To read Jacobean skepticism into Elizabethan plays is very uncertain. The earlier plays tend to make their moral intentions very clear, if they mean to have them. It is merely necessary to remember, by way of example, the only slightly earlier case of *Cambises*, in which one is beaten insistently over the head with a sledgehammer of moral lessons. Marlowe is adventurous intellectually but, I think, seldom original. He envisions a great deal and thinks less. We would expect visionary inspiration from him rather than carefully reasoned philosophy, or even morality. We should expect that he will plunge off into new intellectual waters, to see how they feel, and how deep they are. But we do not necessarily expect skepticism in such minds. That he was restless, perhaps even rebellious, is possible, even likely. But it seems to me that he was more likely credulous of new ideas than skeptical of old, and that this would have caused what rebellion was in him, what antagonism to established ways of thinking.

He has written, then, a spiritual exemplum, an adaptation of medieval religious dramatic form which is also the essential Elizabethan play. And it seems to have taken a vision similar to Bruno's, that of a magus who combines the old faith with the new eye for its practical uses in this world, to inspire him to the task. Under this inspiration, form and idea fit each other perfectly.

The inspiration was soon to fade.

CHAPTER III

TAMBURLAINE, *PART TWO:* *CRISIS AND DESCENT*

But, fortunately, it had not yet faded.

Marlowe had taken his man and woman to perfection in the physical world. Now he had, in his sequel, to show what it was like to be perfect on an imperfect planet, to explore how much further they could extend or prolong their perfection. In a way, this sequel is the ultimate challenge to Marlowe's poetic powers. After this play, he seems never to have been the same.

It is, of course, a subject which haunts all idealists, this difference between the perfection of their vision and the finite transience of that very vision which brings glimpses of eternity. For this young, restless man who was less mystic than adventurer, more trying on a vision than committing himself to it, how difficult it must have been to accept this incongruity. Of course he abandoned it at last, and then reacted against it.

But the attempt is interesting. The critical history of the play is not unlike that of *Tamburlaine*, Part One, and we need spend little space on it here. The fuller treatment of the critics' views of the earlier play indicates the specific lines of opinion. It is generally taken as a tragedy which shows the limits of man's powers; as a play which condemns the hero, at least implicitly, for trying to go beyond those limits; and therefore condemns him also for losing philosophic perspective about his place in the universe. These condemnations may be explicit or implicit, weak or strong, but are almost universally agreed upon.[1] Even A. D. Hope is forced to consider the possibility that Tambur-

laine's death contradicts the assumptions about his heroic powers which Part One, in his view, espouses.[2] Those with a
stronger taste for moralistic readings are, of course, more likely
to condemn Tamburlaine more strongly. Roy W. Battenhouse,
indeed, takes Part Two as such a condemnation of the supposed
immorality of the hero that he finds it necessary to read Part
One as merely the first half of a ten-act play; thus he avoids an
otherwise blatant incongruity between the moral views of the
two.[3]

However, one may see the play rather as a statement of a
religious paradox, that in this world perfection is mortal and in
flux. In addition, one may recall what Jan Kott has recently
reminded us, that death in tragedy sharpens our sense of absolutes, and therefore gives life its values.[4] And indeed, we see
again and again in tragedy that death has the ability to exalt
those values which the dead have lived for; *Romeo and Juliet*
and *Antony and Cleopatra* are prime examples. We may then
raise ourselves above the plane of morality again, and consider
Marlowe's higher orientation.

One of our major encouragements to do so is the degree of
continuity and similarity between Parts One and Two. The
largeness of the arena of action is similar in each Part. The
geography of the whole world, as well as the gods who govern
it, serve as the cosmic backdrop for the hero. Tamburlaine's
ambition, and even some of the events, seem almost modelled
on the first Part—the concubines' treatment is reminiscent of
the virgins' in seemingly unmerited cruelty, the pathos of
Olympia's death recalls this aspect of Zabina's, and of course
the "pampered jades of Asia" were anticipated by Bajazeth's
humiliation as stepping stool.

The hyperbole continues too, both for describing the beauty
and power of Zenocrate, and also for describing his own
prowess. At one point he compares himself to the titans:

> Thou [Jove] hast procured a greater enemy
> Than he that darted mountains at thy head,
> Shaking the burden mighty Atlas bears.

> (II, ii, 52-54)

Or again, to Phoebus, when addressing his "pampered jades":

> The horse that guide the golden eye of heaven
> And blow the morning from their nosterils,
> Making their fiery gait above the clouds,
> Are not so honoured in their governor
> As you, ye slaves, in mighty Tamburlaine.
>
> (IV, iv, 7-11)

In moments of greater significance, his passion is signified by greater boasts still:

> . . . Techelles, draw thy sword
> And wound the earth, that it may cleave in twain
> And we descend into th'infernal vaults,
> To hale the Fatal Sisters by the hair
> And throw them in the triple moat of hell,
> For taking hence my fair Zenocrate.
>
> (II, iv, 96-101)

To the Governor of Babylon, however, one gets the same boast of power:

> Should I but touch the rusty gates of hell,
> The triple headed Cerberus would howl
> And make black Jove to crouch and kneel to me.
>
> (V, i, 96-98)

Even when he is near death, he finds it possible to ask,

> What daring god torments my body thus
> And seeks to conquer mighty Tamburlaine?
> Shall sickness prove me now to be a man?
>
> (V, iii, 42-44)

This view of his power, relative to the gods, is hardly conventional, except for villains, yet in all of his battles Tamburlaine remains victorious. The forces of the universe still favor him, even at the end as, victorious, he maps out what is left for his boys to win. And his boys, mainly on their own, have beaten Callapine's army. Tamburlaine, true to his boasts, is still the hero; his charm still is good.

And of course the model for such views of the hero is still someone like Bruno. In the fifth dialogue of *The Infinite Universe and Worlds*, Bruno explains the hero's relationship to the universe and to the gods in terms which would justify haling "the Fatal Sisters by the hair." Of the enemies who, failing to perceive the knowledge and wisdom of the hero, try to attack, he says:

> the more they conceal him [ignorance] within the depth of thought, the more he will torment them. Just so the infernal Worm based on the bristling hair of the Furies, seeing that his design against thee [the hero] is frustrated, will furiously turn on the hand or the breast of his impious factor.[5]

So the man of proper mind can control his relationship with the Furies, Bruno thinks. Indeed, the relationship between informed men and the gods is in general not so clear-cut as conventional belief would have it, according to the *Hermetica*:

> Man takes on him the attributes of a god, as though he were himself a god; he is familiar with the daemon-kind, for he comes to know that he is sprung from the same source as they; and strong in the assurance of that in him which is divine, he scorns the merely human part of his own nature.[6]

Further,

> even as God is the maker of the gods of heaven, so man is the fashioner of the gods who dwell in temples and are content to have men for their neighbours. Thus man not only receives the light of divine life, but gives it also.

Again,

> just as the Father and Master made the gods of heaven eternal, that they might resemble him who made them, even so do men also fashion their gods in the likeness of their own aspect.[7]

If one were to seek a system of thought which would make a man open to the charge of what is conventionally called blasphemy, no more likely system of thought than Bruno-Hermes could be found. It is tempting, therefore, to look at still one more famous conception of Marlowe's, the famous "pampered jades of Asia" spectacle. Bruno, thinking perhaps of his recent disastrous experience at Oxford, or perhaps only partly of that plus all the other European universities which had not made him welcome, says in the *Cause, Principle and Unity* that a particular university is no worse than others which, through their doctorate, conceal "asses adorned with diadems."[8] A "jade" is a horse, but the beast of burden connotation is the same in each phrase, and the kings of Africa in metaphor are beasts, uninformed of the higher philosophical meaning of existence, whose low natures have indeed been hidden, ere now, beneath their jeweled crowns. Indeed, in *Cabala del cavallo Pegaseo*, Bruno makes the connection between horse and ass in his imagination more explicit still. The great steed Pegasus is the ideal form of earthly ass, and represents the perfect asininity into which men have fallen despite their divine potential.. Tamburlaine makes this idea clear visually, onstage, through action and spectacle, showing us the righteous point of view, and in a scene with a remarkable resemblance to the observations of Bruno.

Marlow pursues his ideas beyond the boundaries of Part One, however, while remaining consistent with Bruno. In particular, Zenocrate's death forces a new philosophical realization on Tamburlaine.

It is therefore worth noticing how the subject of death is treated. At the beginning, in the Prologue, there are no moral implications suggested, even when we are told that

> . . . death cuts off the progress of his pomp
> And murderous Fates throws all his triumphs down.
>
> (4-5)

Death just happens, the conclusion to a remarkable life. Nor is he ever, in this play, in physical danger, either in battle or war. His earthly power is undiminished. And those who profess honor, even when they are Christians, if they fight against Tamburlaine they often turn dishonorable. So Sigismond breaks his oath of alliance with Orcanes. Moral condemnations of Tamburlaine in Part Two require the application of assumptions which the play does not encourage. Indeed, even in Act One, one can already see the play working, instead, in the direction we have already indicated for *Tamburlaine*, Part One.

Even at his most barbarous, therefore, as early as Act One, Tamburlaine makes it clear that some higher vision operates within him. With his sons he emphasizes the importance of inner virtue which one has for oneself, each man a king by virtue of his own qualities, nothing else, not birth. This it is which may force the murder of Calyphas: the demonstration that one's personal virtues, not the privilege of birth, are crucial in a man's fate.

So Tamburlaine says that

> Of all the provinces I have subdued,
> Thou shalt not have a foot, unless thou bear

A mind courageous and invincible;
For he shall wear the crown of Persia
Whose head hath deepest scars, whose breast most wounds.

(I, iv, 71-75)

The scars are not signs of cruelty, but of aspiration, of spirit, of high desire. They show a disregard for the body except as an instrument of the "mind courageous and invincible."

His two brave sons' replies are calculated to show that disregard more than they are to show cruelty:

> CELEBINUS . . . if his chair were in a sea of blood,
> I would prepare a ship and sail to it,
> Ere I would lose the title of a king.
> AMYRAS And I would strive to swim through pools of blood
> Or make a bridge of murdered carcasses,
> Whose arches should be framed with bones of Turks,
> Ere I would lose the title of a king.

(I, iv, 89-95)

The blood imagery is appalling, to be sure, but that need not make us appalled at the characters. The reason these sons can envision such grisly scenes is because their souls, like their father's, are restless, pursuing the beyond at any cost, even this.

It is true that occasionally boast overcomes inspiration, as when Tamburlaine gloats that "half the world shall perish in this fight" (I, vi, 44). But this is hardly enough to erase the total commitment of his forces to the aspirations of a restless soul. What is more difficult for the modern mind, with its horror of violence, is to get beyond the surface of violence to its deeper significance. Acts One and Two show the same inspiration as Part One, but demonstrated in such extreme terms that the modern audience may at times have trouble adjusting to it.

Thus when, in Act Two, Tamburlaine cries that

> This cursed town will I consume with fire,
> Because this place bereft me of my love;
> The houses, burnt, will look as if they mourned;

(II, iv, 137-139)

we may at first think him merely vengeful. We have not had the long build-up which Part One gave to its cruelty. We must superimpose its value system on these events: Tamburlaine has lost Zenocrate, who has represented beauty to him, the

91

ultimate beyond, value beyond value. The restless soul cannot be without her, or at least cannot be without what she has signified. The physical world is merely a symbol for the mind of man. Towns can be burned because, if the spirit rules, the physical universe in this situation ought to mourn, ought to seem black, ought to be without life. For only the spirit can give life to lifeless matter. Tamburlaine's wish is appropriate. He is responding to a higher inspiration than morality or love of physical life can give.

Subsequently, this interpretation is clearly justified. The same idea occurs again and again. In III, iii, Tamburlaine makes a ceremony of drawing blood from himself, and then tests the bravery of his sons. It starts out as cruelty, badgering the sons into manhood, but finally he comes to his main idea when Celebinus offers his arm to be cut:

> It shall suffice thou dar'st abide a wound.
> My boy, thou shalt not lose a drop of blood.
>
> (III, iii, 136-137)

It is the mental attitude, the willingness, that matters. Physical things are symbols as well as realities, standing for higher realities still. And sometimes, the symbol can be bypassed, the mind's virtue seen directly, as in this case.

The scene of greatest cruelty by some lights—when this virtue is less easily seen—is of course the one in which Tamburlaine kills his own son. This is, however, merely the most personal and forceful of his demonstrations of higher spiritual inspiration. We must remember what kind of boy Calyphas is. Not only is he incapable of killing:

> . . . . . to kill a man;
> It works remorse of conscience in me.
>
> (IV, i, 27-28)

He is not above, but below, the aspirations or inspirations of other men. He says to his brother,

> Take you the honor, I will take my ease;
> My wisdom shall excuse my cowardice.
>
> (IV, i, 49-50)

He will play cards (IV, i, 59) and, later, take advantage of the fruits of other men's courage. He will play cards to see

Who shall kiss the fairest of the Turks' concubines first, when my
father hath conquered them.

(IV, i, 63-64)

He is uninspired, lazy, cowardly, willing to let others die for his
pleasure. He is the worst kind of son of a great man, and Tamburlaine must show that one must demonstrate his worth
through virtue and spirit, not mere birth. He rejects any appeal
to mercy for his son, and explains:

Here, Jove, receive his fainting soul again,
A form not meet to give that subject essence
Whose matter is the flesh of Tamburlaine,
Wherein an incorporeal spirit moves,
Made of the mould whereof thyself consists,
Which makes me valiant, proud, ambitious,
Ready to levy power against thy throne,
That I might move the turning spheres of heaven,
For earth and all this airy region
Cannot contain the state of Tamburlaine.

[HE STABS CALYPHAS.]

By Mahomet, thy mighty friend, I swear,
In sending to my issue such a soul,
Created of the massy dregs of earth,
The scum and tartar of the elements,
Wherein was neither courage, strength, or wit,
But folly, sloth, and damnèd idleness,
Thou hast procured a greater enemy
Than he that darted mountains at thy head,
Shaking the burden mighty Atlas bears.

(IV, ii, 36-54)

Tamburlaine has the same spirit as Jove himself (line 5), and
that spirit gives ideal form to his flesh. Calyphas has the same
matter, derived from his sire, as Tamburlaine, but not the inner impulse to ideal outward expression. He has a "form," an
inner soul which gives shape and identity to his physical existence, which is unworthy of the idealized physical presence of
his father.[9] The unworthiness of Calyphas is a religious matter,
in the same way that the seeming blasphemies and rebellious-
ness of Tamburlaine are—which he also justifies by saying that
his readiness "to levy power against thy throne" is a gift from
Jove himself. Tamburlaine, because he is "made of the mould
whereof thyself [Jove] consists," is in his greatness a compli-
ment to Jove, a true son of the highest deity. To worship is to
make of God's gifts the most one can. Which means aspire,
aspire! And for the unaspiring, the unworthy, for him whose

soul is not fit for heroes, and therefore whose physical abilities are similarly limited, who is not fully alive as Tamburlaine ever strives to make himself alive, death is appropriate. Indeed, let the bad one be thrown back to Jove; perhaps the next try will do better with the same material. It is an act of reverence to Jove to bury his mistake.

His next speech, indeed, pretty much makes this self-justification:

> . . . these terrors and these tyrannies—
> If tyrannies war's justice ye repute—
> I execute, enjoined me from above,
> To scourge the pride of such as heaven abhors;
> Nor am I made arch-monarch of the world,
> Crowned and invested by the hand of Jove,
> For deeds of bounty or nobility;
> But since I exercise a greater name,
> The scourge of God and terror of the world,
> I must apply myself to fit those terms,
> In war, in blood, in death, in cruelty,
> And plague such peasants as resist in me
> The power of heaven's eternal majesty.
>
> (IV, ii, 71-83)

Here is his justification, put literally into the mouth of the hero. He is doing God's work in purifying, perfecting the world—putting the inspiration of divinity into practice on earth. The sense of worldly perfectability, of the underlying unified inspiration which enlivens the earth and would have it perfect in spite of its myriad forms, the sense not only of the recalcitrance of matter but also of its perfectability—all the key ideas of the Tamburlaine plays are here in shorthand form. If we have listened up to this point, we understand well. Tamburlaine works God's will on earth through his independent use of the spiritual inspiration which God has given him. Cruelty is a necessary part of the operation. Tamburlaine is a metaphoric creation to demonstrate the divinity in man, and its potential for perfecting material existence until it is ideal. He will continue

> . . . till by vision or by speech I hear
> Immortal Jove say 'Cease, my Tamburlaine.'
>
> (IV, ii, 124-125)

Perhaps if one is pure in honor and faith, it is inevitable that one will be merciless in prosecuting his mission. In this context, it does not seem so much blasphemous as natural when he hurls out at his "pampered jades":

> The horse that guide the golden eye of heaven
> And blow the morning from their nosterils,
> Making their fiery gait above the clouds,
> Are not so honored in their governor
> As you, ye slaves, in mighty Tamburlaine.[10]

His vision of his progress involves them, too:

> If you can live with it, then live, and draw
> My chariot swifter than the racking clouds;
> If not, then die like beasts, and fit for naught
> But perches for the black and fatal ravens.
>
> (IV, iv, 7-11; 20-23)

To be greater than Phoebus' horses is no mean placement in the universal hierarchy. And if one does not aspire to greatness, and have the capacity for it, then he might as well be dead in body, as he already is in soul. This comparison of himself with Phoebus, making himself the guider of the sun, is not essentially different from his saluting the grandeur of Jove by rebelling against him. Tamburlaine's orientation to divinity is generally consistent.

Thus in precisely the same vein he justifies throwing the captured concubines to the lust of his soldiers:

> Save your honors! 'Twere but time indeed,
> Lost long before you knew what honor meant.
>
> (IV, iv, 86-87)

A bit of sarcasm for the kind of people who value honor only when it is convenient. A person is treated by Tamburlaine as his spiritual life deserves. Those without honor will have this fact made public in deed. Mercy or cruelty is not the issue; the issue is truth, as seen from the high perspective of the magus.

However, it can be wondered if such truth-demonstrating is consistent with deceit? When the Governor of Babylon offers money for the saving of his city and life, Tamburlaine is predictable:

Then, for all your valor, you would save your life?

(V, i, 119)

he mocks. Still, he takes the gold, and also goes "forward with execution" (V, i, 124). From Tamburlaine's point of view, of course, the man who fails to recognize the spiritual sovereignty of Tamburlaine, or who fails to bow before that sovereignty, is spiritually dead, and deserves therefore a physical death to demonstrate his situation perfectly. But should the hero accept the money, the bribe, and then commit the execution? Is he perfectly ruthless, perfectly self-centered, thinking of gain more than honor? Or is it that a spiritually dead man can have no honor, and thus cannot be violated by its misuse? Knows nothing of the higher kinds of truth, and so has no relation to it here? Perhaps these ideas are what Tamburlaine demonstrates in this passage. We feel in the play that a man who claims the title of honor, but ends offering a bribe for his life, cannot be further debased. Tamburlaine senses this, and piles indignity upon death.[11]

Subsequently, with this man hanging on the walls of his city while the Kings of Natolia and Jerusalem are harnessed to Tamburlaine's chariot, the visual and symbolic expression of his mastery of the world can go no further. Tamburlaine not only has a full victory, but also money, men, slaves, territory. He has both the real (the knowledge of superiority which victory gives him) and the apparent (physical) fruits of victory. Like a god, the idea in his mind is bodied forth in deed and material form; idea and act, spiritual impulse and physical reality, are one.

It is clear, then, that this progressive capturing of the world, like that of Part One, is also a spiritual quest, for in V, i, he turns to

. . . . . the Turkish Alcoran.
And all the heaps of superstitious books
Found in the temples of that Mahomet
Whom I have thought a god? They shall be burnt.

(V, i, 171-174)

Because this "god" did not show his power to translate ideas into deeds, Babylon was not saved. Therefore, Mahomet is a lesser god, if he is one at all. Tamburlaine himself is greater, and will demonstrate this fact by burning his rival's books. As the hero observes,

> In vain, I see, men worship Mahomet:
> My sword hath sent millions of Turks to hell,
> Slain all his priests, his kinsmen, and his friends,
> And yet I live untouched by Mahomet.
> There is a God, full of revenging wrath,
> From whom the thunder and the lightning breaks,
> Whose scourge I am, and Him will I obey.
>
> (V, i, 177-183)

He advises the soldiers to

> Seek out another godhead to adore—
> The God that sits in heaven, if any God,
> For He is God alone, and none but He.[12]
>
> (V, i, 198-200)

Marlowe, at this point in the play, wants us to associate Tamburlaine's course of world conquest with a search for knowledge and true religion. This pure but untutored spirit must learn by keeping his eyes open to the world and by listening attentively to his soul. Marlowe continues to ask, will such a man understand and use the universe well? His deeds therefore have a higher spiritual purpose than mere conquest, though regality is its ornament and physical expression. Tamburlaine's primary existence is of the mind. His physical perfection, in appearance and deed, are his signatures, the stamps of his higher identity. He is the divine man.

This concept of the physical expressing spiritual reality with precision has, indeed, been so well taught to his officers that, upon his weakening and approaching death, it is in these terms that Theridamas expresses himself:

> Weep, heavens, and vanish into liquid tears!
> Fall, stars that govern his nativity,
> And summon all the shining lamps of heaven
> To cast their bootless fires to the earth
> And shed their feeble influence in the air.
> Muffle your beauties with eternal clouds,
> For Hell and Darkness pitch their pitchy tents,
> And Death, with armies of Cimmerian spirits,
> Gives battle 'gainst the heart of Tamburlaine.

Now in defiance of that wonted love
Your sacred virtues poured upon his throne,
And made his state an honor to the heavens,
These cowards invisible assail his soul
And threaten conquest on our sovereign.
But if he die, your glories are disgraced,
Earth droops and says that hell in heaven is placed.

(V, iii, 1-16)

It is assumed that if the physical universe were so perfect as Tamburlaine (which it is not), it would perfectly reflect its own spiritual state—which is, at the moment, very low because of the imminence of Tamburlaine's death. It should rain and be black, weep and mourn. Further, since Tamburlaine's soul is so great, his physical death is a reflection of the lack of glory in Heaven itself, in the source of his soul and model for its perfection. It has turned out that he is less than immortal, at least in his present form. Thus, the power that made him, its most perfect physical creation, is "disgraced." Absolute perfection was impossible even for the Heavenly powers. The darkness of hell should be in Heaven, as black should be earth's color. Indeed, this sense of Tamburlaine's death implying imperfection in divinity becomes a refrain, repeated by Usumcasane:

For, if he die, thy glory is disgraced,
Earth droops and says that hell in Heaven is placed.

(V, iii, 40-41)

In this context, with the gods somewhat discredited and universal principles, centering on Tamburlaine's life, being tested, the apparently blasphemous complaint is made:

What daring god torments my body thus
And seeks to conquer mighty Tamburlaine?
Shall sickness prove me now to be a man,
That have been termed the terror of the world?

(V, iii, 42-45)

These questions *are* blasphemous and egocentric; in a normal man under normal circumstances, they would be laughable; and in a conventional tragedy, tragic, showing completely his lost perspective about human limits.

But in this play, what are human limits? Are there any? From one point of view, of course, death is a limit, and this idea will be discussed shortly. But from the point of view of the glorious moment of full physical powers which reflect perfectly a pure soul, what limits does Tamburlaine have which are not also imposed on the gods? Certainly he has been more than the normal idea of "man," as his conquests alone demonstrate.

It is, then, in a final attempt to affirm this fact that he utters his ultimate blasphemy:

> Come, let us march against the powers of heaven
> And set black streamers in the firmament
> To signify the slaughter of the gods.
> Ah, friends, what shall I do? I cannot stand.
> Come, carry me to war against the gods,
> That thus envy the health of Tamburlaine.
>
> (V, iii, 48-53)

Or again,

> Come, let us charge our spears and pierce his breast
> Whose shoulders bear the axis of the world,
> That if I perish, heaven and earth may fade.
> Theridamas, haste to the court of Jove;
> Will him to send Apollo hither straight
> To cure me, or I'll fetch him down myself.
>
> (V, iii, 58-63)

It might sound ludicrous for a man to say such things, were they in a different play. Here, all is straightforward and serious. We are not meant to laugh, and that in itself is an index of how seriously we are meant to take Tamburlaine's spiritual, as well as physical, excellence. As we have seen, if Tamburlaine falls, imperfection in the divinity may be implied. The greatest of its creations has failed, at last. Tamburlaine is not immortal. His rebellion is therefore a reflection of Jove's own greatness, and is Tamburlaine's greatest worship and righteousness. In not admitting his own imperfection, he refuses to admit to Jove's.

Because he has all the powers potential in the world, he is its absolute microcosm. His failure is also its failure. His "mind courageous and invincible"

> . . . being wroth sends lightning from his eyes,
> And in the furrows of his frowning brows
> Harbors revenge, war, death, and cruelty.
>
> (I, iv, 73; 76-78)

His very facial expressions, like Jove's in more conventional writings, body forth acts, events, values of the most extreme kind. He bears the signature of his divine identity so clearly in his face, his soul and its power show so clearly through his appearance, that he is more than an analogue for the universe; he is in every literal way "a little world." He it is who

> . . . with the thunder of his martial tools
> Makes earthquakes in the hearts of men and heaven.
>
> (II, ii, 7-8)

by the testimony of even an enemy, Orcanes. So Tamburlaine says to his "good" sons,

> . . . . . tell me if the wars
> Be not a life that may illustrate gods,
>
> (IV, ii, 3-4)

and is answered,

> AMYRAS. Shall we let go these kings again, my lord,
> To gather greater numbers 'gainst our power,
> That they may say it is not chance doth this,
> But matchless strength and magnanimity?
>
> (IV, ii, 7-10)

The battle is not valuable in itself, but rather has value as a test and demonstration of inner spirit, as a sign of virtue. In various ways, then, we see in the play that Tamburlaine and his deeds mirror the ideal of the world and universe in physical terms, even so well as to approach the power of the gods.

Indeed, his very creation is explained as being the most perfectly harmonious act of the universe, in which

> Heaven did afford a gracious aspect,
> And joined those stars that shall be opposite
> Even till the dissolution of the world.
>
> (III, v, 80-82)

Higher powers create unusual greatness, even out of shepherds, and so too may all the world be raised. In such a magical world, the vision that inner soul may express itself more and more perfectly in physical terms exists. The ultimate design in this regard may be Tamburlaine's:

> When heaven shall cease to move on both the poles,
> And when the ground, whereon my soldiers march,
> Shall rise aloft and touch the hornèd moon,
> And not before, my sweet Zenocrate.
>
> (I, iv, 12-15)

will he leave off battles.

Fighting, then, is both test and proof of his inner spirit, and also a mode of creating perfection, not only in oneself by constantly raised aspirations, but also in the universe. War is to Tamburlaine the same kind of self-consecration that, for example, the search for the Holy Grail, or the best ideals of chivalric knighthood, required. When all move with Tamburlaine, to his inspiration, the very earth itself will be raised and stabilized, become more like the Heaven. It is a holy mission whose physical means, spiritual aspirations, and hope for the most perfect possible union of soul and matter, aspiration and physical reality, are one with those of the magus.

It is not surprising, therefore, that there is a pervasive sense in the play that its universe is suffused with a spirit which is clearly reflected in outward events. The magic is not Tamburlaine's alone, but is available to be tapped by any sufficiently noble spirit. When Zenocrate first becomes ill, Tamburlaine hurls out this speech:

> Black is the beauty of the brightest day;
> The golden ball of heaven's eternal fire,
> That danced with glory on the silver waves,
> Now wants the fuel that inflamed his beams,
> And all with faintness and for foul disgrace,
> He binds his temples with a frowning cloud,
> Ready to darken earth with endless night.
> Zenocrate, that gave him light and life,
> Whose eyes shot fire from their ivory bowers,
> And tempered every soul with lively heat,
> Now by the malice of the angry skies,
> Whose jealousy admits no second mate,
> Draws in the comfort of her latest breath,
> All dazzled with the hellish mists of death.
> Now walk the angels on the walls of heaven,
> As sentinels to warn th'immortal souls
> To entertain divine Zenocrate.
>
> (II, iv, 1-17)

Even the heavens respond to the movements of her soul.

101

In such a magical universe, it is generally believed that soul is immanent in even the most dumb of nature's shapes. Thus Orcanes, in going to fight against the treacherous Sigismund, expects that his enemy's

> . . . barbarous body [will] be a prey
> To beasts and fowls, and all the winds shall breathe
> Through shady leaves of every senseless tree,
> Murmurs and hisses for his heinous sin.
>
> (II, iii, 14-17)

All of these hopes and expectations exist because of the play's belief in one all-suffusing Spirit in which the whole world participates. Orcanes, in his fury at the treachery of his supposed ally, rages:

> Open, thou shining veil of Cynthia,
> And make a passage from the empyreal heaven,
> That He that sits on high and never sleeps,
> Nor in one place is circumscriptible,
> But everywhere fills every continent
> With strange infusion of his sacred vigor,
> May, in His endless power and purity,
> Behold and venge this traitor's perjury!
>
> (II, ii, 47-54)

There are differences about the name of this source of "sacred vigor," and also about what virtues most harmonize with it, but no one in the play doubts its existence. Among conflicting claims, obviously, he who most effectively uses this vigor, Tamburlaine, must be assumed to be most harmonious with the world-soul.

Thus because Tamburlaine is in tune with this unifying spirit which, to the informed eye, creates harmony out of diverse, physical shapes, he can split up his world into parts, each harmonious with the others, each governed inwardly by his sons' reflections of their father's unifying and inspiring soul. They each

> . . . . . shall be emperors,
> And every one commander of a world.
>
> (I, iv, 7-8)

When Zenocrate dies, Tamburlaine wishes always to remember, even at the height of his victories, the inspiration and glory which her love represents, the comprehensiveness of soul which he has now gained. He will have his followers

> Over my zenith hang a blazing star,
> That may endure til heaven be dissolved,
> Fed with the fresh supply of earthly dregs,
> Threatening a dearth and famine to this land!

(III, ii, 6-9)

His physical exploits from henceforth exist to feed that spiritual, higher inspiration which the memory of Zenocrate represents.

It is this sense of the world-soul behind the flux of physical events, glimpsed most fully by Tamburlaine and therefore giving him the power to unify the parts of the world, to believe in the eternal qualities of Zenocrate even in her death, and in his own, which allows Marlowe to emphasize the idea of his divinity in the face of these physical evidences of mortality.

In other physical respects, Tamburlaine has been perfect. He has never lost a drop of blood from the power of other men. Never has he been wounded in battle. Thus he can assert the absolute power of his own will over his earthly destiny when, for the first time, he deliberately cuts himself, demonstrating his bravery, his willingness to be wounded. He then bids his sons,

> Come, boys, and with your fingers search my wound,
> And in my blood wash all your hands at once,
> While I sit smiling to behold the sight.

(III, ii, 126-128)

The three boys are invited to partake of the father's blood, a bleeding self-inflicted to force upon them his fierce demand for their virtue. They are judged by their response, and one, Calyphas, is sickened by the sight of the blood. He cannot see beyond the physical outpouring to the spiritual fact it represents. It is a scene mildly but clearly reminiscent of the Christian communion. The terms are far more barbarous, the values less meek, but the spiritual orientation, the generosity of the father, and above all the communion of giver and proper recipient are essential ingredients, and all are here. Marlowe does not, it is clear, make Tamburlaine a Christ. However, a man rep-

103

resenting divinity within humanity must inevitably resemble Jesus in some important ways. The suggestion of parallels with Christian communion in this scene are tactful enough not to force a common identity on the two, but are similar enough to endow Tamburlaine with a borrowed aura of majesty to add to that he has already achieved on his own.[13]

As magus who unites spiritual and physical existence, he is tellingly represented (in III, ii, 53 ff. and III, iii), when he sets forth his wisdom in the arts of war. This, he makes clear, is a wisdom which involves the basic principles underlying the ways of the world—of understanding geography and the land's topography, and knowing what weapons and architectural principles are most effective in a given type of topography, even including lakes and pools. One must understand the principles on which enemy buildings are built so that one can erect other constructions to destroy those of the foe. One must, in other words, understand the mind of the enemy, as well as the qualities of building materials, and have the practical ability to put this wisdom to work. One must be able to see into the inner mysteries of things, and come out with practical uses of them. Indeed, Tamburlaine so thoroughly is master of these skills that he has been able to teach them in turn to his captains who, in III, iii, demonstrate this skill in some detail.

The importance of this wisdom is suggested by the fact that John Dee, well-known magus and prominent Elizabethan intellectual, in his preface to his 1570 translation of Euclid into English, brings the principles governing geography and architecture into a unified set of ideas.[14] Therefore, Tamburlaine's long disquisition on the architectural skills called for in war may well be one of Marlowe's methods for indicating his magus-like powers, and for showing the metaphysical and mental significance of the profession of warrior. He is a type of magus whose physical exploits, to the popular mind, will seem more immediately spectacular and inspired than would the slow, arduous study required of the great architect.[15]

This union of soul and matter is even emphasized in the lament over Tamburlaine's corpse:[16]

> AMYRAS: Meet heaven and earth, and here let all things end,
> For earth hath spent the pride of all her fruit,

And heaven consumed his choicest living fire.
Let earth and heaven his timeless death deplore,
For both their worths will equal him no more.

(V, iii, 249-253)

His union of heaven and earth, however, was demonstrated not only in himself, but also in his choice of women.[17]

She first appears significantly in II, iv (in I, iv, she merely serves to give Tamburlaine occasion for his extended justification of the warrior's life). She is in bed, about to die. Before the end of this scene, her life is over. And in her death she forces Tamburlaine to recognize that even for him there are limits, that not everything he wills can occur. Her sickness and death force a more philosophical cast to the play than it seemed to have in Act One. The very cosmos must have changed its aspect, he thinks, for his Zenocrate to be near death. It affects his soul, as this cosmic change must affect all the world:

Proud fury and intolerable fit,
That dares torment the body of my love
And scourge the scourge of the immortal God!
Now are those spheres where Cupid used to sit,
Wounding the world with wonder and with love,
Sadly supplied with pale and ghastly death,
Whose darts do pierce the centre of my soul.
Her sacred beauty hath enchanted heaven.

(II, iv, 78-85)

She is part of him; the darts which wound her also "pierce the centre" of his soul. In this fact he sees a contradiction in the plan of the cosmos, the paradox that "the scourge of the immortal God" is now himself being scourged. It is a threat to himself as well as to his love, and to the universe as he has known it. Is there more to this existence than he has realized?

Tamburlaine is here confronted with an anomaly, from his point of view. Zenocrate, the earthly emblem of absolute beauty whose power can charm the soul and even the gods, will die. How can one come to terms with the death of an absolute? Can it remain an absolute if it is mortal?

At first he tries to maintain a vain hope of earthly immutability:

Though she be dead, yet let me think she lives
And feed my mind that dies for want of her.

105

> Where'er her soul be, thou [*to the body*] shalt stay with me,
> Embalmed with cassia, ambergris, and myrrh,
> Not lapped in lead, but in a sheet of gold,
> And till I die thou shalt not be interred.

(II, iv, 127-132)

He tries to keep her with him in spite of all. Still, even in this vain attempt to preserve her physical presence, he realizes that her soul has an independent existence, now somewhere else, and that it is her ability to "feed my mind" that matters most. Clearly, here, Tamburlaine shows that mental values beyond physical appearances are primary. But it is difficult for him to come to terms with the separation of body and soul, since he is used to their perfect harmony. So he will use the arts which this world knows to preserve a little longer the beauty of her outward appearance.

By III, ii, however, Tamburlaine has very clearly made the necessary mental transition. Zenocrate, and artifacts which represent her—a "mournful streamer" (line 19), a tablet to "register / . . . all her virtues and perfections" (23-24), and the "sweet picture of divine Zenocrate" (27)—are quite obviously symbols emblematic of her spiritual powers and her union of them with physical beauty. More obviously than before, he has accepted through Zenocrate's death the transience of earthly perfection. But perfection it was; it did exist. And in that fact lies proof of human divinity and power. He memorializes this fact, and believes in the continued power of her talismans, as a magus would. She comes to be a charm, to represent the principle of his own power in the world.

> And when I meet an army in the field,
> Those looks [of Zenocrate's picture] will shed such
>   influence in my camp,
> As if Bellona, goddess of the war,
> Threw naked swords and sulphur-balls of fire
> Upon the heads of all our enemies.

(III, ii, 38-42)

The spirit indeed is powerful and inspiring, even in the physical world. Indeed, her picture

> . . . . . will draw the gods from heaven,
> And cause the stars fixed in the southern arc,
> Whose lovely faces never any viewed

That have not passed the center's latitude,
As pilgrims travel to our hemisphere,
Only to gaze upon Zenocrate.

(III, ii, 28-33)

The hero himself, still charmed, will keep her within the perfect "circle of mine arms" (line 35), as if he were the greatest of the spheres, holding his star within him so that the other spheres, the other stars, must come to her as the center of universal attraction and attention. She is the supreme astral talisman and charm, the supreme emblem of the magic art, indicative of the extreme profundity of Tamburlaine's understanding. This comprehensiveness of soul was, in another way, equally underlined by Zenocrate at her death when she advised her sons:

. . . . . In death resemble me,
And in your lives your father's excellency.

(II, iv, 75-76)

When on earth, the superb union of soul and body which Tamburlaine so clearly demonstrates through battle is appropriate. The less active spiritual and mental qualities—mercy, pity, the "softer" aspects of love—need less violent physical expression to show themselves. The righteousness of Tamburlaine, the importance of the many-sided soul, the complementary nature of the Zenocrate-Tamburlaine relationship, all are suggested in these two lines. In addition, the passage serves to justify Tamburlaine's next scene, III, ii, when he begins teaching his sons about war, a process that culminates in the pitiless murder of one of them.

And by the end, Zenocrate's prior death has taught Tamburlaine to hope even as he faces his own death. His desires no longer need physical objects, but only the illumination of the soul. The spiritual expansion of Part One continues to its conclusion here. As the hearse of Zenocrate is brought to him on his own deathbed, he says:

Now, eyes, enjoy your latest benefit,
And when my soul hath virtue of your sight,
Pierce through the coffin and the sheet of gold,
And glut your longings with a heaven of joy.

(V, iii, 224-227)

107

He recognizes that his continued physical existence blocks him from seeing his love-object in reality; although he takes some pleasure from the symbols of her, he now needs this reality. His own soul has a purer thirst than before. Or, perhaps, as his body's powers wane and it becomes a less and less perfect expression of the soul's desires, it becomes more and more necessary for him to escape this body. The soul is clearly his main motivating faculty, as it has been throughout. And Zenocrate has helped cultivate and maintain this orientation. Bruno explains:

> The chief lesson love teaches him is to contemplate the shadow of the divine beauty. . . . We become enamored of the body because of a certain spirituality we see in it, a spirituality called beauty.[18]

We can see two main changes which this final attitude of Tamburlaine represents. One is the idea that in this world the body, at last, cannot perfectly reflect the soul. In the long run, a magician cannot sustain his power, and must return to the Platonic view that a particular physical reality can only be an imperfect representation of the Ideal. Consistent with this new view in the Tamburlaine plays is the second change in belief, to the thought that the constantly and necessarily rising aspirations of the soul may lead to a metamorphosis into a new kind of being on a new plane of existence, once the old is either exhausted, or no longer receptive to his spiritual power.

Tamburlaine's problem in the latter parts of the play, then, is how to continue to affirm his earthly divinity, his magic— to be worthy of metamorphosis to a higher plane of existence —in the face of all this.

The first phase of this dilemma is the recognition that there is a power of destiny which is beyond Tamburlaine's ability to alter, despite his human godliness. Things begin to go wrong, as they never did in Part One: not only does Zenocrate die, but Almeda turns traitor and allows a prisoner, Callapine, to escape; one of his sons, Calyphas, is ignoble and must be executed to preserve the purity of the family and its blood; we even feel that Callapine may have some justice on his side in wishing to avenge himself on his father's killer. The enormity of the tests of Tamburlaine's virtue is also hard for Marlowe to maintain. More and more he is difficult to outnumber. Orcanes, for example, sees that "he brings a world of people to the field," that "all Asia is in arms with Tamburlaine" and, yet again, that "all Afric is in arms with Tamburlaine" also (I, i, 67; 72; 76).

Further, he begins to recognize the disparity between this world in which he must live, and himself. When Zenocrate is about to die, he speaks of "this loathsome earth" (II, iv, 19), and she of "this base earth" (II, iv, 60). Although he is a godlike figure on earth, his world is imperfect. Now that he rules, the wars he fights are not all for new conquests. He must fight Callapine and his allies, for example, in a civil war, to put down a rebellion. It is potentially ironic that the great hero who was the most successful of earthly rebels now must defend himself against other rebels. But Marlowe does not treat the situation ironically. He takes Tamburlaine too seriously to have such a comprehensive view. The rebels fail, and that is the measure of the validity of their hyperbole, as always in these two plays. Marlowe is forced into this situation because Tamburlaine is running out of land to conquer, yet must finish out the five-act pattern. Marlowe is not, however, prepared to face the philosophical implications of this dilemma of the great rebel who has finally run out of villains and must now fight other rebels.

Or perhaps he did not face it because he did not think it necessary. The obvious inference to be drawn from this situation has something to do with the flux of the physical universe, the transience of individual power and existence, and therefore the question of whether perfection on earth is possible, as Tamburlaine alleges. Perhaps Marlowe could dismiss the ironic implications of the battles because he felt he was facing them more directly in the other aspect of Tamburlaine's problem: that he must face the fact that he personally will die, a fact he is prepared for by the earlier death of Zenocrate.

In any event, when Zenocrate has died Tamburlaine clearly sees the dual inconsistencies of his position: he is perfect, but the world he governs is not; and he is perfect, but he will die.

The final stage of this problem's solution begins at the end of V, i, when he feels himself "distempered suddenly" (V, i, 216) by an unknown cause. We are told by Theridamas that Hell and Darkness and Death "invisibly assail his soul" (V, iii, 13). This imminent death of course also implies the flux of the physical universe, and questions therefore the viability of believing in earthly perfection. Marlowe, then, raises the questions while seeking not to diminish Tamburlaine's stature as warrior, nor to diminish the power even of his name, since his sons put his foes to rout. The answer will not be that earthly perfection is impossible.

Indeed, it is not imperfection of the flesh that causes Tamburlaine to wane. The physician says,

> The humidum and calor, which some hold
> Is not a parcel of the elements,
> But of a substance more divine and pure,
> Is almost clean extinguishèd and spent.
>
> (V, iii, 86-89)

Rather, it is the "cause of life" (V, iii, 90), the spiritual principle which endows matter with life, which has run out. The spirit, not the flesh, dictates still. Tamburlaine's flesh, in which he puts such store, does not fail him. The flux and transience is not, at least in his case, caused by his material elements, but by the movements of the divine soul. The analogue to his sons' belief is clear:

> AMYRAS. Your soul gives essence to our wretched subjects,
>   Whose matter is incorporate in your flesh.
> CELEBINUS. Your pains do pierce our souls; no hope survives,
>   For by your life we entertain our lives.
>
> (V, iii, 164-167)

It is clear, shortly, that they have souls of their own. But Tamburlaine, at this moment, is still so commanding a figure that his soul seems to work on theirs—almost, it seems, as God does on his own.

Tamburlaine knows that this is only seeming, and that the thought occurs to the boys only because of their love. Theridamas counsels Amyras that

> . . . you must obey his majesty,
> Since fate commands and proud necessity.
>
> (V, iii, 204-205)

And Tamburlaine acknowledges the power of Death and the worm by referring to this

> . . . monarch of the earth,
> And eyeless monster that torments my soul.

(V, iii, 216-217)

How are we to confront this fact of the hero's death? Is it, as many scholars have thought, a moral condemnation of the hero, such as occurs to Cambises in *his* play, for example? Or is it instead a further philosophical challenge to the soul of Tamburlaine, and to us? Is it possible for Marlowe to combine a belief in transience, in Destiny, with an ideal of earthly perfection obedient to the soul?

In the *Hermetica*, Hermes says to Tat,

> Nay, my son, the rational man has not committed adultery or murder, yet he must undergo what is destined, as the adulterer and the murderer undergo it. It is impossible for a man to escape from his destined death, just as it is impossible for him to escape from his destined birth; but from wickedness a man can escape, if he has mind in him.[19]

This belief is consistent with the view that man is like a god, as enunciated again in these books: "Man takes on him the attributes of a god, as though he were himself a god."[20]

It is in the "Asclepius" that Trismegistus defines Destiny. It

> is the force by which all events are brought to pass; for all events are bound together in a never-broken chain by the bonds of necessity. Destiny then is either God himself, or else it is the force which ranks next after God; it is the power which, in conjunction with Necessity, orders all things in heaven and earth according to God's law. Thus Destiny and Necessity are inseparably linked together and cemented to each other. Destiny generates the beginnings of things; Necessity compels the results to follow. And in the train of Destiny and Necessity goes Order, that is, the interweaving of events, and their arrangement in temporal succession.[21]

There is an order to things which is created by a complex process, ultimately caused by God, by the unitary soul of the world. Tamburlaine, like all men, even the godlike, must be part of that order. And it is clear, both in Bruno and in Marlowe, that part of that order is the flux and transience of earthly existence for individual things like a particular man. The world *is* ultimately mundane, imperfect, and even for Tamburlaine contains many of the faces of earthly Nemesis. Occasionally his passion and his boasts attempt to maintain his physical stature, but ultimately he must die. Not fail, nor fall. His magic works till the end, when under his influence even his sons can find great triumph in battle. He is perfect, then is no longer alive. His Destiny simply has other plans for him now.

It is in understanding this fact that both Tamburlaine and we can see how death implies not earthly flaws, but metamorphosis.

And it is as we see Tamburlaine grow into this enlarged vision of the human soul that we see him continue in a role consistent with his status as magus. For as magus he must be able to see into the order of things and souls which God has arranged, and to work within that order to good effect.

It is near the point of death that this vision is given to characters in the play. Zenocrate explains that

> I fare, my lord, as other empresses,
> That, when this frail and transitory flesh
> Hath sucked the measure of that vital air
> That feeds the body with his dated health,
> Wane with enforced and necessary change.
>
> (II, iv, 42-46)

And again asks,

> But let me die, my love; yet let me die;
> With love and patience let your true love die.
> Your grief and fury hurts my second life.
>
> (II, iv, 66-68)

She believes in another life after this one—certainly not a Christian one—which is dictated by necessity: it is a "necessary change" in physical existence, and a change in form, but not the end of all. Death is a transition from the old identity to a new.

It is Tamburlaine who suggests more clearly that this new identity involves a closer union with the gods, and that it may in some way be formed in response to the kind of prior life one led:

112

. . . in my coach, like Saturn's royal son
Mounted his shining chariot gilt with fire,
And drawn with princely eagles through the path
Paved with bright crystal and enchased with stars,
When all the gods stand gazing at his pomp,
So will I ride through Samarcanda streets,
Until my soul, dissevered from this flesh,
Shall mount the milk-white way, and meet him there.

(IV, iv, 125-132)

Tamburlaine, who dared greatly, who strove to stretch not
only his soul, but also its tangible expressions, his words and
deeds, to the ultimate human dimensions, even to those of the
gods, expects in his next identity to have that ambition more
fully realized still.[22]

In a playful mood, one might almost be tempted to recall
Bruno's *Expulsion of the Triumphant Beast*, an allegorical
treatise in which Jove is featured as the expeller of sin and
the inculcator of virtue and understanding in the universe. He
and his significance are thus described:

> We here, then, have a Jove . . . something variable, subject to the Fate
> of Mutation. . . . it will eternally continue to incur many other worse
> and better species of life and of fortune, according to whether it has
> conducted itself better or worse in the immediately preceding condi-
> tion and lot. . . . they have been or are about to be pigs, horses, asses,
> eagles, or whatever else they indicate, unless by habit of continence,
> of study, of contemplation, and of other virtues or vices they change and
> dispose themselves otherwise. . . . [Thus the] repentance of Jove
> [since he] changed himself into these various subjects or forms in order
> to indicate the mutation of the various affects that Jove, the soul, and
> man incur, finding themselves in this fluctuating matter. That same
> Jove is made the governor and mover of heaven in order that he give
> us to understand how in every man, in each individual, are contemplated
> a world and a universe where, for governing Jove, is signified In-
> tellectual Light.[23]

The belief in the flux of physical existence, in metamorphoses
according to the merits of the previous life, in a world-soul
pervading this physical flux, the essential divinity of man
which can be expressed physically in many outward shapes—
all are here in Bruno, as indeed all but the last idea are clearly
in Marlowe.

Less playfully, then, we see clearly in this passage from
Bruno's *Expulsion* a view of the soul and of metamorphosis

113

and of the immanence of the soul in all created nature which is consistent with Marlowe's plays about Tamburlaine.[24] The passage, like the plays, presents the philosophical resolution to the problem of maintaining earthly perfection while accepting the power of Destiny and Necessity and also the inevitability of death—in general, the flux and transience of those outward forms for which the magus can claim perfection to be possible.

Indeed, the idea of imparting spirit into other physical entities is taken in still another direction by Marlowe when Tamburlaine, near the end, proclaims,

> . . . sons, this subject, not of force enough
> To hold the fiery spirit it contains,
> Must part, imparting his impressions
> By equal portions into both your breasts.
> My flesh, divided in your precious shapes,
> Shall still retain my spirit, though I die,
> And live in all your seeds immortally.
>
> (V, iii, 168-174)

It is as if Tamburlaine here is not a soul about to find a completely new identity, but is rather a god, the dispenser of spiritual identity, who will disperse a bit of himself to his sons. This may be part conventional father, hoping that his example will be followed by his family. But, given the context of the play, this attitude also clearly shows that Tamburlaine conceives the soul as transportable into other outward entities than its original recipient. There is behind all a spirit, a soul which gives life and identity to transient individuals of all kinds.

It is, indeed, a standard solution to the problem. As Muriel C. Bradbrook points out in her *Marvel*, "The whole Spenserian tradition, in which metamorphosis is the poetical answer to the decay of beauty and the triumph of time, is behind the exultation of this transformation."[25] She was not writing of Marlowe, but she makes it clear that Marlowe's adoption of metamorphosis was not unique.

In addition for us, it is interesting that this adoption is perfectly consistent with Bruno. But at last he seems to back away a bit. If the adoption of metamorphosis was both Brunoesque and conventional, it was also hesitant. Marlowe more and more strongly, as the play nears its end, leaves this physi-

cal world and places more and more emphasis on a purely
spiritual existence. The tendency is not consistently main-
tained, but it clearly exists; to the extent that it does, it turns
away from the view of the magus as the divine man, and toward the more conventional Christian view: that one must
ultimately turn for solace and strength to a sphere of existence
not in which soul and body are merged, but in which soul can
exist in its own pure essence. Worship is always important to
a magus, but it is balanced by self-confidence in the worldly
efficacy of that worship—in the sense of divinity one feels within
oneself, and the power that intuition gives over earthly things.
The balance sometimes seems gone in Part Two. It may be
for this reason that Tamburlaine's final speeches often sound
like his hyperbolic version of the conventional wishful thinking
which fathers and lovers go through when near death, hoping
their sons will carry on the old traditions, and hoping to meet
the lover in the next world. But his terms are philosophical,
as we have seen, and suggest thought as well as sentiment.
That these thoughts lead to rather conventional conclusions
may simply be the sign that Marlowe, faced with the paradox
of universal flux, and with the desire to unite soul with body on
earth in the person of magus, could no longer carry the burden.
At last he could resolve the problem only by returning to a conventional heaven *beyond* the fluctuating forms of the universe.

The expressions of rather conventional spiritual belief, without significant regard for the physical, are several:

With Zenocrate on the point of death, Tamburlaine imagines
the preparations of the Heavens for her arrival. He concludes,

> And in this sweet and curious harmony,
> The God that tunes this music to our souls
> Holds out his hand in highest majesty
> To entertain divine Zenocrate.
> Then let some holy trance convey my thoughts
> Up to the palace of th'imperial heaven,
> That this my life may be as short to me
> As are the days of sweet Zenocrate.
>
> (II, iv, 30-37)

This world is no longer of value, with Zenocrate soon to be
gone. Nor is this life. All concentration is on an existence with
God, outside of present or physical experience. Any conven-

tional Christian might say the same in such a moment. Or again, contemplating the possibility of his own death, he hopes that

> . . . Jove, esteeming me too good for earth,
> Raise me to match the fair Aldeboran,
> Above the threefold astracism of heaven,
> Before I conquer all the triple world.

(IV, iv, 60-63)

A self-righteous man of conventional stripe might very well have such thoughts. They clearly devalue this world of physical life for another of indeterminate nature. We hope for an afterlife, making the insoluble problems of this world, the unfinished tasks, unimportant and therefore at least bearable.

The wisdom which this hope allows him for this life is also conventional, on occasion. For if all value is vested in the next world of spiritual awakening, then the limits of this one are easier to see. So Tamburlaine can warn his son Amyras against overconfidence: "tempt not Fortune so" (IV, ii, 11). And well before his actual death, he clearly sees that "I shall die" (V, iii, 66). He sees his limits, the inevitable limits imposed on all men's ambitions by the very nature of this world. This is the kind of idea which conventional tragedy applauds: the blind, arrogant, ambitious man finally sees that it was those very qualities causing his success which also cause his ultimate downfall, that man must be moderate and have some humility. And the like. But it is the kind of wisdom which he would have rejected in Part One, and in his more powerful moments in Part Two. As the divine man, he had no limits, neither to his physical abilities and perfections, nor to his physical and spiritual aspirations. His acknowledgement of his limits is an indication of how he dwindles into conventionality, from time to time in this play. He does not continue as a divine human being.

The problem is well illustrated by his speech in the last scene when he acknowledges,

> But I perceive my martial strength is spent,
> In vain I strive and rail against those powers
> That mean t'invest me in a higher throne,
> As much too high for this disdainful earth.

Give me a map; then let me see how much
Is left for me to conquer all the world,
That these, my boys, may finish all my wants.

(V, iii, 119-125)

Here is the recognition of limits on earth, the ascription of "higher" value to the "throne" of the afterlife, the belief that "those powers" have sovereignty over him. None of these beliefs are inconsistent with the kind of natural magic which a Christian, or any kind of religious, magus might practice. But none of them suggests the unity of physical and spiritual realms of existence in this world, or the divinity of man, which the Renaissance magus from Agrippa and Paracelsus and Ficino and Pico, to Bruno and Campanella, felt and adopted as one of the definitive and characteristic marks of his thought.

On the other hand, there are vestiges of the magician still here, near the end. There is Tamburlaine's unwillingness to give up to these higher powers, to leave this earth even if it is "disdainful." And there is the call for the map, the emblem by now of his penetration into the ways of the world. Also the assumption that his spirit in his boys will allow them to continue his conquests. The human spirit is not dead, will not be even after he is gone. Perhaps it is not fair to accuse Marlowe, and/or Tamburlaine, of conventionalism. Perhaps in the nature of such philosophical speeches it is inevitable that at some time the emphasis will seem too spiritual to suggest the full reach of the man's beliefs.

In the same way, for example, Bruno has Teofilo say in *Cause, Principle, and Unity*:

> . . . only outer forms change and are even destroyed, since they are not things, but of things; they are not substances, but accidents and circumstances of substances.[26]

It is as if Bruno wished to argue not only that the world-soul, or the divine mind behind it, creates an Ideal which is the only reality, but also wished to argue that therefore the physical forms of this world are without value. But he does not wish to defend this point; his emphasis on the spirit behind and within matter, giving it life and form, simply lends itself to more conventional theology than Bruno would espouse if he had bothered

117

to state the full case explicitly. He does not, nor does Tamburlaine, every time.[27]

So this may explain what seems to be Tamburlaine's conventional falling back on an easy resolution of the paradox of his experience: the paradox that although perfection has been possible in this world, in physical forms, it has occurred nonetheless in a world of flux and change. Its most perfect man must die. The eternal vision is finite.

Benvenuto Cellini has observed, "Here then are the elements necessary to resolve his [Marlowe's] spiritual crisis, and here certainly is the genesis of *Tamburlaine*."[28] Whether or not it was Marlowe's spiritual crisis, or merely Tamburlaine's, is of course arguable. But the possibility that his vision occasionally slipped below the highest inspiration suggests that the author did not find it an easy problem to resolve.

There is, then, a third possibility in trying to account for these lapses into conventionality. Cellini suggests again that there exists

> . . . the contrast between the hyperbolic aspirations of the hero, which often assume a transcendental value, and the inadequacy of their realizations, which can seldom get around the fact of the material plane of existence.[29]

Possibly the artistic problem of representing the highest spiritual inspiration in physical terms exceeded Marlowe's ability as an artist. The metaphor of the great conqueror-king-lover for the ideal man at last has its limits, and cannot at every turn adequately express Marlowe's intentions.

We must look to the ending for a statement of these intentions. They may clarify our perspective on the full play, and on the character of Tamburlaine.

That he is exalted in death, rather than diminished, is clear from his last speech. Marlowe certainly does not intend us to view Tamburlaine as a sinner, suffering perhaps from false pride, who gets at last and inevitably what he deserves. The view is larger than that, more directed toward the idea that destiny, though inevitable in the nature of things, exalts rather than diminishes the great man, victim or no.

For at the end Tamburlaine is noble enough to justify a glorious new life. He is also wedded to the values of this earth he has conquered, whose vibrant life he still feels and respects. He leaves, but does not repudiate, this world; yet he values and is worthy of the next. His final speech, and the final eulogy by his son, emphasize these qualities of the hero:

> TAMB. Now, eyes, enjoy your latest benefit,
> And when my soul hath virtue of your sight,
> Pierce through the coffin and the sheet of gold,
> And glut your longings with a heaven of joy.
> So, reign, my son; scourge and control those slaves,
> Guiding thy chariot with thy father's hand.
> As precious is the charge thou undertak'st
> As that which Clymene's brain-sick son did guide,
> When wandering Phoebe's ivory cheeks were scorched,
> And all the earth, like Ætna, breathing fire;
> Be warned by him; then learn with awful eye
> To sway a throne as dangerous as his;
> For if thy body thrive not full of thoughts
> As pure and fiery as Phyteus' beams,
> The nature of these proud rebelling jades
> Will take occasion by the slenderest hair
> And draw thee piecemeal, like Hippolitus,
> Through rocks more steep and sharp than Caspian cliffs.
> The nature of thy chariot will not bear
> A guide of baser temper than myself,
> More than heaven's coach the pride of Phaëton.
> Farewell, my boys! My dearest friends, farewell!
> My body feels, my soul doth weep to see
> Your sweet desires deprived my company,
> For Tamburlaine, the scourge of God, must die.
>
> (V, iii, 224-248)

He begins with the philosophical acceptance of the stoic: in this life, and for Tamburlaine particularly right now, at his weakest moment, spiritual vision is blocked by the physical senses. This moment is one of high aspiration and expectation: in moments he will possess a "heaven of joy." Thus more than ever, now he feels the opposition of body and soul which may have been implied in some earlier speeches, seeming to emphasize a conventional view of the afterlife. Zenocrate is spiritual perfection; he must get beyond the golden hearse to the spirit which exists still, alive. She is both inspiration and goal.

These four lines, however, lead him to a consideration of the virtues needed to combine soul and body, idea and act. He

119

compares the relationship between himself and his sons to the relationship between Phoebus and Phaeton. This is a reminder that physical strength, that wisdom and a knowledge of a map of the heavens, are necessary. But also it must be a body which thrives "full of thoughts / As pure and fiery as Phyteus' beams." Purity of mind and, clearly implicit in the invocation of the great god Phoebus, purity of spirit are necessary for the body to thrive. "If thy body thrive not full of thoughts . . . ." The thoughts permeate the body, inform it, give it its perfection. Inner vision and virtue determine outer success. In this comparison, indeed, may lie the key to the pampered jades of Asia, the kings who earlier acted as Tamburlaine's horses. The boys' chariot, driven by these "jades," is potentially very dangerous indeed. Only a strong ruler can keep great kings as subjects. This metaphor was vividly enacted onstage in Act Four.

His final speech, then, is a summary of what we have often seen before in this play about the union of spirit and matter, mind and body, idea and act. He seems consistent with this high vision at the end.

His son, in his concluding eulogy, makes this attitude equally clear:

> Meet heaven and earth, and here let all things end,
> For earth hath spent the pride of all her fruit,
> And heaven consumed his choicest living fire.
> Let earth and heaven his timeless death deplore,
> For both their worths will equal him no more.
>
> (V, iii, 249-253)

The same note, the wedding of spirit and matter, of heaven and earth, is struck. Here is the magus-type, spelled out in his basic attributes, the divine man, the fire of heaven in the fruit of earth.[30] One is reminded of the advice Bruno gives himself:

> Though deeply rooted you are held by earth,
> Mount, lift your summit to the stars in strength.
> A kindred force from the height of things is calling,
> Mind, making you the bound twixt hell and heaven.
> Maintain your rights, lest, sinking to the depths,
> Assailed, you drown in Acheron's black waters.
> Rather go soaring, probing nature's lairs;
> For, at God's touch, you'll be a blaze of fire.[31]

120

This could be a description of Tamburlaine, as indeed it is intended to be of Bruno. Held hard by earth and earthly ambition, with limitless aspiration, awake to the voice of the heavens, boundary and meeting place for heaven and hell, soaring, becoming at last "a blaze of fire," as indeed he is: heaven's "choicest living fire." It is at times tempting to consider Tamburlaine as a warrior-king model of Bruno: the Renaissance intellectual firebrand raised to metaphoric heights in martial and political terms. The descriptions fit both.

To the extent that he is exemplum of anything, then, he is hardly a negative moral exemplum. Surely he is a positive one—if not of what we all should literally try to be, at least of what we all metaphorically might be if we were more capable and willing to be our truest selves, our divine identities. Johnstone Parr writes that Tamburlaine died from his astral destiny combined with a fatal flaw: passion, which was influenced by celestial bodies. The physical cause then was an excess of heat which dried up his vital fluids.[32] But we have seen that no man escapes destiny, that all men die, that the nature of this world is to be in flux physically. Therefore, that Tamburlaine is condemned by destiny and influenced by celestial bodies argues nothing against the values he espouses and enacts.

And excess passion is not vice either, in the context of this play. Here, it is no sin to listen hard to the gods.

Indeed, near the end of the play an ever-enlarging identity is suggested for Tamburlaine, even in this world he prepares to leave. When his son Amyras flirts with suicide because of his sadness at the imminent death of his father, and because he, Tamburlaine, is unable to command immortality with prayers, the father counsels:

> Let not thy love exceed thine honor, son,
> Nor bar thy mind that magnanimity
> That nobly must admit necessity.

(V, iii, 199-201)

We are reminded of the end of Part One, and the need to balance honor and love nicely. But we are reminded, too, of

121

the new problem introduced in Part Two, that of reconciling the divinity within humanity with necessity, immortality with mortality, full human power with the existence of a higher power. Marlowe is even less up to arguing this problem's solution in detail than was Bruno, but his solution is like Bruno's, in essence. One "admits," does not submit to, necessity. And that admittance is termed "magnanimity," a species of charity, as if the spirit wills necessity to govern, as if for the will in harmony with the universe there can be no conflict between the purposes, or even the methods, of the creator, or other higher powers, and those of the hero. The two wills are one. Tamburlaine is prepared for a higher destiny. In this preparation, his soul has become so comprehensive that it embraces the ultimate challenge to his identity and existence, and makes of it no longer a challenge, but his ally. His final faithfulness to Zenocrate, as he has her hearse brought to his side, merely underlines this comprehensiveness. Love, of which charity for necessity—that force which also brought Zenocrate's life to an end—is a part, is a major factor in his identity. In it, he includes all things, even acceptance of his own limitations.

Clearly we are being shown a spiritually powerful man, one to look upon with awe and admiration, not with condemnation. We are encouraged to see the large outlines of his nobility, not the narrow details of a moral code irrelevant to such a play-world.

As Jan Kott has observed, belief in death and other absolute values defines the limits and the seriousness of man and of life. Without such belief, there would be no meaning. Without it, we could play with life and non-death, love and war, as the classical writers often portrayed their gods as doing.[33] But there is an end. At last, then, unless we are absurdists, we try to find meaning in our brevity. In death, Tamburlaine assumes for us his full monumental proportions. We value him most in losing him. He pursues his vital urge beyond good and evil, to the completion of his earthly destiny. He reaches self-realization, and triumphs over that, resolving the paradox of the finite vision of infinity, of the divine man who is mortal. He is beyond tragedy, as Amaresh Datta defines it; unlike the tragic hero, he does not resist that destiny, but embraces it.[34] It is an heroic play. The great man drives ever forward, unravelling his destiny as he fulfills his identity and, by fulfilling it, finding it. The idea of the man is his acts. The two are in this man indissoluble. It is a great spiritual lesson, perhaps most clearly taught in the usually-tragic situation of his death.

When this hero seems conventional, therefore, we should remember the problems of the artist in portraying such a figure in drama. First, the thing must be done dramatically: onstage, with minimal explanations, by a human character and his actions. Thus Marlowe chooses a metaphoric persona. But the ideas are many, subtle, interrelated—a complex intellectual system. It may be argued that at times the speeches do not clearly imply this full system, and that the metaphor is not always adequate for the full range of the ideas. Perhaps. However, given the context of the play generally, and the consistency of its ending, it seems more sensible to recognize the artistic difficulties than to believe in Marlowe's intellectual failure in *Tamburlaine*, Part Two.

This may become clearer still by a further examination of the resemblance of the ideas in this play with those of Giordano Bruno. We have seen that Tamburlaine bears similarities to Bruno's concept of the great man. We have seen, too, the world's combination of spirit with matter; and that the spiritually informed man has the power to alter matter—indeed, that this power implies spiritual insight. The idea of metamorphosis we have also briefly seen.[35] As Robb puts it, "Visible things must be loved since they alone recall the vision of pure beauty, but to see that vision and try to reveal it to men [in the case of Marlowe, we might say, 'to try to maintain that vision'] is to know that matter is forever at enmity with the spirit."[36]

An attempt to solve this spiritual crisis is at the base of the Tamburlaine plays;[37] the solution is to merge the conventional with the less conventional. The wheel of fortune idea has been, in traditional tragedy, wed to conventional morality. One falls because he went too high. But Marlowe changed the formula. One cannot go too high, if one is pure in spirit. In order to accept mortality, the most obvious conclusion to the earthly wheel of fortune, he wed it instead to the idea of metamorphosis. One existence ends so that another can begin. Thus the wheel of fortune continues to be valid as a description of terrestrial fortunes, and continues to be a positive teaching image, but its lesson is optimistic in a new way which does not cancel out the glorification of earthly ambition advanced earlier in the play. As Bruno puts it in a poem taken from Ariosto,

> The more depressed is man
> And the lower he is on the wheel,
> The closer he is to ascending,
> As with it round he turns.
> A man who but yesterday
> To the world gave laws,
> Now upon the block
> Has placed his head.[38]

But, line three makes clear, the block is not the end of it, not the final comment on earthly ambition. For all men fall in this world, and the poem is partly a contemplation of that fact. Then they rise again. The "block" is not final; rather, it clears the way for a new beginning.

It is, I believe, in this context that we should remember Tamburlaine's death. Just before it, as we have seen, he has least spiritual insight. But he is confident that with death the dross of his physical senses will be cleared away, and his full spiritual vision will return—nay, perhaps improve.

To see that vision more clearly in the play, it is useful to examine Marlowe's imagery and how he develops it, and also some of the ways in which his imagery is similar to Bruno's.

The principal images are celestial, specifically of the sun and the moon. Bruno typically equates the sun with divine intelligence and vision;[39] he sees the moon as the embodiment of the physical flux which masks, but also participates in, the real and essential unity of the cosmos. "The active and actual intellect," as distinct from the inferior one, "influences every individual and is comparable to the moon which is always of the same species and whose aspect ever renews itself as it turns toward the sun, the first and universal intelligence."[40] The moon is therefore like the phoenix, constantly changing and renewing itself in its old identity, ever finding new life through the power of the sun. The moon is essentially an image of stability behind superficial change, of the spirit enduring behind matter; its overtones of rebirth are also consistent with, though not the same as, the ideas of metamorphosis already discussed.

In the play, even enemies to the hero like Orcanes seem to share this exalted view of the moon. It is the physical veil over spiritual vision, yet somehow represents the passage to that vision—almost, it sometimes seems, as if it contained that vision itself for those who can see. For Orcanes, it is the veil nearest the vision and power, which once opened will reveal all:

> Open, thou shining veil of Cynthia,
> And make a passage from the impereal heaven, . . .
>
> (II, ii, 47-48)

Such glorifications of the moon are reasonably frequent throughout the play. (See II, iii, 29-30; II, iv, 18-21; III, i, 65-67; IV, iii, 28-32; V, ii, 46-47.) Further, the virtues of Zenocrate are associated with whiteness (I, iv, 25; 35), as they were in Part One, and this too is the color associated in both plays with the moon (II, ii, 47; II, iii, 30; II, iv, 18-19).

It is interesting, in this context, to see Marlowe connecting Zenocrate in his imagination with the moon. For it is Zenocrate who first in the play changes her physical situation completely, by dying. This example of the flux of physical existence, in turn, encourages Tamburlaine to begin thinking in terms of the spirituality behind even his apparently unchanging dominion over physical worlds. He thus learns to anticipate another life, and to accept the flux of this world— most clearly in his recognition of his own mortality.

Even in Act I, when he is still confident of his mastery of the world, when he need hold no doubts, he already views the moon as a kind of ultimate place. It has high enough inspirational value to represent Zenocrate and her qualities; at the same time it is fundamentally like this world: tangible, not out of reach and intangible and of the spirit only. When

Zenocrate begs him to stop his wars and he indicates the enormity of what she asks, he may in fact be anticipating the level of perception which she comes to represent at last.

> . . . when the ground, whereon my soldiers march,
> Shall rise aloft and touch the hornèd moon,
> And not before, my sweet Zenocrate.

(I, iv, 13-15)

He will in fact cease when his Zenocrate, in her change to death, rivals the heavens' brightness—when earthly values clearly merge with celestial ones. And indeed, in Part One Zenocrate, too, was identified with the moon.[41]

But the moon is not always Zenocrate, nor she it. The value which Bruno gives the moon in philosophical terms, on the other hand, is universally ascribed to it by various characters in the play, of whatever side, from Orcanes to Tamburlaine. It is an image working in the mind of Marlowe, but perhaps unconsciously, not carefully limited to the perceptions of the hero, nor to the virtues of Zenocrate. On the other hand, since the moon is described consistently throughout, it is significant that Marlowe allows Zenocrate to be associated with it. The moon image not only indicates one similarity the author shares with Bruno in idea and image, but also gives us a clue to the character of Zenocrate as Marlowe conceived her. She represents flux, the spirit behind that flux which sometimes shines through, and the rebirth into new life which the spirit makes possible and which the flux makes necessary, since otherwise life would end.

In his *Heroic Frenzies*, Bruno uses another moon image, this one consistent with the other usage and also with Marlowe's, but making a more precise connection with the power of the sun. He gives an image of "a full moon with the motto, *Talis mihi semper et astro* [such is it always to me and to the sun]." This "means that to the star, that is, to the sun and to him the moon is always such as it is here, full and clear in the entire circumference of its circle."[42] In human terms, it means that to the informed spiritual vision of the divine man,

> by means of the constant application of my intellect, memory and will
> . . . it is always such [full] to me, and . . . is entirely present and is

never separated from me by distraction of my thought, never obscured by any deficiency of attention, for there is no thought that turns me from its light, no natural necessity that compels me to attend it less.[43]

Although to earthly eyes the moon seems to vary in its phases, in fact it is always receiving the same amount of light from the sun, and from that higher point of view its real constancy is seen. The relationship between Tamburlaine, the sun of Part One, and the moon, Zenocrate (see pp. 168-172 below), is obvious and very similar to Bruno's vision of it. The same motif is repeated in Part Two. In a dozen passages Tamburlaine makes of himself a kind of earthly god, below the ultimate divinity, but a divinity nonetheless in himself, capable in this world of whatever he will. And he does so by comparing or identifying himself with the sun. At Zenocrate's death he commands

> Appollo, Cynthia, and the ceaseless lamps
> That gently looked upon this loathsome earth
> Shine downwards now no more, . . .
>
> (II, iv, 18-20)

Later, railing at the kings of Asia ("ye cankered curs of Asia"), he complains that they

> . . . will not see the strength of Tamburlaine,
> Although it shine as brightly as the sun.
>
> (IV, ii, 57-59)

When he warns his sons of the need for strength, he compares the strength needed to that of Phoebus (V, iii, 229-240), and asserts that Phaeton was not strong enough in the skies, nor would he be with the pampered jades of Asia. The same idea is used when he screams at those same pampered jades earlier, telling them that they should be honored to serve him:

> The horse that guide the golden eye of heaven
> And blow the morning from their nosterils,
> Making their fiery gait above the clouds,
> Are not so honored in their governor
> As you, ye slaves, in mighty Tamburlaine.
>
> (IV, iv, 7-11)

His consistent view of himself is as a kind of sun (see also IV, iv, 115; and V, iii, 115-116), one who embodies the greatest earthly power and possesses the certain knowledge that he alone knows what is just, what is spiritually pure, on earth. This certainty is clear in his self-righteous statements as well as in his arrogant deeds. And this view is of course consistent with Bruno's view that the sun is an appropriate image of the pure, active intellect which sees into the secret truths of the world: sees the myriad shapes and phases of this world in flux as a whole, sees that they are only superficially imperfect, that behind all is the stability of the divine soul. Tamburlaine seems to be Bruno's, as well as Marlowe's, sun.

Marlowe, however, does not stop here. As, in Part One, Tamburlaine had to combine within himself those values which Zenocrate came to represent in order to grow into a fully comprehensive soul, so in Part Two Tamburlaine wishes to continue that union with Zenocrate. This forces him to acknowledge her inspirational value, to acknowledge the purity of her soul and of the spiritual vision which she represents,[44] to wish to rise from this life on earth to which he still clings, into his next life, with Zenocrate.

It is perhaps not surprising, then, that in Part Two Zenocrate, as well as Tamburlaine himself, is sometimes described as equal to the sun, as being a sun, and the like. She is described as she who

> Gives light to Phoebus and the fixèd stars,
> Whose absence makes the sun and moon . . . dark.
> (II, iv, 50-51)

Or again, after her death, when she is beyond the physical world, she is

> A greater lamp than that bright eye of heaven,
> From whence the stars do borrow all their light.
> (IV, iii, 88-89)

She is a greater sun than Tamburlaine's, when she is beyond this world, and he recognizes this in the inspiration he derives from her. We have, then, a moon (Zenocrate) whose changes (to death and into new life) do not eclipse the sun's (Tamburlaine's) vision of her consistent spiritual purity, and whose change translates her into another dimension of existence, into a higher and brighter sun. Marlowe uses the perspectives and essential images of Bruno, with only minor changes to fit his particular dramatic situation and its particular philosophical problems.

Marlowe uses other images to emphasize this pattern, however, which are less clearly derived from Bruno, though they are used in ways consistent with his ideas. In Marlowe's imagery, for example, are found echoes of his handling of the sun. In it, we can find Brunoesque ideas about the essential spiritual power which suffuses the universe, and also the more specifically Marlovian equation of Zenocrate with the sun and even with God.

Tamburlaine refers to the eyes of the men he considers worthy to rule like himself, as he discusses the failure of his son Calyphas. Such a man,

> . . . being wroth sends lightning from his eyes,
> And in the furrows of his frowning brows
> Harbors revenge, war, death, and cruelty.
>
> (I, iv, 76-78)

Isolated, and from the mouth of another, we might take such a statement as conventional hyperbole. But we know by now that Tamburlaine means this as nearly literal metaphor. The eye image here shows both Marlowe's concept of the eye as indicator of god-like powers akin to those he uses the sun image to express, and also as the sign of the deification of Tamburlaine. Later, just before Zenocrate's death (II, iv), he tells her of divinely inspired crystal springs

> . . . whose taste illuminates
> Refinèd eyes with an eternal sight.
>
> (II, iv, 22-23)

The eyes, properly inspired, have a power to see into the infinite. The sun in Bruno's image can see the permanence behind the apparent flux of the moon; the eye in Marlowe's play has similar power. Also Marlowe gives it, like the sun, inspirational ability. They can create passion in the observer:

> . . . my heart, thus firèd with mine eyes.
>
> (IV, ii, 18)

129

This idea, in turn, might be associated with Ficino's theory of love and the divine inspiration it requires, and also with Leonardo's theories of light as being the key to seeing into the essence of things.[45] Both are magical in their leaning and inspiration.[46] Also Campanella: perhaps an orientation which values the sun as a symbol of the ultimate power and knowledge possible in this world inevitably sees the eyes in this way. Perhaps it is a sign of a writer's magical, or semi-magical, orientation.

However, again, it is not only Tamburlaine's eyes, nor only his sons', which are referred to in this way. As in Marlowe's treatment of the sun, so with his handling of eyes: Zenocrate too is deified.[47] Her ultimate union with Tamburlaine, and present ability to inspire him, is therefore prepared by these images.

Tamburlaine himself refers to her in I, iv, as

> . . . . . the world's fair eye,
> Whose beams illuminate the lamps of Heaven,
>
> (I, iv, 1-2)

combining eye and sun images in Zenocrate, and making their conjunction as clear as can be. The fact that she is enhearsed under "a sheet of gold" (II, iv, 131) may add a color-association to her connection with the sun. And Tamburlaine's attribution to her of great power, when he asserts that by "dying, [she will] be the author of my death" (II, iv, 56), reinforces her stature in our minds.

Indeed, in this same scene she is described by Tamburlaine in her relationship to the sun:

> Zenocrate, that gave him light and life,
> Whose eyes shot fire from their ivory bowers,
> And tempered every soul with lively heat.
>
> (II, iv, 8-10)

Her stature, and the identification of sun and eyes, are very clear again.

Thus, in her pure spirit, which the eye-sun images encourage us to see, she is described in much the same way that Tamburlaine is. We are prepared for their merging in the next plane of existence, to be achieved after the play is over. The imagery encourages us to believe that such a metamorphosis will occur, and that in part Zenocrate will have inspired Tamburlaine to that high plane on which he may achieve it.

Color imagery also reinforces this general view of the characters, their meaning in relation to one another, and their place in interpreting the full play. In Part One, Zenocrate is associated with whiteness and mercy,[48] whose color still is borne out in Part Two by Tamburlaine's changing flags on successive days of a siege. The first day's white banner signifies mercy. This, and the gold with which she is associated after her death in Part Two, both light colors, combine to reflect her qualities of the sun and the moon, just as her death reflects the flux which the moon superficially represents. She is in these respects identical to Tamburlaine in his merciful side (not prominently displayed in Part Two except by his devotion to Zenocrate's memory), and in his kinship with the sun and divinity. Tamburlaine, however, is also associated with the red of blood, of his flags on the second day of a siege, and of his arrows burning like meteors; he is associated with black as well, as exemplified when he complains of his sons:

> Their hair, as white as milk, and soft as down—
> Which should be like the quills of porcupines,
> As black as jet, and hard as iron or steel—
> Betrays they are too dainty for the wars.
>
> (I, iv, 25-28)

He will later alter his opinion of two of them, but here shows his connection with that black color which also marks his flags on the third day of a siege. It may be that these three colors represent the stages of life: innocence and youth (white), blood or fiery passion and maturity (red), and finally death (black). Certainly this would be consistent with their significance in the sieges, and with traditional Christian symbolism. Also, Marlowe may have been suggesting Tamburlaine's essential kinship with Zenocrate, and foreshadowing the flux of his outward existence also.

131

Color imagery, then, reinforces the concepts expressed by imagery of the sun and moon, but it is finally these latter two images, and their parallel in Marlowe's use of the eyes (borrowed from the followers of Petrarca and modified to his own uses or, perhaps as likely, with the modification also borrowed from a specific Petrarchan follower, Giordano Bruno) which carry the essential points of the play. Through them we see the flux of outer existence, the unchanging spirit within, the magus-like hero's attempt at perfecting the outer world into correspondence with the inner idea, at last the completion of that process and the need to seek a higher plane of existence through a belief in metamorphosis. Tamburlaine, the divine sun, sees the inner perfection of the moon; is inspired by it when its outer flux and inner spirit merge, changing, metamorphosing into the higher plane, the beyond-the-sun, Zenocrate in death.

This is a change from Part One, both imagistically and, in a corresponding way, in idea and scheme of action. In Part One, there is a clearer split between Tamburlaine and Zenocrate. Zenocrate is white or pearly, Tamburlaine associated with more brilliant colors: she is Juno, moon, day; she is peace, mercy, coolness, calm. He is fiery, Jove, sun; he is cruelty, violence, the heat of action. However, several images in Part One signify the same thing in Part Two. Eyes are the agency by which one penetrates the infinite. Similarly, the sun and moon do not signify different things, although each is exclusively associated with a different character. And there is nothing in the heavens beyond the sun. For in this fiery play, the major concern is with what can happen on this earth, and on this earth we are mainly concerned with how comprehensive Tamburlaine's soul can become. Zenocrate needs to represent a whole different set of characteristics, therefore, from those with which Tamburlaine begins the play, so that he may come to absorb those characteristics by the end. And since in this earlier play the fact of the hero's death is not considered, no consideration of a higher plane of existence, or of metamorphosis as an answer to this fact, is required. Zenocrate needs to be no higher sun; nor does a meeting in another life require their imagistic unification, their each nearing common description as both sun and moon.

The characters in Part Two, then, are not described as they are in Part One. But the descriptive *terms* are the same— sun, moon, eyes, colors, etc.; and they are used in essentially the same ways, with essentially the same meanings, as in Part One. This perception lets us see, further, that these ways of using similar images in each play are like Bruno's usage; the images are often those used by Giordano Bruno, and the meanings are always consistent with the essential ideas of Bruno. It is then reasonable to believe that Marlowe's two plays are two progressive steps in his adaptation of Bruno's ideas, or at least of ideas that he develops in ways perfectly consistent with those of Bruno.

Part Two, however, represents a more complicated, more sophisticated world-view—one which Marlowe has some difficulty expressing with consistency. He sometimes falls back on conventional formulations of a vague afterlife. It almost seems at times that the author's imagination breaks down under the strain of resolving the paradox of life which is this play's great perception: that the vision of the infinite, during which a man seems to hold eternity in his mind, is itself transient. More, that the seer of such visions is mortal, though gazing at a realm without time or mortality. Further, that in spite of transience and mortality, the vision of the ideal and one's personal sense of divinity are valid. At last, having carried the paradox and its resolution as far as he can, he is forced to recognize the difference between this world and the next. In a way, Marlowe seems prophetic here. In Part One he pushed the idea of the divinity of man, his limitlessness, his absolute power, to its ultimate extreme. Here, in Part Two, trying to push it further still, he begins to show in cracks, between the lines, as it were, the limits of this world and of the Hermetic superman views which Bruno had so heroically championed throughout Europe. In trying out this enthusiasm and coming up, perhaps, a bit short, Marlowe is anticipating the verdict of his age as it matured. The broad neo-Platonic-Hermetic revival gradually died as men took to themselves its emphasis on empiricism, on practical experiment and experience, but rejected its supernaturalism. The intransigence of this world, its requirement to sensible men that first they pay attention to their experience here—in the case of Tamburlaine, to the facts of Necessity and Destiny and Death—finally forced men to recognize, as the earlier neo-Platonists had, how imperfect this physical world of ours is. The high promise of magic seemed unfulfilled. The new promise of the Age of Reason swept it aside.

Marlowe's purpose in Part Two, however, seems clearly not to be to debunk magic, but quite the reverse, to show how it can solve even this intransigence, and make it part of an optimistic theory of the cycle of universal life.

Therefore, here again, as in Part One, we have hyperbolic images, whole worlds at stake in battle, even the stars as active participants (at least in the characters' minds), characters relatively simple in their characterization—the hero and heroine idealized. There is not the feel of our own mundane reality about this play, but rather the glitter and high passion of a larger universe, another dimension of existence. And this is, of course, the point. "Reality" in our narrow modern sense is not. The soul *is* worth large worlds, and the spiritual man *does* live in another dimension; on such a dimension, our hyperboles become reality. Like Part One, it is a poetic play. It conforms to Sidney's view, in his "Apologie for Poetrie," of what its strengths should be: precisely that it is unfettered by physical requirements (as none of the sciences, nor even history, are) so that it can with absolute freedom invent ideal existences, and so teach what ought to be, perhaps what is, behind this mortal and mundane realm of physical appearances. Muriel C. Bradbrook senses that perhaps "all the power of *Tamburlaine* is only a transparent veil for a power which is not physical."[49] Perhaps, as in Part One, we have a spiritual exemplum, a teaching device, a merging of Renaissance and medieval dramatic conventions in a poetic play which, because of its greater philosophical complexity, may seem more strained, less fully successful.

But the tendency to poetic and symbolic drama, to inventive and hidden seeking for the essence of things behind the surface action, is consistently Marlovian in these two plays. It was his early and his most natural dramatic note. It was also consistent with the age. The symbols of Lyly are obvious. So is it that Shakespeare was seeking for something—one could debate endlessly what—behind his realistic action and characters. Perhaps when we unfavorably compare contemporaries like Marlowe to Shakespeare on the basis of that surface verisimilitude, or of "true" psychological types, we are misreading Shakespeare and doing an injustice to the others. What we should look for, rather, is an inventive, symbolic drama in which the principle of harmony is carefully operative, and in which this principle leads the informed audience to pursue some deeper understanding of the principles underlying this world than it had before. Thus appearances must mask, yet ultimately imply, the spirit within. Their form must deceive (perhaps be mundanely real, but that is only one possibility), yet represent the Ideal. Spenser's famous allegory does these things, but without worrying much about the realism of the masks, of the physical appearances.

Everywhere in the Renaissance, indeed, one reads of this stress on what is within. Even Bacon, who eschewed magic and mathematics, believed that with his empirical method he was searching into the inner mysteries of the universe. And Edgar Wind demonstrates this same concern in Renaissance painters like Botticelli. The double resemblance of Raphael's "School of Athens" makes the case in another obvious way, since his Greek characters are modeled after the likenesses of Raphael's own contemporaries—specifically those who might be thought to be the modern Plato, the new Aristotle, and the like. To the informed viewer, Raphael was saying that Florence is the new Athens at the flower of its civilization. We see too Michelangelo defining love as

> an idea of beauty imagined or seen within the heart of a friend who possesses strength and grace. . . .[50]

He strives in his visual representations to achieve passions which suggest the ideal behind the physical manifestation. Leonardo sees accurate painting of physical appearances to be dependent on mastering the way light suffuses an object. Accurate painting requires that the artist see into the full reality of the object.[51] Garin writes:

> The magical point of union between the science of painting and the science of nature, for both of which the mind of man 'transmutes itself into

a similitude of the divine mind'; that in this ideal—which is the same soul as that in the thinking of Leonardo—one finds the true roots of the Platonic-Ficinian philosophy.[52]

In this context it should not be surprising to read Benvenuto Cellini's view of the character Tamburlaine:

. . . probably one deals with a symbol—and any other would be unfit, considering that it is Tamburlaine who speaks—with a symbol of the greatest conquest of the spirit, the attainment of divinity, toward which the Middle Ages, from the vittorini to Bonaventura, from Bagnoregio and to Dante, inclined by means of a mystical enthusiasm, and toward which the Renaissance, from Ficino to Pico della Mirandola, from Bruno to Campanella, tended more naturalistically by means of an intellectual process.[53]

The whole Renaissance tradition of using symbolism to seek the ideal is here seen behind Marlowe, and helps to define his artistic and philosophic stance.

We may now see even more clearly than before that the world-view which allows belief in the magus-figure is also a world-view which encourages what we have come to call the essential Elizabethan dramatic form: poetic drama. This term does not refer only to the well-known unlocalized stage whose sets must be painted by the dramatist's verses. It refers to the idea as well that a play is a metaphor for the inner secrets of life, is itself a poem cast in dramatic form and delivered to its audience in a playhouse. Thus to ask interpreters to accept the use of the term "magus" is to pose in an obvious way the most crucial aesthetic problem presented by the drama of this age, and perhaps preeminently presented by Marlowe's Tamburlaine.

Part of our problem, too, is that the metaphor is never meant to be obvious to the spiritually blind. Campanella, Marlowe's longer-lived contemporary (he was four years younger), makes that clear.[54] Indeed, the Renaissance audience expected that there would be hidden meanings which it would have to guess at for itself. In fact this assumption seems to have been so widespread that, for example, the unknown author of *Willobie, His Avisa* plays on it. He pretends to try puzzling out the allegorical meaning of the narrative, and the identity of the characters in real life, in ways so absurdly simple-minded as to indicate clearly that he is commenting on contemporary writing and critical practices.[55] We have seen again and again the need for literary detectives to unearth the meaning contemporaries might have assigned to particular Elizabethan literary works.

However, in *Tamburlaine*, the references are not to specific people (unless to Bruno, in Part One), but to a more broadly-based concept of the divine man. A general orientation to the aesthetics and philosophy of the Renaissance, rather than a particular curiosity about specific people, is the cause of the search in this case and, I believe, of its solution.

The term "magus" is crucial in these basic issues. It emphasizes through its sensationalism the tie to Bruno, and to the system of values which he upheld. In addition, no other word so fully comprehends the divine nature of man in all its manifestations and implications. The play *Tamburlaine* was assertive, even argumentatively so. In the England which prepared for and then defeated the Armada, it found a receptive audience. What could a young Englishman not then believe he could do? Its acceptance asserts the importance of the magus in the thought of the age.

Marlowe's contemporary defines the breadth of this term:

> All that which is done by scientists who are imitating nature, or who are helping her with unknown arts, seems not only to the low plebians, but to the larger community of man, to be the work of magic.[56]

It comprehends that double vision which is the trademark of the Renaissance: both symbolic and, in some way, tangible and real in its expression; aware simultaneously of the human limits and the divine possibilities of man. In Leonardo's famous "Annunciation," a religious scene is dominated by a receptive Mary whose equanimity suggests that she is well aware of her great virtue. She seems to feel not humility, not the enormity of the gift and of the responsibility of becoming Christ's mother, but rather that she deserves such recognition. Or in Donatello's young "David," whose foot rests on top of Goliath's severed head. Viewed from one side, he grins as one would expect a boy to do, proud and happy. But the other side of his face is sober, as if in awe at the way God's unseen power has used his weakness to overthrow such strength.

Marlowe, in *Tamburlaine*, Part Two, tries to explain how

137

this is possible, although he seems more confident, the explanation easier, in Part One. And he does so in terms consistent with those of Bruno, the very personification for his age of this two-sided vision of man as god and animal, the magus. The basic thrust of the play is Brunonian as well: not Chapman's stoicism, though it is true that Chapman too owes a debt to Bruno.[57] But the cosmic scope of aspiration, the insistent urge to success instead of stoic resignation, the refusal to bend to the view that although virtue is of greatest value, it cannot finally triumph in this imperfect world; all this stamps the influence as like Bruno's. Marlowe did not get this inspiration from Chapman, but rather more directly. That he knew Bruno cannot be proven, though the circumstantial evidence that Marlowe knew *of* him seems overwhelming. If this conclusion is valid, then whether Marlowe admired this Italian for himself and his personal magnetism, or because he was the most available and loudest spokesman for Italian Renaissance culture and ideas, including that of man's divinity, can also not be known. But it is clear that many in this "reformed" England were ripe for Italian thought, and were therefore ready to embrace Bruno and his ideas. Marlowe is in the forefront.

However, by the end of Part Two he had carried Bruno's ideas forward as adventurously as his abilities allowed. If there are signs of the banner's faltering, the turn Marlowe then takes to more secular plays, and to more conventionally religious ones, represents the total break-up of his vision. In the plays to be considered in the next chapter, the union of heaven and earth, of divine and human, is thrown asunder in various ways. The two sides of the most powerful Renaissance vision, which in itself held potentially opposing ideas in delicate but arresting tension and balance, these two sides separate.

And if the Renaissance is to be seen as the transition between medieval and modern, then here too Marlowe is ahead of his time. He quickly exhausts the compromises of his age, and turns to the schizophrenia of the modern world, in which the true philosopher-magus no longer exists.

Shakespeare, becoming gradually more and more aware of the grand meaning of art in the theatre, culminates his career with a glorification of the magus in the character of Prospero.

Marlowe penetrates more quickly; university-trained, unmarried, traveling quickly and without excess baggage, he sees beyond the magus to the modern world-centered universe within a couple of plays. A quick study he was, and a brilliant writer. But, had he lived, it is a fair question whether he would have had the patience and tenacity and, ultimately, the profundity to explore all the nuances and implications of the stances toward life he notices. In the Tamburlaine plays, he seems rather to paint in brilliant, bold, but swift strokes, and then be ready to move on. An explorer, a pioneer, rather than a man of whom enduring and solid structures are to be expected. But in these two plays, and particularly in Part One, he found his most natural note immediately, as if by intuition.

CHAPTER IV

DOWN FROM OLYMPUS

Part One

THE SUPERMAN PLAYS:
Dido, The Jew of Malta, and *Dr. Faustus*

These three plays span Marlowe's career.[1] The earliest, *Dido*, probably written with Nashe while at Cambridge, and for a boys' company, the Chapel Royal, is perhaps least suggestive of his genius. In it, however, we can already see several important tendencies that he would develop later.

It is an heroic play in which Aeneas, like Tamburlaine in Part One, gets what he wants. The admiration for his power which the play invokes, his connection with Venus and therefore with a source of both divine power and wisdom (she tells him he is fated to return home to Troy, though only after hardship), the ennoblement of man—all are themes to be more fully developed in *Tamburlaine*, Part One. The sudden changes in the characters, too—to love, by both Aeneas and Dido, and to leave, by Aeneas—suggest the primacy of inner impulse, as if some superior power from within the characters suddenly inspired them. This is a characteristic which comes also to be associated with the ideal hero in his later development. Bussy D'Ambois and Dryden's Almanzor are obvious examples.

But there is a difference here. Marlowe has not yet fully developed his ideas of the superman, or at least is not yet taking them seriously. The hero is too obviously self-seeking to be wholly admirable. He is motivated neither by his conception of the wills of the gods, nor by an ideal conception of himself. Therefore, although the action is set in a legendary situation which suggests great scope and significance, the main characters' motives are petty and self-willed. The verse which tries to puff up the importance of the action seems, as a result, merely artificial rant.

Similarly, the heroine is not seen by the hero as an ideal; rather, in order to write a tragedy, Marlowe uses her and then discards her. She becomes, therefore, an object of pity, and this feeling also encourages our condemnation of Aeneas.

We have seen that in the Tamburlaine plays Marlowe began to look more seriously at the ideas implicit in this early experiment, and to simplify the plot pattern so that the hero is always admirable and never seriously challenged, as Aeneas is by Dido. He merged power with wisdom—and with beauty, the heroine becoming the hero's ideal rather than his pathetic toy. He created a man so lofty that his wisdom is godlike, his motives never petty but embracing the noblest conceptions of the dignity of man himself. The hyperbolic verse, in this changed framework, seems appropriate rather than artificial.

After *Tamburlaine*, Part Two and its difficult problems, he returned to a jaundiced view of the hero, but this time he had thought it out from the beginning. He was working out the implications of the view that man is a demi-god, a superman, a law unto himself needing to trust only his inner inspiration, confident that that inspiration was heaven-sent. He complicates the plot when he moves into *The Jew of Malta*. Marlowe adds the Bellamira and Ithamore sub-plot, and engineers several plot-reversals near the end which involve both the sub-plot treachery against Barabas, and the Turkish-Jew-Maltese treacheries of the final act. We are given neither leisure nor encouragement to contemplate an idea about man; rather, we are thrust into the world of the play, concentrating on each new turn of the plot and each new ambiguity or outrageousness of character.

The nature of the main character, Barabas, is consistent with this kind of play-pattern. He is at first somewhat justified in deceit, since Ferneze has treated him unfairly. But soon he becomes a monster, so openly wicked (from our vantage point) that we can no longer take him seriously. Whether we should in fact actually laugh at him, or instead be appalled, is a fair question. But at any rate here ideas are not at issue; tone is. Barabas is obviously the hero with the hero's virtues perverted. He accepts his inner impulses without question; he acts on them, however outrageously, and until the end always with success. He has the power and the assumption of self-righteousness of the legitimate hero. Further, his success is based mainly on his assessment of other men's weakness and corruptibility. Power is married to wisdom, as in the greater heroes.

There are, however, crucial differences above and beyond the fact that Barabas' motives and actions, unlike Tamburlaine's, are patently unworthy of the hero. The motifs which we found essential in the Tamburlaine plays have here been debased or lost. The sense of a union between heaven and earth, and between the wills of the gods and of the hero, is irrecoverable. The view of the world and of men generally as not only malleable, but as basically inferior in virtue and wisdom and stature to the hero, is lost. Barabas, corrupt as he is, is no more so than Bellamira or Ithamore or—despite his smooth speeches—the man who at first and last rules Malta, Ferneze. Barabas is not in this sense above his world, but very much sunk in it, made of its very texture.[2]

The concept of metamorphosis was also important in the Tamburlaine plays, particularly in Part Two. Marlowe tried to make it his vehicle for justifying human divinity in the face of morality. Here Barabas, thrown over the wall as if dead, returns to life. He disguises himself and his designs, as do others. To change shapes and appearances becomes a scheme, a mere device for playing deadly practical jokes on people. No longer given philosophic meaning, it has become trivialized into a dramatic stage convention, the equivalent of a sight-gag.

Thus, the inspiration for this play, as the prologue and many critics have noticed, is Machiavelli. The "high astounding" ideas of Bruno and Plato and Tamburlaine are gone. In this drama, the game of life is played out on a reduced field, with no heavens for inspiration; visibility is nearly zero.

It is for this reason, perhaps, that critics have had such difficulty seeing it clearly. It cannot be a conventional tragedy, for the main character is unsympathetic. Nor can it be a conventional comedy: the victor, Ferneze, is equally unsympathetic, deserving to win no more than Barabas does. One wonders if the play as a whole then becomes a parody of Elizabethan revenge tragedy. Fredson Bowers could take it seriously; there are numerous resemblances to the type.[3] Then too we could see the ending as farcical with T. S. Eliot,[4] and see that such a tone at the end would be thematically appropriate: in a cheap world with such a debased hero, what response could be more appropriate than laughter?[5]

The wild laughter which is possible at the final *coup de theatre* is, then, not completely irresponsible. Harry Levin has pointed out that because of his soliloquies and our amusement at his cleverness, we are "in collusion with Barabas,"[6] are indeed the "worldlings" to whom he speaks. But the shock of Ferneze's unjust victory stifles our laughter, forces us to think, to try to understand how such a thing can be. The context of the play is suddenly altered, and we must orient ourselves to this new context. A conventional moral framework has not been restored. Although evil in the person of Barabas has destroyed itself, there is no reason to believe in Ferneze's virtue. There is no clear pattern of justice here. In effect, Ferneze has merely revealed himself as another, perhaps more clever, version of Barabas. Between Jew and Christian there is little to choose, morally. And we auditors who, in Elizabethan times, are Christians and who have been amused by the Jew, who are we? As we end our laughter, must we not remind us of ourselves and our too easy self-righteousness?

It is almost as if Marlowe, having written one sequel to *Tamburlaine*, Part One in a serious and moral mood, decided to write another from quite another point of view. In it, he demolishes the myth of the superman by bringing the hero down to earth, into a land smoking with corruption of which he himself is a part. The plot becomes more complicated, even

143

as the intentions are devious. The language is more and more changed for the situation in which it is found; its diction becomes more and more colloquial.[7] Instead of bringing the materials of his play up to the transmuting level of "high astounding terms," Marlowe here has paid more attention to the propriety between language and form of action on the one hand, and subject and character-types on the other. He is moving toward realism. He is concentrating more in this world. He is using Machiavelli, the master of politics in this world, the man who separated politics from religion, as his guide.[8] For Marlowe, Tamburlaine and his vision are dead.

And so, a couple of years later, *Dr. Faustus*. It is not a sequel or continuation, but it is a final answer to the questions posed by the character Tamburlaine. For in this play Marlowe does not evade the problem of the relationship between the hero and the heavens. In this play, that relationship becomes the central subject of exploration.

As in *Tamburlaine*, so in *Dr. Faustus* we have an aspiring, heroic figure, a man stretching the limits of the human sphere, a man of great abilities, and in these senses noble.[9] He is often a man, too, of self-righteousness, one who can see only from his own point of view; his long opening speech makes this side of him clear. Too, like the earlier heroic plays, Marlowe connects the idea of a divine level of wisdom, of insight into the nature of things, with power (C. L. Barber has argued, for example, that power is the prime attribute of Helen).[10]

The limits of these ideas are in this play seriously discussed, within a moral and psychological framework. The pattern of the plot is simplified to a kind of objectified psychomachia,[11] in which various objective manifestations of the two sides of Faustus' moral sense are presented: bad angel, the seven deadly sins, and the like are balanced by the good angel and the old man. It is a kind of morality play, a familiar plot line, in which Faustus struggles between wilfullness and obedience to God. Mephistophilis is his alter-ego;[12] Faustus tempts himself, and does not need the devil's servant for that. But when Faustus has second thoughts, Mephistophilis is the other side of his personality. That is why he does not lie, but does not tell the whole truth either. On one level Mephistophilis behaves

144

within the devil's design, but on another, he is silent about the ultimate mysteries because Faustus himself is ignorant.

Faustus, then, is everyman on a grand scale—given the stakes he plays for, the size of his egotism, the scope of his ambition, the scale is comparable to Tamburlaine's. And he is cast in a familiar plot pattern which, despite the enormous cast of characters and variety of events, allows our minds freedom to concentrate on the implications and subtleties of the main idea and the character who represents them most centrally. The sense of recurrence which might give the pattern of action a ritual sense is not present, as it was particularly in *Tamburlaine*, Part One, but perhaps is clearly implicit in the well-known parallels of the morality play, and in the Christian audience's sense of its repetition in each of their lives. It is a recurrent part of the Christian view of the cosmos.

In concentration through plot and through characterization, then, *Dr. Faustus* is conceived very much as a sustained *Tamburlaine*-like statement. But there are obvious differences. As soon as the action is placed in a Christian frame of reference, Christian morality applies to the hero and his aspirations are immediately condemned. We are forced to see Faustus as self-seeking, therefore, without the self-righteousness which we could believe in for Tamburlaine, since for the earlier hero it is never undercut. His magic is black, not the Hermetic natural magic of Tamburlaine. And therefore, although at last in *Tamburlaine*, Part Two we are shown the physical limits of the hero by his death, it is not until *Dr. Faustus* that we see his spiritual limits as well.

The dichotomy between the scope of his aspirations and his personal limitations as a man is also emphasized in other ways. Marlowe has been praised for developing a new dramatic verse in this play, wedded to the personality and situation of the speaker. There are many short lines; the rhythms are colloquial.[13] The language does not enlarge the main character to the level of Tamburlaine, but rather emphasizes his humanity, that side of him which he holds in common with all of us.

This reduction of Faustus to would-be hero is perhaps most remarked by critics in the drama's use of illusion. The high-philosophical use of the ideas of metamorphosis and metempsychosis, of changing forms and phases of existence, here becomes unreal and merely illusory. Dr. Faustus, who at first at least knows the difference between illusion and reality (he tells the German Emperor, "These are but shadows, not substantial."—IV, ii, 54), at last himself believes in the illusions he himself creates, asking, "Sweet Helen, make me immortal with a kiss" (V, i, 101). Zenocrate could do that for Tamburlaine, perhaps; Helen, in a Christian play, is insubstantial—a shadow; she cannot do it for Faustus. Finally, this Doctor does not know reality from mere appearance, does not know his true relation to God, does not know the difference between the phantoms of his mind and the cosmos in which he lives. For him, having chosen to live by personal will in a Christian universe requiring personal obedience, the world is a hall of mirrors.[14] Everything seems substantial, but nothing is; he is lost in a labyrinth of his own making, of his own mind.

The morality play pattern of events, structured as an objective psychomachia, emphasizes this inner fact about Faustus' mind. He exists in a cosmos in which devils and angels do literally exist, and do literally present themselves in the finite universe. But the right cast of mind can sweep the devils aside and exalt the angels. They exist not only objectively and literally, but at the same time as projections—symbols, if you like—of the inner life of Faustus. In this sense, the play is both realistic and symbolic, just as Dante's *Commedia* is; this fact should remind us of the essentially medieval quality of Dr. Faustus. It should remind us at once of how richly suggestive every act is, yet how simple, almost formulaic, the essential pattern of action is. Arguments about whether Faustus was condemned at the start or only at the end, whether the play is realistic or symbolic, are irrelevant. This is a play in which the same aesthetic spirit operates as in *Tamburlaine*. It simplifies plot to emphasize the subtleties of its ideas. That is why there are so many characters and events, and why so many critics have been able to argue and analyze its essentially simple but subtly elaborated ideas so much.

However, the formula of this simple framework has changed in various ways from its form in *Tamburlaine*. The point of view is more complex: Faustus sees himself unclearly, is indecisive, but we see him and his universe from the outside, clearly. We are in the realm of what Northrop Frye would call the ironic mode. Whether this disqualifies him from being the scapegoat hero of a powerful tragedy which C. L. Barber sees,[15] and makes him instead a moral spectacle—the fullest human portrait in any morality play, in the greatest morality play in English—is too large a question for this work. It requires a definition of tragedy, before one can begin an answer, and the present work is going in another direction.

What we must see here is that in this play it is not the hero who must go beyond the normal confines of this world; rather, the world makes the demand of Christian obedience, but offers the reward of Christian salvation. Faustus fails to measure up. The equation of *Tamburlaine* has been fully reversed. Metamorphosis is no longer part of Marlowe's philosophy. Nor is magic. The hero is dead. Man is limited. The optimistic questions raised by Tamburlaine have been definitively answered, and in an orthodox way.[16] No further religious statement is necessary about man's limits, and Marlowe chose not to explore the positive aspects of Christianity.

Instead, he returns to the ground of *Tamburlaine's* bitterly comic sequel, *The Jew of Malta*. And in the realm of politics, with characters and action planted firmly in this physical world, he continued his exploration of human limitations. He never achieved a positive view again in drama. In the words of Tamburlaine's famous, but less consistent descendant, Bussy D'Ambois, man is thenceforth to Christopher Marlowe "but penetrable flesh."[17]

Part Two

POLITICS AND VILLAINY: MACHIAVELLI
Massacre at Paris and *Edward II*

Both these plays

> deal with historical personages and events; in both Marlowe deserts the
> legendary world of Faustus, Tamburlaine, and Aeneas for a world of
> political reality; in both a powerful and revolutionary noble overcomes
> a wanton king only to be deposed himself; and both contain ambitious
> queens[18]

who also, it should be noted, end badly. It is therefore reasonable to consider them together, in spite of their considerable
differences. Both reduce the frame of dramatic reference to
the political world.

Indeed, in *Massacre at Paris* there are scarcely any astral
or magical references. Thus Irving Ribner not only assumes it
to be a play about politics, but has suggested that the deaths
of the Guise and the king show the "futility of all policy."[19]
However, although the main Machiavellian characters are in
the end defeated, this suggestion is true only on one level.

The Guise is a powerful man who aspires to still greater
power. He is, to us, openly hypocritical, hiding his selfishness
behind great schemes like the protection of the Roman Catholic
faith, and the patriotic protection of country from the weak rule
of a lascivious king (ii, 34-110). He is the aspiring hero turned
Machiavel, somewhat in the manner of Barabas in *The Jew of
Malta*. The spectacle of horrors in scenes v-viii also suggests
the barbarity of *The Jew*. It is true that when the conventionally religious Protestant, Henry of Navarre, triumphs over the
Machiavellian Catholics, the play does condemn Machiavellian
political tactics far more clearly than does the *Jew*, while at the
same time praising the Anglican settlement. However, in the
broader sense, this is a Machiavellian play. Its subject is politics; its range of ideas is political. When religion comes into the
play, it is as a political fact, one of the motivating forces for
civil war in France, rather than for the inherent virtues of one

148

religion over another. Religion is not discussed on its own terms; it is merely taken for granted that sincere belief is a virtue.

Marlowe in *The Jew of Malta* showed the horror of the hero governed not by morality or even inspiration, but only by self-seeking and the skills which Machiavelli seemed to teach. *The Massacre at Paris* is far more deeply Machiavellian in its inspiration. Its frame of reference, the very terms in which it views its world, are those of the politician. If the religious man wins, his religion is not seriously considered. There are no new ideas to supplant either Hermeticism or its stalking-horse successor, Machiavellianism. Marlowe in this play is reduced to writing propaganda. His world, his frame of dramatic reference, is smaller, no longer cosmic. The events he describes are contemporary. He is fast into fact and detail, lost in its mazes much as Faustus was in his. The center of his strength as a dramatist, his strong sense of a controlling idea, is gone.

Edward II is a far better play: its characters are taken more seriously as personalities; we can feel some sympathy and antipathy for them. In this regard, Act V is superb; it evokes pity for Edward in spite of everything mean and petty about him. Indeed, it is this fifth act that makes one wonder if a longer-lived Marlowe would have developed as Shakespeare did. But this is not the point here.

What is to the point is that this play, too, separates politics from the ideal order and harmony of the world, studies it without reference to larger or higher ideas, and is a history play without any moral view of history[20]—quite unlike the plays on the same subject by Shakespeare, Marlowe's exact contemporary.

Individualizing the characters is therefore of the essence. There is no other level of attention. The speeches are perhaps in this play most carefully modulated to the personalities and situations of the individual characters.[21] Possibly as a result of this attention to natural-seeming dialogue, there is no overall pattern of images to encourage us to see a pattern of ideas in the political events and characters (the sun-king images are an exception, but conventional).[22]

Similarly, there is not one central figure who absorbs our

attention in the way that Tamburlaine, Barabas, and Faustus do. The main character, Edward II, is an artist in his aesthetic sensibility and in his ability to create illusions to deceive others.[23] He could be construed as a dim echo of the godlike Tamburlaine if we take the idea of the artist as a kind of god seriously, a man who gives his airy imaginings tangible form. This is a teasingly interesting interpretation of him, but not, unfortunately, one which the text of the play encourages.[24] Rather, in this play our attention is divided among several important and diverting characters: Edward, Gaveston, Mortimer and Isabella at the least, none of them acting as satellites for one major figure as in many of the other plays, but all demanding attention in themselves. This distributed attention, coupled with the weakness of the king, suggests a psychological emphasis in the play which is reinforced by our pity for Edward in the last act. But this psychological emphasis is not rewarded. Edward does not grow in interesting ways; he changes from sensualist to active man too late, then subsides into childish whimpering. Gaveston never changes; once we understand his nature, our interest in him is secondary. Both Mortimer and Isabella do change, and radically—or are better hypocrites in the first two acts than they are later. Her change from loving but wronged wife, and his from outraged patriot, both to ambitious self-seekers and, in Act V, to unfeeling monsters in their treatment of Edward II, could be interesting. However, Marlowe does not show us the process of their change. Instead, he simply presents them in Act IV with their new characteristics. They are either inconsistent with their earlier selves; or consistent and unchanging, yet with their full natures only gradually being brought out; or changing in some way which would be understandable if we were told what that principle of change was. Instead, since the transition is not shown, they are simply ambiguous. The psychological interest of the play is not rewarding because that theme is not carried through by the playwright.

In seeking alternatives, one can look for larger political themes, about the nature of the state and a proper ruler, which would justify or give direction to the interaction of these unsatisfactory characters. J. B. Steane observes that the strong,

Mortimer, wins, and the weak, Edward, is scorned.[25] Finally the prince, who is in a still stronger position, and with a strong will as well, casts Mortimer down. But we know the prince too little to be sure that his apparent wisdom is more than what he knows convention requires him to speak. "Might makes right" is not an uplifting theme.

There are some negative ideas, if Marlowe can be believed to have intended to imply them. Weakness even with proper hereditary right to rule fails in Edward. Strength without humanity eventually becomes outrageous, and it fails too in Mortimer. The good king, presumably, needs both strength and humanity; however, no such good king is presented to illustrate the point. No image pattern nor clear sense of morality in history encourages us to think in these terms. We are left with a kingdom which is a jungle, an uncharted place in which people leap out from positions of power to depose others. It is a series of clashes between petty individual wills.[26] The reader, now, not the character as in *Dr. Faustus*, finds himself in the labyrinth of modern consciousness, the hall of mirrors of the earth-bound mind, in which one is lost. More clearly even than in *The Massacre at Paris*, where at least Marlowe satisfied himself with a conventional ending, here we need direction.

If we can recognize the temptation to find psychological interest in the play *Edward II*, and equally recognize that this view is a dead and unsatisfying end; if we can recognize the temptation to look for some overall idea about history or the state, and find again a dead end there—in short, that there is little pattern in the play, few clear cause-and-effect relationships—then we may be ready to see Marlowe moving, consciously or not, toward a peculiarly modern reaction to the dilemma of modern consciousness.

Like the characters (and audience) of *Waiting for Godot*, we must accept the impossibility of making sense of this play's pattern or theme. We must, instead, by Act IV, give up on this hope. It was a false lead. The history plot is a thin thread of convention, like the waiting in *Godot*, on which to hang a series of individually interesting confrontations between characters. This is an absurdist point of view about the universe. But I do not believe that Marlowe is Beckett; he does not have the temperament for it. Perhaps no Elizabethan could truly accept the proposition that one cannot make sense of his cosmos. Thus instead of cynical laughter, we have Act V, a last attempt to save the play, to make us forget it has no pattern, to make it a tragedy if as history it seems somewhat tentative and weak. Marlowe and his age must cry, not laugh, at the absurdity of the cosmos.

But Marlowe has run out his string. After losing the living hope for man on earth as demi-god, he has gradually turned the flux of outward forms in metamorphosis into disguise, illusion, and finally into real but inexplicable change in character. From creating a great hero who must arise from the mundane earth, he has finally found a way to place man in harmony with that earth: not by exalting man's setting, but by diminishing his hero until he can no longer fill even a stage, and requires several major characters instead.[27] The pattern of plot and character interaction then becomes more and more confusing, the language less and less heroic. The thematic influence changes from Hermeticism to a Machiavellianism which is broadened gradually to that world-limited consciousness in which nothing is certain.

In Act V of *Edward II* Marlowe shows again his dramatic skill. He rages in the confines of his world, an idealist without a vision.

CHAPTER V

CONCLUSION—MARLOWE'S PLACE IN HIS AGE

Like most of his contemporaries, Marlowe began his dramatic career very much under the influence of Italian ideas. Rather than working his way out from under them, however, he simply changed from one inspiration—from the set of conceptions about man associated with Giordano Bruno—to another, to that way of seeing the world which is generally associated with Nicolo Machiavelli. Not so much skeptical as unoriginal, he was able to absorb the ideas of others and to be inspired by them. In *Tamburlaine*, he absorbed an idea which lent itself admirably to his talents as a writer. Marlowe unreservedly adopted the ideas represented by the magus-figure as a human ideal. Yet, when he had to cast these ideas aside, he found no similarly affirmative inspiration to follow. It is not, as Ribner would have it, that Marlowe is a skeptic about conventional religious beliefs.[1] On the contrary, he is suggestible about unusual beliefs like those of Bruno and Machiavelli, but subsequently skeptical of them as well. Yet to be skeptical of one's inspiration is perhaps to be grounded in some basic belief, or at least in common sense, about the nature of human existence in this world.

He was, then, a quick study, seeing at once the possibilities in a new strain of thought, working it out swiftly, seeing its limits, passing on to something else. This essentially mercurial nature has in part been responsible for many critics' emphasizing the poetic rather than the dramatic side of his genius and talent.[2] However, Frank B. Fieler has demonstrated how clev-

153

er a dramatist Marlowe actually was. He took a hero, Tamburlaine, who violated so many of the common Elizabethan precepts about how a man ought to act and feel and think that to make him admirable to a popular audience would seem impossible. Yet he succeeded, and did so by skillfully placing emphasis on other, heroic characteristics. His handling of this emphasis by deftly juxtaposing a scene of one tone against a contrasting one, and the like, is fully shown by Fieler.[3]

However, it is not necessary to deny his gifts as a dramatist in order to assert that Marlowe's essential inspiration and genius is poetic. In his greatest play, *Tamburlaine*, Part One, Marlowe develops his metaphor for the idea of man's semi-divinity, the great warrior-conqueror-emperor, as far as he can before ending the play. None of the usual forms of dramatic interest are given primary emphasis here: conflict between characters, within a character's mind, between man and the gods, etc. Rather, this play does what a poem normally does: it states an abstract idea about the nature of man in terms of a metaphor. Then, like Donne, for instance, Marlowe develops that metaphor until its proportions are so huge that it can go no further (*Tamburlaine*, Part Two proves this point). It is the logic of the metaphor, not of the human action or even of the human dilemma as an idea, which dictates the shape and length of the play itself. Since the action is essentially a repetitious series of victories, any one of them could satisfy ambition and clarify motive and idea. Their continuation for five acts is largely arbitrary, from any but the metaphoric point of view. Thus it is precisely when Marlowe starts to develop "dramatic" language in which the quality of speech is suited to the character and his situation that his plays become less powerful and clear.

In his greatest play, the dramatic structure is simple and repetitive in the way that a religious ritual is. Its stem, its essential framework, is straight, its direction transparently clear. If Marlowe is a poetic dramatist, then this play is a dramatized religious poem. The hero's egotism and self-righteousness are appropriate, because he *is* great and virtuous. The hyperbolic language is nearly literally accurate when it describes his massive dimensions. Although Tamburlaine has sometimes been compared with Machiavelli in his ruthless cruelty,[4] in fact he is simply blind to the affairs of this mundane earth. He is as un-Machiavellian, from this larger perspective, as is possible. He listens to a higher inspiration than that of this earth. His cruelty is merely a sign of his absoluteness in whatever he does—a sign, that is, of his semi-divinity. His conquests are merely a worldly and communicating metaphor for his inner virtue and wisdom which, within the Hermetic tradition of the magus, convert almost immediately to power.

The mundane world of other people, of course, opposes him. But as the challenges become greater and greater, Tamburlaine expands, becomes more and more inclusive without sacrificing his absoluteness in any sphere. He continually metamorphoses himself into greater and greater identities.

When the inspiration is lost, the dramatic poems become less and less powerful. When, in *Tamburlaine*, Part Two, he admits that the great man must die, Marlowe descends to conventional platitudes about the comforts of the next life. Gradually, in the succeeding series of plays, he debunks the superman idea as self-defeating, unjustifiably egotistical, irresponsible. The ideas, vaguely merged, of metamorphosis and metempsychosis, no longer offer hope for preserving man's greatness; the main characters turn to baser forms of change: disguise, illusion, and the like. At the same time the structure of the plays becomes less clear; more central characters get involved; the language is more "realistic"; the mundane world no longer is more corrupt than the "hero," if such there is. Thus some see Marlowe as mainly skeptical,[5] or indeed as showing even in the process of *Tamburlaine* the kind of egotistical, false humanism which leads finally to a death-wish in *Edward II*.[6] He ripened into "a gradual recognition of the sternest facts that govern the whole of life."[7] But this is to see the pessimism, or anyway lack of affirmation, in the later plays, and to assume that Marlowe progressed in as straight a line of development as happened internally in *Tamburlaine*, Part One by itself. If we look at this early play on its own terms, we see something quite different, and therefore see Marlowe's development quite differently, albeit ending in the same abyss.

We can see in the first *Tamburlaine*, both in its simple and linear plot development, and in its devotion to one controlling idea, the religious origins of English drama: the mystery plays, with their simple, chronological progressions. When we think of the theatre for which the play was written, we contemplate a theatre reflecting the world in literal physical terms as well as in the famous metaphor of Shakespeare's Jacques. There were two levels of acting, the heavens above with their zodiacal signs, the square stage within the round interior, the audience composed of all classes—the theatre was a microcosm of the world, like man himself. As his inner struggles are cosmic in their importance and universal in their repetition in the "real" world in every man, so the cosmic framework within which men act out their parts was always clearly physically present.[8] Like the cosmic history of the miracles, *Tamburlaine* too, engaging ultimate intellectual and religious issues in such a theatre, must seem to be engaged in telling cosmic history. Marlowe is in this play the proto-Elizabethan dramatist, the bridge between the primitive and the sophisticated.

He is also, in this play, the essential poetic dramatist in an age, we are often told, which wrote above all poetic drama.[9] The purest form of this mode of play must, as we have seen, surely be *Tamburlaine*, Part One. In it, although there is an intellectual and spiritual idea developing around the degree to which Tamburlaine's soul can expand and aspire, there is no serious attempt by Marlowe to engage our attention with the conventional kind of plot in which we observe conflicts among men. It is because of the almost supernatural aura of greatness with which the hyperbolic verse of the play enwraps the hero that these conflicts seem unimportant, their outcomes foreknown. In this respect, as well as in its overall metaphoric structure, it is the poetic qualities of the play which create its nature and its success.

In addition, this play is a mirror of its age, one might almost say the ultimate reflection of its age, in other ways. Indeed, it is so protean as to embody not only the characteristics of its age, but also to include within it the age's main lines of development. It is, perhaps, the seminal, the unavoidable, play to study for an understanding of Renaissance English drama, and perhaps of Renaissance England.

156

The parallel of Tamburlaine, the human demi-god, with the Hermetic conception of the magus, for instance, suggests the ways in which Renaissance England (and Italy) was the crossroad where the medieval and the modern met. This magus-type combines the classical scientific knowledge of the medieval scholastic with the new belief in experiment and observation, then uses the product of this combination to solve physical problems in the physical world. At the same time, it is the humanist tradition, having opened up the study of classical belles lettres and religious writing, having shown the parallels among Egyptian, Roman, Greek, Christian and Hebraic religions, which allowed the Renaissance intellectual to take a more liberal attitude toward his Christian faith. It became theoretically possible to have a direct spiritual relationship with God, and therefore to believe that one saw the world more truly than could others, who were less spiritually informed. With this humanist neo-Platonism came too the Hermetic books, carrying this high view of man's spiritual potential further, asserting the possibilities of natural magic as a form of worshipping God. Thus in a man like Tamburlaine, and in the conception of man which lies behind him, is the full complexity of the age, and the many strands of belief and learning which will finally coalesce into the Age of Enlightenment, the modern age. The magus, as Frances Yates has suggested, is the bridge between the old and the new.[10]

This centrality of the magical tradition—Hermeticism—has important implications for Renaissance aesthetics. In general, it comes at a time in the development of the arts which is ripe for it. And it may help to account not only for the so-called "poetic drama" mentioned above, but for the nature of poetry and the other arts of the time as well. Indeed, we may see from this viewpoint that poetic drama in England is only one manifestation of a much broader aesthetic movement. And when we remind ourselves further that the aesthetic of an age—the way people look at a work of art of any kind in any given time-period—is a reflection of how they look at their surroundings generally, then it becomes clear that poetic drama is simply one manifestation of the intellectual orientation of the Renaissance as a whole.

Johan Huizinga describes *The Waning of the Middle Ages* and the rise of the Renaissance in the following terms:

> . . . medieval thought frequently yielded to the inclination to pass from pure idealism to a sort of magic idealism, in which the abstract tends to become concrete.[11]

A symbolic art is then developed; at a later stage still, the symbols become more and more lifelike, and more and more details are added to them, as an embellishment of the symbol.

> Now this scrupulous realism, this aspiration to render exactly all natural details, is the characteristic feature of the spirit of the expiring Middle Ages. It is . . . a sign of decline and not of rejuvenation. The triumph of the Renaissance was to consist in replacing this meticulous realism by breadth and simplicity.[12]

One thinks of many of the works of Dürer and Brueghel and especially the Van Eycks as examples of such realism, such dispersion of the central inspiration into a large number of details.

By contrast, one can see in Raphael's "School of Athens" a large group of men, but all arranged carefully in accord with their place in the development and classification of schools of philosophy, as the artist interpreted them. The design is dominated in an obvious way by a controlling idea. Further, the artist makes a comment on his own contemporary world, as well as on Athens and human thought generally, by drawing Socrates, Aristotle, Plato, and others in the likenesses of Renaissance counterparts—Ficino, Pico, Leonardo, etc. The design and its detailed working out are complicated, but the artist never lets us lose sight of his central idea, and all details converge on it. More simply, behind the equestrian mural of Sir John Hawkwood in Santa Maria del Fiore, Florence, lies Paolo Uccello's ideal geometry as the basis for all shapes, ideas, and forms in this world. Whether the surface texture is simple or complex, the inspiration behind the work of Renaissance art is always a unifying agent. The unity of the work lies in this inspiration. There is coherence on the surface; it is interesting in itself, but it is also meant to lead us to the inner intellectual life of the work.

There is a kind of transparency to great Renaissance art of

all kinds. The details are intended as guides to their inner source; they are intended to reveal what is within, as well as to stand as themselves. T. S. Eliot has observed of Ben Jonson that one of his chief skills was his ability to do without a plot.[13] This observation is precisely to the point. It is the unity of the world of characters, at least in his best comedies, which gives us our most satisfying pleasure.[14] To argue, therefore, about the plays of another Jacobean, John Webster, that his characters and even his plots are sometimes inconsistent, is to speak of irrelevancies. There is a poetic unity of design in a play like *The Duchess of Malfi* which has nothing to do either with realism, or with our normal ideas of cause and effect in this world. When the implausible and—some feel—unnecessarily sensational masque of the madmen assaults the Duchess in Act Four,[15] we must understand that this act is metaphoric. The surrounding world is morally corrupt. The madmen express the madness of the surrounding world which intrudes on the Duchess' inner chamber. Her brother wishes her to fall to corruption before she dies; he wishes to degrade her. But she remains sane (moral): she is "Duchess of Malfi still!" Instead, the corrupt brother goes mad, nailing the point home. Madness is a pervasive metaphor in the play which causes us to see the relationship between sanity and morality, between insanity and corruption. This central perception in the play causes us to feel, even in the depths of such a pessimistic drama, that it is after all God's world, that the moralists were right, that virtue does give its own reward—internal equilibrium.

Somewhat later, in the 1630's, John Ford was to develop this aesthetic idea to its logical extreme. In his final play, *The Lady's Trial*, he casts both language and form of action in the image of a proceeding at law, though in essence his subject is the jealousy-trust theme of *Othello*. In this play, drama has moved from using a controlling idea to govern the nature of the dramatic metaphor, as in *The Duchess of Malfi*, to using a metaphor more for its own sake, as inspiration as well as unifying principle. This is as far as poetic drama can go. Beyond this point it is merely playing with words. Thus even in Ford's title, the word "Trial" has three meanings: there is a literal testing of the wife's guilt; there is the form of this testing, which is like

159

a trial; and there is the form of the whole play, as well as the nature of its vocabulary and imagery, which suggests in fuller dimension a proceeding at law. The title refers, then, to the nature of the main conflict, to the form which the action of that conflict takes, and also to the structural principle of the whole play. A somewhat similar case is *The Changeling*; as Karl Holzknecht has pointed out, its title has indeed not three, but four meanings, each corresponding to a different level or kind of action. This word-play too controls the nature of the action, and gives the clue for what unity the play as a whole possesses.[16]

This metaphoric elaboration may very well be Renaissance English drama's equivalent to the medieval development in art toward the proliferation of details which Huizinga described above. Here, in *The Lady's Trial* and in *The Changeling*, however, the profusion has become metaphoric rather than realistic. It is the earlier, simpler metaphoric plays which have more dramatic concentration: the relationship between action and meaning is clearer and more direct; their aesthetic equilibrium and their unifying inspiration are more coherently expressed. At the beginning, helping to prepare this period of supreme metaphoric drama, there is *Tamburlaine*, Part One.

The time was ripe with Marlowe's youth. The theatre was conceived physically as a microcosm, a place in which man could play his cosmic drama. Aesthetically, the tendency was toward simplicity of inspiration, to metaphoric expression of that inspiration. Philosophically, humanism, scholasticism, and Hermeticism had merged in the new thought of the new age. This Hermetic sense of the immanence of the spirit in all things, of the ability of the demi-god man to perceive this inner quality and to see all the world as God's metaphor for his own divine Mind; simultaneously, the recognition that we must live within this metaphor, that its details are important to us; these two tendencies, Hermetic in their conjunction, give the artists of the age an ability to image the material world flexibly, to distort, to manipulate, in accord with an inner idea which governs their works of art. In the same way, the Hermetic philosopher believed that by seeing beyond the metaphor of the world to the eternal Mind and its laws, he could change that metaphor, alter the physical conditions under which men actually lived. Creation was a divine poem, continuously under revision. The magus could participate in that revision. Tamburlaine, with his "pen," reorganized, remapped, and renamed the world.

Marlowe, then, created in *Tamburlaine* the great and simple image of the Elizabethan age's optimistic beliefs. In his short career, however, he also anticipated the change the age would take. Having most fully and positively stated the extreme Hermetic position about man's semi-divinity, he next had to ask what limits there were to this position. One of the first to see the internal labyrinths of the human mind when deprived of outside perspective, he was also one of the first to be lost in them. He is reminiscent of Giovanni Pico della Mirandola who, a century before *Tamburlaine*, in 1486, had said:

> Man is the most fortunate of creatures and consequently worthy of all admiration

because his rank in the Chain of Being is "to be envied not only by brutes but even by the stars and by minds beyond this world."[17] At twenty-four Pico, in this frame of mind, had challenged all the scholars of Rome to debate. Marlowe at twenty-three asserts man's grandeur with similar audacity. They are both *enfants terribles*. Even the ages in which each lived could think their respective cities, London and Florence, to be the new Athens. The flame of the Renaissance and its inspiration had been sent across the sea. Yet, within eight years of his famous "Oration on the Dignity of Man," Pico wrote his *Argumentum Versus Astrologium*, renouncing much of this view. And Marlowe, in the five or six years left him, wrote plays which also sharply questioned his earlier optimism.

However, before the inevitable cycle turned, at precisely the right moment, Marlowe made *Tamburlaine*, Part One the trumpet call of the first half of the English Renaissance. The reverberations of its note reached into every field of endeavor, and at the same time heralded the approach of what was to come. Pico's spirit was reborn in a northern clime.

APPENDIX A

FURTHER SPECULATIONS ABOUT THE MARLOWE-BRUNO RELATIONSHIP: TAMBURLAINE, PART ONE

We saw in Chapter II that *Tamburlaine,* Part One can be interpreted in ways consistent with Bruno's ideas. It is interesting in addition to notice the similarity in tone and image between the two; it is as if they were, for a few months, men of similar temper and imagination, even as they held similar ideas—almost as if in that age it was the temperament which made such ideas possible.

There is, for example, a group of images used by both writers which are broadly associated with idealized or Petrarchan love conventions. This similar orientation is suggested by the very nature of two of their books: Bruno's *Heroic Frenzies* combines love sonnets and their verbal images into emblems which represent ideas about heroic love and about the nature of the hero; Marlowe's play, as we have seen, is also about a hero and his idealized love for the ideal woman who is his human complement.

Like these common themes, their similar images themselves are common enough for Marlowe to have found in many places. It is not only their presence, but the nature of their use, which reveals a parallel temperament and imagination in the two writers.

One is the image of fire. Muriel Bradbrook suggests that Marlowe borrowed the idea of fire as central to existence from Heraclitus.[1] It "is not change, but changing, and the changing is Fire. For fire never rests and it is the element of animation which engenders all and consumes all."[2] We have already seen that Bruno believes physical existence to be in flux, and that Marlowe portrays life through the hero of *Tamburlaine*, Part One as a process of becoming, at least in the awakened soul.[3] We have likewise seen that both writers believe in a force of permanence behind the flux, to which the soul of man is allied. Muriel C. Bradbrook, although not agreeing about the basic philosophical similarity, observes that Marlowe did take the image of fire for his use "as a poetic symbol," and was "very ready to take [his] own 'raptures' as inspired."[4]

Bruno too uses fire images frequently. He refers in general to the "divine spark" which can inspire men, and to "burning desires" when referring to love.[5] Indeed, of the twenty-eight major emblems in the *Heroic Frenzies*, twelve involve fire, and two others smoke or sparks. In more specific terms there is, first, the Petrarchan image of the burning arrow, with the motto, "Where does the new wound strike?" Bruno explains that "when all the affections are completely converted to God, that is, to the idea of ideas, by the light of intelligible things, the mind is exalted to the suprasensual unity, and is all love, all one, and it no longer feels itself solicited and distracted by diverse objects, but becomes one sole wound. . . . To the perfect, if it is perfect, there is nothing that one can add." Thus it is useless "*to try to kill one who is dead*, that is, one who is deprived of life and insensible to other objects, so that he can no longer be *stung* or *pierced* by them." Such a man is "cut off from the multitude."[6]

The similar implication of an absolute beyond the ability of the uninformed to fathom is paralleled by Tamburlaine:

> So shall our swords, our lances, and our shot
> Fill all the air with fiery meteors.
> Then, when the sky shall wax as red as blood,
> It shall be said I made it red myself,
> To make me think of naught but blood and war.
>
> (IV, ii, 51-55)

Swords, lances, and shot are not arrows, but they will flame, and fill the air, and forcibly represent a power which will seem supernatural, beyond the enemies' grasping. And the emblem's motto refers to a "wound," as Tamburlaine has his fiery missiles turn his mind toward blood. Image and idea in both writers are working in similar veins.

A like parallel with Marlowe exists in Bruno's second image, which is not so clearly derived from a common source. The four colors of the sun's rays fall to earth; the motto is "always and everywhere the same."[7] This image and idea are quite similar to Tamburlaine's triple colors, the white, red, and black banners which are progressively shown to enemies. As we have seen, the different colors reflect the degree of hardness of soul which the enemy has displayed to Tamburlaine, the judge of spiritual awareness. The three colors then show different facets of Tamburlaine's character which exist in potential simultaneously together. Given the right stimulus, he can be either merciful or bloody or wholly destructive at any given moment, depending on what his foe deserves, and without canceling out his potential for the other qualities, should one deserving a second or a third response also be present. Indeed, this is exactly what his mercy for the Soldan shows: that he holds several absolute qualities in balance at the same time. Thus the three colors demonstrate to us that Tamburlaine's many-faceted nature is always the same, always absolute in several simultaneous directions. In this, he is like the spiritual power demonstrated in Bruno's emblem. The world has many colors, many forms, but all reflect the same universal soul within—just as with the fire of Heraclitus.

From these emblems of the universe and power, we can move further into Bruno's treatment of love. We have already noted that this passion is often associated with fire, as in Petrarch; it follows Petrarch into the realm of paradox also. In the same sonnet which refers to "burning desires," Bruno ends:

> My heart throws off sparks, while my eyes distil water; and I live and die, laugh and lament; the waters remain living, and the fire does not die, because I have Thetis in my eyes and Vulcan in my heart.[8]

The fire of passion is associated with the heart, and the watery tears, expressing the pain of unfulfilled love, are associated with the eyes. Both tendencies are immortal, like Thetis and Vulcan. Together, they represent in another way the ability of the inspired person to contain opposites simultaneously within him. This perception is consistent with, and includes the idea of love within, Tamburlaine's expanding absolutes, his three progressive colors, and Bruno's image of the sun's rays.

We can now see that although the images of Bruno and, to a large degree, those of Marlowe are from the Petrarchan tradition of love and religious poetry, they are used to suggest a different truth. For although the beloved of Petrarch, like that of Dante, becomes in the lover's mind an image for the idea of perfection beyond this physical world, Bruno's and Marlowe's ideas are of another kind. Bruno, rather, advocates "a renunciation of neither the corporeal nor the spiritual element, but bringing both into harmony. . . ." Instead, his Diana becomes "the finite mode of the infinite being."[9] She is worthy in herself of worship. We know that the same absolute principle seems to animate Tamburlaine's thoughts of Zenocrate, and their proposed marriage at the play's end seems to represent Tamburlaine's achievement of this harmonious state of balance. We can now see, that is, how Bruno and Marlowe twist the same essentially Petrarchan poetic inheritance in essentially the same new direction.

This general orientation, with its combination of spiritual aspiration and worldly love, is clear in Bruno's *Heroic Frenzies* in his seventh emblem, "two stars in the shape of two radiant eyes and the motto, *Mors et vita* [death and life]."[10] There is in the following explanation a reference to the pain of being able to see the eyelids but not the eyes of the loved one's soul.

> Thus he [God] shuts out the light with his eyelids, and does not bring calm again to the murky sky of the human mind by removing from it the shadow of enigmas and similitudes. . . . the divinity can bring him death by the light of its eyes and by the same light can give him life; but if it bring him death, he pleads that it be not by shutting out the endearing light with its eyelids.

Here again is the Petrarchan paradox of wanting to see Beauty but fearing it also; yet being full of pain without this vision, while still alive and in hope. However, Bruno explains, "he begs that beauty in the name of his own love, which is perhaps equal to it." Until the vision of love is achieved, the lover's "soul exists only in potency and aptitude without the accomplishment of that perfect act which awaits the divine dew."[11] For the great man, spiritual perception is not by itself sufficient. It must be actualized physically. We have seen this to be true as well for Marlowe. The physical level of existence is highly exalted, then, to the point where love and spiritual aspiration are one. The normal operations of the human mind, bringing only "murky sky" and "the shadow of enigmas and similitudes," is inadequate for contacting the source of spiritual knowledge and inspiration. Spiritual knowledge exalts, and the metaphor both for what is to be known, and for the means of knowing, is the eye, the act of seeing. This is Petrarchanism raised well above its normal bounds. And everywhere, sight and eyes are identified with light and with stars and with radiance.

And so with Tamburlaine, whose "fiery eyes . . . conquered with thy looks" (I, ii, 157; 227) Theridamas, and gains with spiritual power, control of men and land. It is like Bruno's love, which also combines physical and spiritual ideals. Tamburlaine says shortly after that, "These are my friends in whom I more rejoice / Than doth the King of Persia in his crown" (I, ii, 240-241). Ficino's view of friendship—a variation on the high-minded love which Bruno expresses—may well have been in the back of Marlowe's mind here. Or again, in his eyes are "the fury of his heart, / That shine as comets" (III, ii, 73-74). Eyes are one with the feelings of the heart, reflecting the inner inspiration of the man. The association of eyes with celestial bodies is also developed. Indeed, Zenocrate's eyes, which obviously have the ability to inspire Tamburlaine, are also "brighter than the lamps of heaven" (III, iii, 120), and in the evening are bright enough to make "The moon, the planets, and the meteors, light" (V, ii, 87). Their outward comparison suggests the larger harmony between the universe itself and the inner man. Marlowe uses the brightness and inspiring and spiritual power of eyes for the spiritual aspirations of Tamburlaine, both by describing his eyes and also those of his beloved; they are remarkably like the eyes which Bruno describes, and are used to convey essentially the same meaning.

Marlowe once uses another image for Tamburlaine's eyes, one which more fully suggests this internal-external harmony. Menaphon speaks of

. . . his piercing instruments of sight,
Whose fiery circles bear encompassed
A heaven of heavenly bodies in their spheres,
That guides his steps and actions to the throne.

(II, i, 14-17)

Here are eyes not only fiery, but circular and containing in them more circles, circles within circles, an image of the Ptolemaic cosmos of spheres. Tamburlaine's eyes are in the shape of the universe, carry the same signature, the same ultimate identity. They reflect this universe which, implicitly, is the spiritual identity he holds in common with it. He is a microcosm, a little universe, and his eyes mirror that forth. More, this circle within his circular eyes "guides his steps and actions." He is attentive to his inner spirit. There is a power which moves the power of his eyes.

This receptiveness to the power of the smaller circle within, which guides the larger, his eyes, to their aspirations in the outer universe, the still larger circle which the inner circle reflects, here suggested by the reference to the throne—all of this is strongly reminiscent of Bruno's image VII in *The Heroic Frenzies*: the "figure of the sun with a circle inside it and another circle outside of it."[12] The sun moves within the larger circle, and is moved itself by the smaller circle; it touches all the points of both circles at each moment. In the combination of motionless and moving circles, the principles of rest and movement coexist. "Representing eternity itself and therefore in perfect possession of all, it [the sun's circle] comprises the winter, spring, summer, the autumn, the day and the night together, for it is wholly everywhere and in all points and places."[13] The sonnet accompanying this emblem makes it clear that the lover would like to be as stable and perfect as the sun. Therefore "so hot is my desire, that I am easily moved to contemplate that lofty object for which I burn so much, that my ardor throws off sparks to the stars."[14] Tamburlaine, though full of sparks and ardor and restlessness, is not so imperfect. In the process of becoming, his spirit would wither if it remained motionless. He is more like the sun in Bruno's image, moving always, with an inner inspiration guiding him, containing all kinds of potential, winter and spring and the rest, always and fully within himself. We have seen this from other images. And, like the sun, giving heat and inspiration to others, but with still greater and more motionless objects for his desire, ultimately, like the sun and all other spheres, looking up to the "imperial Heaven," the *primum mobile*. Tamburlaine is a more perfect lover than the one Bruno depicts in his commentary on his image. Marlowe has created a lover closer to those more fully inspired ones which Bruno elsewhere portrays. Here, he uses Bruno's image to describe the earthly sun, Tamburlaine.

This image of the sun, and its importance, are often used by Bruno, and indeed by his Hermetic sources. Its significance may be clearest in this passage from the *Hermetica* in which Hermes explains to his son Tat

> That God is hidden from sight, and yet is most manifest. . . . If you wish to see Him, think on the Sun, think of the course of the Moon, think of the order of the stars. Who is it that maintains that order? The Sun is the greatest of the gods in heaven! to him, as to their king and overlord, all the gods of heaven yield place; and yet this mighty god, greater than earth and sea, submits to have smaller stars circling above him. Who is it then, my son, that he obeys with reverence and awe?[15]

So in *Tamburlaine*, Part One we find a close connection between Tamburlaine and this solar deity of the physical world:

> . . . sooner shall the sun fall from his sphere
> Then Tamburlaine be slain or overcome.
>
> > (I, ii, 175-176)

If he is threatened, indeed,

> . . . Jove himself will stretch his hand from heaven
> To ward the blow and shield me safe from harm.
>
> > (I, ii, 179-180)

The comparisons between Tamburlaine and Jove or the sun, almost interchangeably, come thick and fast in the play. Early on, he plans to make conquests as broad, in

> Measuring the limits of his empery
> By east and west, as Phoebus doth his course.
>
> > (I, ii, 39-40)

His bullets are "like Jove's dreadful thunderbolts," his armour is "sun-bright" (II, iii, 19; 22), he is compared in looks to the sun:

168

> As looks the sun through Nilus' flowing stream,
> Or when the morning holds him in her arms,
> So looks my lordly love, fair Tamburlaine.

Indeed, he even rivals the music which reflects the harmony of the universe, over which the sun presides:

> His talk much sweeter than the Muses' song.
>
> (III, ii, 47-50)

And again promises the "stars, that reigned at my nativity," that he

> Will send up fire to your turning spheres
> And cause the sun to borrow light of you.
>
> (IV, ii, 39-40)

Tamburlaine is indeed an analogue in Marlowe's circle image for Bruno's sun. And the sun is clearly the ruler of the physical universe, connected in Marlowe's imagination to Jove, the chief pagan god. Thus the dramatist's imagination sees the sun as Bruno does, though with an added figure in the equation, the heroic figure of Tamburlaine. In Bruno, this sun is sometimes also a symbol that some still higher power exists, even as in Marlowe we have seen frequent, though vague and inconsistent, references to the higher power of fortune. So in Bruno, there is described the man who

> By intellectual contact with that godlike object [the good and the beautiful] . . . becomes a god; and he has thoughts of nothing but things divine and shows himself insensible and impassible to those things which ordinary men feel the most and by which they are most tormented; he fears nothing, and in his love of divinity he scorns other pleasures and does not give any thought to his life. . . . it is a heat enkindled in the soul by the sun of the intellect, and a divine force which sets wings upon him; so that always bringing him closer to the intellectual sun, rejecting the rust of earthly cares he becomes gold proven and pure, acquires the feeling of divine and internal harmony, and conforms his thoughts and acts to the common measure of the law innate in all things.[16]

This is not only a portrait of the ideal hero, to which Tamburlaine rather well conforms. It also indicates another use of the image of the sun: to embody the highest use of the most fully informed intellect. Its heat, the purity of its fire, the inspiration

169

which the highest power within the physical universe can give the spirit, all of these qualities are suggestive. This sun becomes not only an external object, but also internal, subjective, the "sun of the intellect." It is not only the thing to be known, but also the means of knowing, the feeling of inspiration which spiritual desire bestows—just as the image of the eyes is used both to indicate the object of spiritual desire and also the means of perceiving that same spirit. The sun becomes associated with the ardor of spiritual love. It kindles "a heat . . . in the soul." It possesses also the kind of fire which had been attributed to the eyes as well. The circular pattern of eyes in Tamburlaine, and its resemblance to the sun-image of Bruno, suggests another realm of similarity between these two images.

Therefore when we see Tamburlaine of the fiery eyes so closely associated with the sun and Jove, and when we have already seen Zenocrate as the complement to his soul, representing those qualities which he must embrace in order to become more perfect, more comprehensive, it is tempting to look for her as a complementary "lamp" in the heavens. Such a finding would indeed suggest that Marlowe was working on the imaginative wave length suggested above.

She is consistently associated with light color, often with white, and with coldness rather than heat. Tamburlaine, though associated with light when linked to the sun, seldom gets to act the part of white in his banners (until he has taken Zenocrate's quality of mercy unto himself late in the play); he is more associated with red (blood, violence), black (conquest, destruction), and the like. But Zenocrate is

> . . . lovelier than the love of Jove,
> Brighter than is the silver Rhodope,
> Fairer than whitest snow on Scythian hills.

(I, ii, 87-89)

He pictures that

> With milk-white harts upon an ivory sled,
> Thou shalt be drawn amidst the frozen pools,
> And scale the icy mountains' lofty tops,
> Which with thy beauty will be soon resolved.

(I, ii, 98-101)

170

Although associated with snow and ice, though thought of in terms of cold and white, she possesses in her beauty a kind of heat which can thaw ice. We are again reminded of the interior heat of spiritual love (of which her beauty is a physical reflection) which the sun represents in Tamburlaine.

In the same way, she is often compared to that white and cool and precious gem, the pearl. She is "fairer than rocks of pearl" (III, iii, 118), her tears are "resolvèd pearl in showers" (V, ii, 79). (Tamburlaine's face is also compared to a pearl: II, i, 12, but the image is not prolonged, and not repeated later when the imagery surrounding Zenocrate is being more fully elaborated.)

With this coolness is associated calm and the night sky. Her

> . . . eyes are brighter than the lamps of heaven
> . . . .
> That with thy looks canst clear the darkened sky
> And calm the rage of thundering Jupiter—
> Sit down by her [Zabina], adornèd with my crown,
> As if thou wert the Empress of the world.
>
> (III, iii, 120; 122-125)

Which, of course, she will be, as Tamburlaine, the day-star, the sun, conquers it, wearing the day's violent colors, and as the imagery describing her tends more and more to cool calmness, to peace and mildness, to the light of the night sky, with

> Eyes, when that Ebena steps to heaven,
> In silence of thy solemn evening's walk,
> Making the mantle of the richest night,
> The moon, the planets, and the meteors, light.
>
> (V, ii, 84-87)

And, since the moon is, of course, the brightest of the night's luminaries, closely associated in magical belief with the pearl,[17] in effect Zenocrate is taking over its position in the sky, and its effects on the earth. It is consistent with this view that she should be compared with Juno, Jove's consort (V, ii, 447-450), and that only at his cruelest, with Bajazeth, must Tamburlaine command his bright skies to take illumination from him, and "Disdain to borrow light of Cynthia." The moon cannot be heeded when daylight deeds of violence are required and, instead, Tamburlaine compares the operations

171

of his sword to casting "a flash of lightning to the earth" (IV, ii, 35; 46).

Rather clearly in Tamburlaine-Zenocrate we have a set of paired, complementary characteristics and identities: Jove-Juno, sun-moon, colors-white, heat of action-calm and cool, day-night, violence and cruelty-mercy and peace. Thus the need for the magus, given the restless soul of a Tamburlaine, and the awakened "further passion" of Zenocrate who, nonetheless, like Cynthia, retains her chastity during the play. At last she will be married, she will allow her soul to express itself in physical terms, unlike Cynthia; for she has Tamburlaine; for her, complete perfection, not only spiritual, is possible. In each character there is a beauty which reflects in its own unique way and in the most perfect physical terms the world within, outdoing even the beauty of the natural universe. The play's supposed blasphemies are therefore not hyperbolic, but rather a way of stating the need the magus has for finding a physical perfection, a body-soul harmony, which transcends anything nature offers. Therefore, even Zenocrate's speech is "more pleasant than sweet harmony" (III, iii, 12).

Once again, then, both in the nature and meaning of images and of character, and also in their pattern of usage, we have an unusually detailed parallel between Marlowe and Bruno. The central core of fire-sun-moon images, all related to the eyes as reflectors of both inner and outer reality, of the inner virtue and perfect outward object of love, suggests that the imaginations and tempers of these two minds were working along very similar channels in the 1580's.

We can take this similarity a bit further still. The image of the eyes, associated with both Tamburlaine and Zenocrate, and with their transcendence of this world's level of harmony and perfection, is concisely suggested by Theridamas' praise of his chief:

> . . . A Scythian shepherd so embellished
> With nature's pride and richest furniture!
> His looks do menace Heaven and dare the gods.
> His fiery eyes are fixed upon the earth. . . .
>
> (I, ii, 154-157)

Here is the union of heaven and earth, of spirit and body, of the ideal and its outward expression, all visible and obvious in those "fiery eyes." They summarize everything, as does the play's final line, in evoking the ideal of marriage.

Bruno too has an image which cuts through to the essence of these similarities—to the fundamental belief and attitude toward existence which encourages such usage of eyes and fire and of the heavens. It describes the third heroic lover in the *Heroic Frenzies'* gallery of such lovers. He

> carries upon a shield a nude boy lying upon the green meadow. The boy rests his head upon his arm, and turns his eyes to the sky toward certain edifices, houses, towers, landscapes and gardens set above the clouds; and a castle is also to be found whose walls are made of fire, with the motto, *Mutuo fulcimur* [mutually we are sustained.] . . . .
>
> The nude boy represents the frenzied lover . . . who with his power-ful imagination builds castles in the air and, among other things, a tower, whose architect is love, whose walls are the amorous fires and whose builder is himself who says *Mutuo fulcimur*. This is to say, I build and sustain you up there with my thoughts, and you sustain me here below with hope. You would not exist were it not for my imagination and my thought which forms and sustains you; and I would not be alive were it not for the consolation and the comfort I receive because of you. . . .
>
> Magicians can do more by means of faith than doctors by means of the truth.[18]

The power of the mind to reach beyond the forms of tangible things, to be sustained and inspired by intuitions which it knows are self-created, to have faith in the human soul as the source of ultimate power in human existence, is of the essence to a magus like Bruno. But so also is it to Tamburlaine, whom Marlowe makes not a nude and youthful lover, but a warrior wearing armor. Tamburlaine too sees visions beyond the reach of more mundane eyes and, pursuing them, finds that they can be expressed in terms of physical reality as well. He refers to his mind, and those of his men, as such as

> . . . in conceit bear empires on our spears,
> Affecting thoughts co-equal with the clouds.
>
> (I, ii, 64-65)

Or again he is encouraged to

> . . . whet thy winged sword,
> And lift thy lofty arm into the clouds.
>
> (II, iv, 51-52)

He is forever looking at the stars, making his plans and form-ing his ambition on the basis of his higher vision, rather than on his assessment of mundane reality. He is indeed the nude boy with armor on, turned from shepherd to warrior as an image of the power the active mind has, having turned from idle dreams of the beyond to active seeking after it. Imbued with faith and knowledge, the magus-warrior knows few bounds. For such a man, indeed, "Fortune herself doth sit upon our crests" (II, ii, 73)

Ultimately, however, the strongest sense of similarity between Giordano Bruno and Christopher Marlowe may be one of tone. Bruno's self-righteousness—his absolute belief in his and only his right understanding of the universe, his tendency to hyperbole and to metaphoric statements of profoundly believed ideas, his reference to the celestial heavens even when enunciating ideas about the mundane earth, above all perhaps his vaunting optimism in the power of the right-seeing man to create his own world and to make the old one accommodate itself to him, his sense of the mystery and power and spiritual perfection of which man is capable—all of this which characterizes Bruno also characterizes Marlowe's treatment of Tamburlaine. Not only is there a similar complex of images and ideas, but they are developed from essentially the same point of view, the same attitude toward man and the world, and are expressed in essentially the same tone.

When we combine with these images and their ideas, and the tone in which they are expressed, the proximity of the two men in England during a time when Marlowe would have been most receptive to the older man's incendiary thinking, and the circumstantial evidence which suggests that they did know of one another; after all of this, it must still be admitted that we have no proof which requires belief in the theory that Bruno directly inspired the young Marlowe.

However, these similarities and circumstances are great enough to force one to consider the alternative to believing that Bruno had a very great influence on *Tamburlaine*, Part One: that two restless travellers and thinkers, one famous and the other young and ambitious, within a few miles of one another, independently arrived at the same conclusions about the universe, independently found their imaginations returning to the same complex of images to signify the same complex of ideas, independently pictured the same ideal hero. To argue instead that Marlowe might have been influenced by Chapman, who in turn was influenced by Bruno, or that he was influenced by Raleigh's "school of night," is to concede that he was working with the same people as Bruno, and this in fact places Marlowe closer to Bruno than we can demonstrate he actually was.

It is, nevertheless, possible that both men did pick up their ideas and their modes of thought and expression independently, and are two of the age's best separate examples of the optimistic philosophical view of man which belief in magic made possible. There were widespread tendencies in Elizabethan England, and in Italy, which would have encouraged either man independently to come to the views he expresses in the works under discussion. In that case, a study of Bruno's ideas about man and magic becomes a detailed gloss on *Tamburlaine*, to be checked as we have against the play, without indebtedness being implied.

A teasingly related, but quite undemonstrable, theory is that the similarity between Marlowe's thought in *Tamburlaine* and Bruno's occurs because Marlowe, having independently come to his ideas, saw in Bruno their perfect representative, and deliberately wrote his play with the more famous figure in mind. As Edgar Wind has pointed out, for the few enlightened members of an audience there was frequently a "hidden" meaning to a literary work.[19] This aspect of writing would have been likely to appeal to a youthful metaphysician who was very likely also an international spy. Indeed, it is at least an interesting caprice to wonder if Tamburlaine is not Marlowe's portrait of Bruno, portrayed as if he really had the power, in physical terms, which he claimed so vociferously for man in theory.

Or, when we remember the sun-Jove imagery which is frequently used to describe Tamburlaine, we might wonder if there is any connection to Bruno's allegorical suggestion in *The Expulsion of the Triumphant Beast*

> that Jove sometimes, as if he were bored with being Jove, takes certain vacations, now as a farmer, now as a hunter, now as a soldier.[20]

Tamburlaine similarly observes that

Jove sometimes maskèd in a shepherd's weed,
And by those steps that he hath scaled the heavens,
May we become immortal like the gods.

(I, ii, 198-200)

This passage simultaneously suggests the conceit of Bruno, while specifically disclaiming that Tamburlaine is in fact Jove. However, it does leave the possibility open that he could *become like* Jove, which comes close to Bruno's inspiration without literally using it. He has the power and brightness of Jove on earth, certainly. Might this have been an interesting working metaphor of Marlowe's imagination as he wrote? Bruno opens many fascinating questions about *Tamburlaine*.

At last, these questions, and the numerous and striking and interrelated similarities between him and Bruno, make it seem likely that the younger man was, if only for a few months or years, profoundly touched by the older's influence. This seems to me a far more likely hypothesis than the reverse: that the rich vein of similarities is pure coincidence. We cannot, in literary study, compute tables of statistical probabilities, as one sometimes can in sociological studies, for example. But to the spiritually informed mind, mathematics is merely a numerical system for recording the soul's intuitions. Euclid and Pythagoras knew this well, and the Renaissance had not yet lost its feel for mystical ideas in numbers. So although we lack statistics, we should not entirely mistrust the intuition which asserts a close Marlowe-Bruno relationship.

APPENDIX B

THE LOVER, THE EAGLE AND THE PHOENIX IN BRUNO AND TAMBURLAINE, *PART TWO*

Zenocrate's death in *Tamburlaine*, Part Two forces Tamburlaine to face the existence of death and destiny, and finally to conceive the possibility of triumphing over them through metamorphosis. It is interesting that in Part Two, just as in Part One, both her great influence and the conclusion it leads Tamburlaine to, are suggested by visual images and dramatic events which are strongly reminiscent of Bruno.

One image suggests Tamburlaine's resemblance to Bruno's heroic lover in the *Heroic Frenzies*; it expresses the hero's need to unite with Zenocrate on her new, non-physical level after her death, in order to satisfy his soul's desires. It therefore anticipates the greater resolutions to come. He speaks to her as if she were now with Jove and begs:

> Behold me here, divine Zenocrate,
> Raving, impatient, desperate, and mad.
>
> (II, iv, 111-112)

One can only recall Bruno's heroic lover, who has

> frozen hopes and burning desires: at one and the same time I tremble, freeze, burn and sparkle, I am dumb and I fill the sky with ardent shrieks.[1]

It is the tremulous lover who knows he is enamored of a superior ideal, a level of aspiration beyond himself. We must, however, remember that Tamburlaine's earthly power is

177

undiminished; he is, even in this love, heroic, raised to ever higher inspiration, even as in Bruno the anguished spiritual love which this sonnet describes raises the lover to higher and higher spiritual levels.

It is therefore not surprising that Tamburlaine should often be described as an eagle, that most aspiring and powerful of birds, representative of the region of the air, which Bruno describes as "warning all the animals that at his third flight he prepares for destruction,"[2] very like Tamburlaine's three days of progressive warnings. He pictures his aspiring soul's chariot as "drawn with princely eagles" (IV, iv, 127), and Theridamas exclaims that above him, at his

> . . . zenith, clothed in windy air,
> And eagle's wings joined to her feathered breast,
> Fame hovereth, sounding of her golden trump.
>
> (III, iv, 61-63)

One might also be reminded of Dante's Gryphon in the *Purgatorio* (Cantos XXIX, XXX), made half of eagle and half of lion, symbolizing the union of spiritual and physical, divine and human, identities. Or, in the *Paradiso*, the eagle as symbol of the hope for universal law and authority on earth, and as symbol also of the mysteries of Divine Justice (Cantos XVIII-XX).[3] Similarly, we have seen Tamburlaine striving to reduce the world to one unified authority, his own, whose principle of justice is spiritual, righteous, but mysterious to all eyes, requiring above all subservience to his superior vision of the soul.

In this context we have the beautiful Olympia, wife to the valorous captain of Balsera, stabbing her son after her husband is killed, fearful of being taken by Tamburlaine. She then burns the bodies of both her loved ones and prepares to kill herself. Theridamas stops her and begins to praise the virtues of his leader as

> . . . . . a man greater than Mahomet,
> In whose high looks is much more majesty
> Than from the concave superficies
> Of Jove's vast palace, the impyreal orb,
> Unto the shining bower where Cynthia sits,
>
> (III, iv, 46-50)

178

going on until he describes Tamburlaine's fame as having "eagle's wings joined to her feathered breast," so that "the name of mighty Tamburlaine is spread" (line 66). Here is the man of high spiritual aspiration and power, the eagle of the world and of the heavens, imaged in Theridamas' mind as the meeting with Olympia approaches, while nearby the bodies of husband and son burn. (Marlowe is quite explicit about this stage direction.)

One is forcibly reminded of an image in Bruno's *Heroic Frenzies*:

> an image of a flying phoenix toward which a little boy is turned who burns in the midst of flames, and I see the motto, *Fata obstant* [their fates run contrary] [which] . . . shows us that . . . the fate of the phoenix and the fate of the frenzied one . . . are different and opposite.
>
> One knows what the phoenix was and knows what it shall be, but only in terms of many and uncertain metamorphoses shall this lover be able to clothe himself again in a natural form. . . . Besides, the phoenix in the presence of the sun changes death for life, and this subject in the presence of love changes life for death. . . . The difference between the inferior intellect . . . and . . . the active and actual intellect. This intellect . . . influences every individual and is comparable to the moon which is always of the same species and whose aspect ever renews itself as it turns toward the sun, the first and universal intelligence.[4]

The son who burns does so because of his love for his father, himself a bravely heroic captain worthy of love and earthly emulation. The son cries out,

> Mother, dispatch me, or I'll kill myself;
> For think ye I can live and see him dead?
>
> (III, iv, 26-27)

To the unformed, youthful soul, his father's bravery is an appropriate and ennobling inspiration. He will die for it. And Olympia, herself noble and brave, a character whom we admire, she too kills herself rather than have another lord. She must seem noble in order to make the point that she and her son die for a noble cause, in the service of a vision higher than they recognize as still existing on earth. Thus the boy fits Bruno's image in his flames.

However, as we saw above, Tamburlaine's is the higher inspiration; it contrasts with the lower, more personal, less universal inspiration of the boy and his mother.

Tamburlaine is therefore already turning toward the phoenix of Bruno's image, is transformed for this point in the play (III, iv) into the eagle of justice, righteous vision, absolute power and superiority over the earth, because the implications of metamorphosis contained in Bruno's phoenix-image are not appropriate to this part of the play. For Act V Tamburlaine will learn to appreciate the spiritual value and solace in metamorphosis; for the moment, he has not. He is still the eagle, but soon he will transform his death into a new triumph and identity and life. Thus to notice the close identity of the two birds, both of which in Christian iconography represent the idea of resurrection, seems appropriate here. Once more, Bruno's ideas and images combine in ways that suggest an unusual parallel with Christopher Marlowe.

NOTES

INTRODUCTION

1. Besides Eugene Waith, *The Herculean Hero* (New York: Columbia, 1962), several other scholars will grant modified heroic statue. Frank B. Fieler, *Tamburlaine, Part I and its Audience*, University of Florida Monographs in the Humanities, No. 8 (Gainesville: University of Florida Press, Fall, 1961), believes that Tamburlaine was "a man capable of mounting the highest possible level of achievement, but perverting that capability" (p. 64). Nemi D'Agostino, in *Shakespeare e il Rinascimento* (Trieste: Università degli Studi di Trieste, 1959), argues that Tamburlaine is an Elizabethan version of the ideal Renaissance prince (p. 17). Benvenuto Cellini sees him as the apotheosis of heroic will in *Marlowe* (Roma: A. Signorilli, 1937), I, 111. Never is admiration unqualified, however; often, it is grudging.

Thus Michel Poirier, in *Christopher Marlowe* (London: Archon, 1968, reprinted from 1951 ed.), makes the problem clear when he describes the typical Marlovian hero, including Tamburlaine, as "a veritable Nietzschean superman" with a "thirst for the infinite," whose ultimate drive is nevertheless "the thirst for power" (p. 45). "Marlowe's heroes represent all the aspirations of man save one, that of moral perfection. Indifferent to the distinction between good and evil, they thrust aside anything they consider an obstacle to the development of their personality. Their kingdom is of this world" (p. 46).

2. Thus Patrick Cruttwell, in his *The Shakespearean Moment* (New York: Random House, 1969), refers in passing to "a piece of Marlovian hyperbole, such as the description of Tamburlaine," as being "naïve" (p. 78). And Wylie Sypher, in *Four Stages of Renaissance Style* (Garden City: Doubleday, 1955), asserts that "*Tamburlaine* approaches baroque overstatement" (p. 95).

3. Frank P. Wilson, *Marlowe and the Early Shakespeare* (Oxford: Clarendon Press, 1953), p. 53.

4. Una M. Ellis-Fermor, in her introduction to her edition of *Tamburlaine* (New York: Gordian Press, 1966, reprinted from 1930); Paul Kocher in his *Christopher Marlowe: A Study of his Thought, Learning, and Character* (New York: Russell and Russell, 1962, reprinted from 1946); Robert E. Knoll in *Christopher Marlowe* (New York: Twayne, 1969); J. B. Steane, *Marlowe: A Critical Study* (Cambridge, 1964); Lawrence M. Benaquist, "The Ethical Structure of *Tamburlaine*, Part I," *Thoth*, X, 2 (Spring, 1969), 3-19; and Charles G. Masinton, *Christopher Marlowe's Tragic Vision* (Athens, Ohio: Ohio University Press, 1972) all see Tamburlaine as cruel, ruthless, and as lacking any sound ethical standards.

5. Douglas Cole, *Suffering and Evil in the Plays of Christopher Marlowe* (Princeton, 1962), pp. 103, 113.

181

6. Harry Levin, *The Overreacher: A Study of Christopher Marlowe* (Cambridge, Mass., 1952), pp. 30-31.

7. Robert Greene, prefatory epistle "To the Gentlemen readers" to "Perimedes the Blacke-Smith," *The Life and Complete Works in Prose and Verse of Robert Greene*, ed. A. B. Grosart, 15 vols. (New York: Russell and Russell, 1964, reprinted from 1881-1886), VII, 8.

8. Wilbur Sanders, *The Dramatist and the Received Idea: Studies in the Plays of Marlowe and Shakespeare* (London: Cambridge University Press, 1968), p. 35.

9. Roy W. Battenhouse, *Marlowe's Tamburlaine: A Study in Renaissance Moral Philosophy* (Nashville: Vanderbilt University Press, 1941). However, John D. Jump, in his introduction to his edition of *Tamburlaine the Great, Parts I and II* (Lincoln, Neb.: University of Nebraska Press, 1967), argues that "Marlowe apparently meant that [Part I] to be the whole play. He covered in it so much of the career of Tamburlaine as recorded in his sources that, when public demand induced him to write Part II, he had to turn elsewhere for supplementary materials" (p. xiii).

10. M. M. Mahood, *Poetry and Humanism* (New Haven: Yale University Press, 1950), pp. 58-59.

11. Cole, p. 113.

12. Poirier states that "Marlowe starts his dramas in a revolutionary spirit; he concludes them in full conformity with the opinions commonly accepted" (p. 71).

13. Knoll, p. 16.

14. F. P. Wilson, pp. 54-55.

15. Irving Ribner, "Introduction" to *The Complete Plays of Christopher Marlowe* (New York: Odyssey, 1963), p. xxx.

16. Sanders, p. 35.

17. Poirier, p. 71.

18. Frank P. Wilson offers one such alternative, p. 22.

19. Warren D. Smith, "The Substance of Meaning in *Tamburlaine Part I*," *SP*, LXVII, 2 (April, 1970), 156-166.

20. G. I. Duthie, "The Dramatic Structure of Marlowe's *Tamburlaine the Great*, Part I," *Shakespeare's Contemporaries*, eds. Max Bluestone and Norman Rabkin (Englewood Cliffs: Prentice-Hall, 1961), p. 69.

21. Fieler goes so far as to argue that "there is contained in *Tamburlaine, Part I* a comprehensive design of apotheosis which pervades every element in the play's structure" (p. 63). However, he also sees Marlowe as creating a character clearly unworthy of this exalted stature (pp. 64, 67-68).

22. Levin, p. 24.

23. Cole, p. 102.

24. Steane, pp. 63, 80, 83.

25. Waith, *The Herculean Hero*, p. 59.

26. Eleanor Grace Clark, *Ralegh and Marlowe* (New York: Russell & Russell, 1965; c. 1941), pp. 406-407.

27. Ellis-Fermor, *op. cit.*, p. 59.

28. Ellis-Fermor, *op. cit.*, pp. 49-50.

29. Fieler, p. 63.

30. Tamburlaine has "un valore di conquista spirituale, ed egli stesso sia la personificazione di un'ideale eroici, il cui concetto però no era forse ben chiaro nella mente del poeta." My translation from Cellini, p. 116.

31. There is "nel Tamburlaine quasi una infocata versione elisabettiana dell'ideale rinascimentale del Principe. . . ." My translation from D'Agostino, p. 17.

32. A. D. Hope, "The Argument of Arms," *The Cave and the Spring: Essays on Poetry* (Chicago: University of Chicago Press, 1965), p. 120. David Riggs, in *Shakespeare's Heroical Histories* (Cambridge, Mass.: Harvard University Press, 1971), argues similarly that "Although he wins power and titles by his victories, the hero [for example, Tamburlaine] does not fight to acquire kingdoms as such, but rather to exhibit and satisfy his innate nobility of nature" (pp. 59-60). However, Professor Riggs then engages in rhetorical analysis, rather than an exploration of the larger ideas implicit in this observation. Similarly too, Eugene M. Waith argues in *Ideas of Greatness* (New York: Barnes and Noble, 1971) that his great ambition "is ultimately an expression of the vastness of the conquering mind" (p. 55).

33. Greene, p. 8.

34. "Cose tutte create per essere da noi usate; così, non senza fondamento, i Magi credono che noi possiamo agevolmente risalire gli stessi gradini, penetrare successivamente in ciascuno di tali mondi e giungere sino al mondo archetipo animatore, causa prima da cui dependone e procedono tutte le cose. . . ." My translation from Enrico Cornelio Agrippa, *La Filosofia Occulta*, trans. Alberto Fidi (Milano, 1926), vol. I, p. 3.

35. "La Magia è la vera scienza, la filosofia più elevata e perfetta, in una parola la perfezione e il compimento di tutte le scienze naturali, perchè tutta la filosofia regolare si divide in Fisica, Matematica e Teologia." My translation from Agrippa, p. 4.

36. Giovanni Pico della Mirandola, "Oration on the Dignity of Man," trans. Paul O. Kristeller, *The Renaissance Philosophy of Man*, eds. Ernst Cassirer, *et al.* (Chicago: University of Chicago Press, 1948), p. 247.

37. The great mind operates "per un'intuizione che si attua sotto il lume di Dio che sa e pentra tutto il mondo dei corpi e degli spiriti, e che eleva la mente fina a se stesso, in guisa che essa veda non nell'essenza divina, ma nella posteriore ideazione le cose che in un dato momento son necessarie a sapersi da tutti." My translation from Tommaso Campanella, "Magia e Grazia," inediti *Theologicorum Liber XIV*, ed. Romano Amerio, Edizione Nazionale dei Classici del Pensièro Italiano, Series II, No. 5 (Roma, 1957), p. 151.

38. "Non seulement l'intelligence humaine revendique pour elle comme un droit divin de former et de façonner la matière au moyen de l'art, mais encore de transformer les espèces des êtres par son propre pouvoir." My translation from Marsilio Ficino, *Théologie Platonicienne*, trans. Raymond Marcel (Paris, 1964), vol. I, p. 229.

39. The magus "adopera cause naturali che operano in maniera stupefacente." My translation from Campanella, *op. cit.*, p. 165.

40. Pico della Mirandola, p. 225.

41. "Fra le attività umane l'opera magica viene, anzi, ad assumere una posizione centrale, in quanto proprio in essa si esprime in modo quasi esem-

plare quella divina potenza dell'uomo cui Campanella inneggiò in versi giustamente famosi. L'uomo-centro del cosmo è appunto l'uomo che, afferrato il ritmo segreto delle cose, si fa sublime poeta, ma, come un Dio, non si limita a scrivere parole d'inchiostro su carte caduche, bensi inscrive cose reali nel grande e vivente libro dell'universo." My translation from Eugenio Garin, *Medioevo e Rinascimento* (Bari: G. Laterza & F., 1954), p. 151.

42. "L'infinta potenza dell'uomo si raccoglie nell'unità dell'Atto. Ed ecco il sapiente che domina le stelle, il mago che plasma gli elementi; ecco l'unita dell'essere e del pensare, e l'apertura totale della realtà. Questo, e non altro, intendera la difesa della magia, che il Rinascimento inseri nella sua celebrazione dell'uomo." My translation from Garin, p. 169.

43. Frances Yates, *Giordano Bruno and the Hermetic Tradition* (Chicago: University of Chicago Press, 1964) pp. 155-156.

44. Pico, p. 252.

45. Daniel P. Walker, *Spiritual and Demonic Magic from Ficino to Campanella* (London: The Warburg Institute, University of London, 1958), p. 236.

46. William Shakespeare, "A Midsummer Night's Dream," ed. Madelaine Doran, *William Shakespeare: The Complete Works*, general ed. Alfred Harbage, rev. ed. (Baltimore: Penguin, 1969), V,i,16-17.

47. Christopher Marlowe, "Tamburlaine: Part One," *The Complete Plays of Christopher Marlowe*, ed. Irving Ribner (New York: Odyssey, 1963), V,ii,108-110. All references to Marlowe's plays will be to this edition.

Chapter I

1. Frances Yates, *Giordano Bruno and the Hermetic Tradition* (Chicago: University of Chicago Press, 1964). Before this book, the simple lines indicated by E. M. W. Tillyard's *Elizabethan World Picture* (New York: MacMillan, 1944) seemed right, though of course needing amplification and readjustment for the mature student who needs more than oversimplification. Thus one might consult, for example, Paul Oskar Kristeller's *Renaissance Thought*, 2 Vols. (New York: Harper and Row, 1961); Hardin Craig's *The Enchanted Glass* (New York: Oxford, 1936); Hiram Haydn, *The Counter-Renaissance* (New York, 1950); Wallace K. Ferguson, *The Renaissance in Historical Thought* (Cambridge, Mass., 1948); or some other book with alternative or more comprehensive visions. An earlier work on Prof. Yates' general subject, though not concentrating on England or Bruno, is Eugenio Garin, *Medioevo e Rinascimento* (Bari: G. Laterza & F., 1954). Unfortunately, it is not available in English at this writing.

2. Wylie Sypher, "Magical Mystery Tour," *New York Review of Books* (January. 29, 1970), p. 23.

3. Kristeller, II, p. 92.

4. Don Cameron Allen, "Renaissance Remedies for Fortune: Marlowe and *The Fortunati*," *SP*, 38 (1941), 197.

5. See, for example, Josephine Burroughs' essay in *The Renaissance Philosophy of Man*, pp. 185-190. Also Ernst Cassirer, *The Platonic Renaissance in England*, trans. J. P. Pettegrove (Austin: University of Texas Press, 1953), p. 9.

6. Alexandre Koyré, *From the Closed World to the Infinite Universe* (Baltimore, 1957), p. 2.

7. Nikolai Copernicus, *De Revolutionibus Orbitum Celestium*, quoted from Koyré, p. 31.

8. Wolfgang Pauli, *The Influence of Archetypal Ideals on the Scientific Theories of Kepler* (New York, 1955), p. 176. However, a more complete catalogue of such analogues appears in Sir Walter Ralegh's "History of the World," *The Works* (Oxford: Oxford University Press, 1829), II, 58-60.

9. Henry Cornelius Agrippa argues, for example, that since the soul lives, and matter is inert, "one says it is necessary to have a mediator of most excellent abilities to reunite body to soul. And this is the spirit of the world. . . ." ("si dice esser necessario un mediatore più eccelente capace di riunire il corpo all'anima. E questi è lo spirito del mondo. . . .") *La Filosofia Occulta*, p. 27.

Marsilio Ficino agreed: ". . . it is necessary that in all things an incorporeal substance exists and asserts itself, a substance which penetrates through matter and from which are derived the instruments which are the corporeal qualities." (". . . il faut qu'en toutes choses existe et s'impose une substance incorporelle qui pénétré à travers les corps et de laquelle les instruments soient les qualités corporelles.") *Théologie Platonicienne*, I, 48.

Perhaps Agrippa most clearly draws the conclusion that in this world the enlightened man can see spiritual power in every physical thing: "Thus now we know that the position and the character of the celestial bodies are the cause of every active virtue which one notices in the inferior species." ("Dunque ora noi sappiamo che la situazione e la figura dei corpi celesti sono la causa d'ogni virtù attiva che si riscontra nelle specie inferiori"—p. 23.) And therefore, "the virtues of natural things reveal themselves in their effects." ("Le virtù delle cose naturali rivelano i loro effeti"—p. 8.)

It is Pietro Bembo who clearly states the distance between the celestial and the terrestrial sphere: "But so much are those things of more excellent being [in the higher world which is neither material nor sensible], than are these of this world, as among these are the celestial in a superior condition to the terrestial." ("Ma tanto sono quelle cose di più eccellente stato, che non son queste, quanto tra queste sono le celesti a miglior condizione, che le terrene.") *Gli Asolani e le Rime* (Torino, 1932), p. 154. This distance between the two realms, however, does not discourage the notion of correspondences between them, as Agrippa indicates: "The correspondence, the submission and obedience of the substance of things, is produced and generated by the soul of the world. . . ." ("La corrispondenza, la sottomissione e l'obbedienze della sostanza delle cose prodotte e generate dall'anima del mondo . . ."—p. 24.) Thus, he illustrates with "human nature, a perfect and complete image which reflects in itself all the universe, and which contains all the celestial harmony, in which without doubt one could find all the signs and all the characters of all the stars, and in a manner more pleasing." ("La natura umana, immagine perfetta e completa, che rispechia in sè tutto l'universo e che contiene tutta l'armonia celeste, in cui senza dubbio ci sarà dato trovare tutti i segni e tutti i caratteri di tutte le stelle e in modo tanto più efficace. . ."—p. 56.) Indeed, as Jacob Burckhardt summarizes, with reference particularly to the *Orazione* of Lorenzo the Magnificent, but also with general reference to the age, that "the visible world was created by God in love, that it is the copy of a pattern preexisting in Him, and that He will ever remain its eternal mover and restorer. The soul of

185

man can by recognizing God draw Him into its narrow boundaries, but also by love to Him itself expand into the Infinite." *The Civilization of the Renaissance in Italy*, trans. Ludwig Geiger and Walther Gotz, 2 Vols. (New York: Harper and Row, 1958), II, 516.

10. Thus Baldesar Castiglione refers to "the divinity which, I believe, Pythagoras and Socrates attributed to music." *The Book of the Courtier*, trans. George Bull (Baltimore: Penguin, 1967), pp. 121-122. One of his speakers enlarges on this widely-held principle of the universal harmony: "the wisest of philosophers held the opinion that the universe was made up of music, that the heavens make harmony as they move, and that as our own souls are formed on the same principle they are awakened and have their faculties, as it were, brought to life through music" (pp. 94-95).

11. Pauli, p. 156.

12. Pauli, p. 162.

13. Yates mentions this difference in *Bruno*, p. 156. Koyré also suggests a possible cause for this difference, pp. 18-19, 54. Bruno's metaphysical view of the Copernican universe is stressed too by Lawrence S. Lerner and Edward A. Gosselin, "Giordano Bruno," *Scientific American*, 228 (April, 1973), 86-94.

14. Burckhardt goes so far as to argue that "the Platonic Academy at Florence deliberately chose for its object the reconciliation of the spirit of antiquity with that of Christianity" (II, 479). There can be no doubt that Ficino's influential Platonic Theology was such an attempt.

15. The ideal Renaissance man has been defined in various ways. What is important for this argument is to show that all this variety is based on a common assumption about his spiritual depth. Italo Siciliano suggests his diversity in one way: "The new man born with the Renaissance in Italy: with the synthesis of nature and spirit in art and life, with the symbol of Cato (the search for liberty), with the myth of Ulysses (strength and knowledge in balance), with the Platonic ideal of Petrarch. . . ." ("L'uomo nuovo nasce col Rinascimento in Italia: con la sintesi di nature e spirito nell'arte e nella vita, con il simbolo di Catone (libertà vo cercando), col mito di Ulisse (seguir virtute e conoscenza), con l'ideale platonico del Petrarca . . . .") *Medio Evo e Rinascimento* (Milano: Albrighi, Segati & C., 1936), p. 158. Thus "the 'divine' (and the 'omnipotent') man of the Renaissance finds this strength in nature and, above all, in himself, in his intellect." ("Il 《 divino 》 (e l' 《 onnipotenza 》) l'uomo del Rinascimento lo trove nella nature e sopratutto in sè stess, nel suo intelletto." P. 158)

Even when Castiglione seems most to encourage affection for good appearance and reputation in his descriptions of the perfect courtier, there is a larger conception of the man to whom outward grace seems natural. Occasionally this becomes explicit, as when he argues that outward "beauty springs from God and is like a circle, the centre of which is goodness" (p. 330). And when he emphasizes that "if the activities of the courtier are directed as they should be to [a] virtuous end. . ." (p. 284).

This large view of man as ideally tending toward virtue, as seeing Beauty in man and God, of being nearly divine himself, is a common one. Pietro Pomponazzi states that "to man . . . power is given to assume whichever nature he wishes. Hence there are three kinds of men to be found. Some are numbered with the gods, although such are but few," in "On Immortality," trans. William H. Hay, *The Renaissance Philosophy of Man*, pp. 282-283.

Pico says something very similar to man: "Thou shalt have the power, out of thy soul's judgment, to be reborn into the higher forms, which are divine," in "On the Dignity of Man," p. 225. Thus Giuseppe Saitta, in summary, asserts that to the Renaissance mind, "the science of man is like the science of the infinite." ("La scienza dell'uomo [è] come scienza infinito.") *La Filosofia di Marsilio Ficino* (Messina: G. Principato, 1923), p. 156. One must, to achieve this near-divinity, "become almost completely rational," according to Pomponazzi, p. 283. And this rationality in which one sees into the hidden mysteries of things, "this grace, is the greatest achievement of human wisdom and power." ("Questo grazia [è] l'apice dell'operare sapiente e potente dell'uomo," according to Romano Amerio in his "Avvertenza" to Campanella, *Magia e Grazia*, p. 7.)

Of such a writer, Eugenio Garin states, "his transposition of philological and rhetorical humanism to the plane of a metaphysic of man the creator. This is, I believe, the most profound word of the entire Renaissance." ("La sua traposizione dell'umanesimo filologico e retorico sul piano di una metafisica dell'uomo creatore. Che è, io credo, la parola più profonda di tutto il Rinascimento"—*Medioevo*, p. 93.) This high view of man is not only widely held, but perhaps very close to the heart of the deepest meaning of the age.

16.   Thus Castiglione argues that "outward beauty is a true sign of inner goodness" (p. 330). Or again, emphasizing the organic relationship between the inner and outer man: "Nature has implanted in everything a hidden seed which has a certain way of influencing and passing on its own essential characteristics to all that grows from it, making it similar to itself" (p. 54). The courtier's inner grace will be such that he will combine the following external qualities; he will be "enterprising, bold, and loyal" (p. 57) in arms; he must be a good mediator of disputes (p. 62); "an accomplished and versatile horseman" (p. 62); he should be skilled at hunting, swimming, jumping, running and casting the stone, and at tennis (p. 63); he must also be something of a graceful musician (p. 69), writer (p. 92), conversationalist, drawer and painter (p. 96), sculptor (p. 98); and many more things, each performed with an apparently nonchalant grace which seems a natural reflection of the courtier's inward virtues.

17.   Plato's well-known parable of the cave makes this clear, and Pietro Bembo clearly echoes this view in the Renaissance; *op. cit.*

18.   With Bembo and Ficino, then, as with Petrarca and Dante and finally Tamburlaine, we can see the two sides of the Renaissance mind. Bembo sees glory in the higher world of intelligence and spirit, but his contemplation of the Ideal makes him emphasize the imperfect qualities of earth instead of its glories. Ficino tends to emphasize the possibilities for spiritual perfection in this world, by contrast. In single minds, we have Petrarca, who in Laura nearly deifies his love, yet finds himself sinful, an imperfect man, unworthy of her; Dante very much the same with Beatrice. When one reaches *Tamburlaine*, Part One, he is beyond these neo-Platonic views and into Hermeticism. Here both lover and beloved, Tamburlaine and Zenocrate, are deified. They can, as a result, meet on the physical as well as on the spiritual plane. Marlowe brings Renaissance neo-Platonism down to earth in ways consistent with this new set of ideas added to the mixture of Renaissance thought.

19.   Nesca A. Robb, in *Neoplatonism of the Italian Renaissance* (London: Allen & Unwin, 1935), points out how nature is perfectable: "Nature appears to the poet as a fellow artist toiling through years of failure and experiment

to attain perfection" (p. 249). Thus the magus is an editor of God's work, with the Author always as the editor's guide. And therefore Marlowe's contemporary, Tomasso Campanella, allegorically joins idea and act under the aegis of magic, by making the prince of his ideal city a metaphysician under whose control are wisdom, power, and love, including all abilities and knowledge (*La Città del Sole*, a cura di Alberto Agazzi; Siracusa, 1958; p. 20).

20. Henry M. Pachter, *Magic Into Science: The Story of Paracelsus* (New York, 1951), pp. 84, 119-120, 337. For the following idea, see also Paolo Rossi, *Francis Bacon, From Magic to Science*, trans. Sacha Rabinovitch (London, 1968), pp. 15-16.

21. Walter Pagel, *Paracelsus: An Introduction to Philosophical Medicine in the Era of the Renaissance* (Basel, 1958), p. 63.

22. See both Daniel Walker's *Spiritual and Demonic Magic*, and Frances Yates' *Giordano Bruno*, for example Chapter II, and particularly p. 45, where she explains that "The methods and the cosmological background presupposed are the same whether the magician is using these forces to try to obtain concrete material benefits for himself, or whether he is using them religiously. . . ."

23. Yates, *Bruno*, p. 154. Also Koyré, p. 30. Campanella's city of the sun is his ideal place; its name is "Sole." "They [the citizens] honor the sun and the stars like living things, and as statues of God and celestial temples; but they do not worship them, and honor more the sun." ("Onorano il sole e le stelle come cose viventi e statue di Dio e tempii celesti; ma non l'adorano, e più onorano il sole"—p. 52.) Thus perhaps it is that Leon Battista Alberti puts the sun at the top center of his facade for Santa Maria Novella in Florence—a sun with a smiling face in its center. The sun as closest visible thing to the Divine essence is often honored in this way in the Renaissance.

24. Pauli, pp. 156, 161-162.

25. For example, in discussing political controversies, he writes that "one should not only exclude ordinary astrology but also the one which I have recognized as being in accord with nature." Clearly, he sees some kind of astrology as legitimate (Carola Baumgardt, *Johannes Kepler: Life and Letters*; New York, 1951; p. 99). His arrogance and awareness of earlier, magical modes of thought is suggested when he wrote: "I defy the mortals with scorn by an open confession. I have stolen the golden vessels of the Egyptians to make out of them a holy tabernacle for my God" (p. 18). At another time he makes a similar confession: ". . . I too play with symbols; I have started a small work *Geometrical Kabbala*; it deals with the 'ideas' of the things of nature in geometry" (p. 80). He is attracted, at least, to this view of the universe.

26. Pagel, p. 1.

27. Thus D. P. Walker argues that there were important Christian sources for this kind of magic, p. 36. And Eugenio Garin emphasizes that practical use of ideas which this magic represented: "It signifies the rejection of inert contemplation of definite essences: it signifies the hard-won convergence of knowing and doing; it signifies science at the service of the infinite magical transformation of all things." (". . . Significa . . . refiuto di una contemplazione inerte di essenze definite: significa operosa convergenza di conoscere e fare, e scienza al servizio della magica infinita transformazione del tutto" —*Medioevo*, p. 167.)

NOTES

28. *The Complete Poems of Michelangelo*, trans. Joseph Tusiani (New York: Noonday, 1960), from poems #83 and 84, pp. 76, 77.

29. "The Crosse," *The Complete Poetry of John Donne*, ed. John T. Shawcross (Garden City: Doubleday, 1967), p. 352, ll. 33-34.

30. This view is essentially valid for literary artists as well. Writers create their own images of expression, but have the same deep intuition of reality as their subject. In Giordano Bruno's play "Candelaio," appearances are comically manipulated to create and then resolve complications; finally the one man who can see beyond appearance to reality manipulates the surface of things to harmonize it with ideal human society. This character, Gioan Bernardo, says in V, xxiii, p. 199, "My art is . . . to give to the eyes of the mundane the image of Our Lord, of Our Madonna and of the other saints of paradise." ("La mia arte è . . . donar a gli occhii de mundani la imagine di Nostro Signore, di Nostra Madonna e d'altri Santi di paradiso." And so the playwright, by manipulating figures resembling those in our world, tries to show us a vision of the Ideal lying within it. It is in Bruno, a scientist and magician in the noblest intellectual sense, that we see most clearly magic and art combining. Giordano Bruno, *Opere Italiane*, ed. V. Spampanato, 2nd. rev. ed. (Bari, 1923), III.

31. Frances A. Yates, *John Florio, The Life of an Italian in Shakespeare's England* (New York, 1968; c. 1934), p. 256.

32. Yates, *Florio*, p. 108.

33. Yates, *Florio*, p. 335.

34. Frances A. Yates, "The Hermetic Tradition in Renaissance Science," *Art, Science, and History in the Renaissance*, ed. Charles S. Singleton (Baltimore: Johns Hopkins Press, 1967), p. 255.

35. Keith Thomas, *Religion and the Decline of Magic* (New York: Scribner's, 1971), p. 269.

36. Frances A. Yates, *Theatre of the World* (Chicago: University of Chicago Press, 1969), p. 9. See also Peter French, *John Dee, The World of an Elizabethan Magus* (London: Routledge and Kegan Paul, 1972), Chapter 4, and pp. 161-162.

37. Yates, *Theatre*, p. 17. For fuller information on this library, see French, *Dee*, pp. 40-61.

38. French, *Dee*, pp. 126-159. For other propagation of Hermeticism, see A. C. Hamilton, "Sidney and Agrippa," *Review of English Studies*, New Series, VII (April, 1956), which demonstrates that Sidney's "Apologie for Poetrie" takes most of its ideas from the magus Agrippa's critique of reason, *De incertitudine et vanitate scientarum et artium*. Also, the reference to Agrippa in the anonymous *Willobie his Avisa* of 1594, ed. G. B. Harrison, The Bodley Head Quartos (London: The Bodley Head Ltd., 1926), p. 6.

39. Yates, *Florio*, p. 109.

40. Muriel C. Bradbrook, *The School of Night* (New York: Russell and Russell, 1965; c. 1936), p. 71.

41. Bradbrook, p. 72.

42. French, p. 171.

43. One indication of Bruno's universal influence in Europe may be suggested by Fabio Paolini's Accademia degli Uranici, a group of distinguished

189

NOTES

thinkers in Venice, according to D. P. Walker, pp. 126-127, whose Hermetic speculations coincidentally ended when the long Roman arm of the counter-reformation reached out to Venice in 1592 to take Bruno from that comparatively free city to Rome for eight years' imprisonment before he was burned.

44. Giordano Bruno, *On the Infinite Universe and Worlds*, trans. Dorothea W. Singer (New York, 1950), p. 302.

45. For a bibliography of Bruno's work, see Virgilio Salvestrini, *Bibliografia delle Opere di Giordano Bruno* (Pisa, 1926). V. Spampanato, in *Vita di Giordano Bruno*, 2 vols. (Messina, 1921), argues that Bruno often went to Elizabeth's court with the French ambassador, Castelnau, that he was a well-known and controversial London figure, and even goes so far as to speculate that Hamlet was created on his model (I, 346, 349, 362-387).

46. Dorothea Singer, *Giordano Bruno, his Life and Thought, with Annotated Translation of his Work "On the Infinite Universe and Worlds,"* presents a long list of Englishmen with whom he was probably familiar, and the contemporary evidence for such conclusions, pp. 35-44.

47. This influence continued into the seventeenth century on the continent as well. The activities of Kepler and Campanella speak for this fact. The most interesting—but perhaps not fully successful—attempt to trace this theme in Europe recently is that of Frances Yates in *The Rosicrucian Enlightenment* (London, 1972). And Maurice Evans, in his introduction to George Chapman's *Bussy D'Ambois*, The New Mermaid Series (New York: Hill & Wang, 1966), notices that Bruno's "*Spaccio [de la bestia trionfante]* was still well enough known in 1634 for Carew to base on it his masque, *Coelum Britannicum*" (p. xx). In addition, Donne's "The Extasie" has been shown to have close affinities with French neo-Platonism, and even with that of the Florentine Academy, by Merritt Y. Hughes in "The Lineage of 'The Extasie'," *Modern Language Review*, XXVII (January, 1932), 1-5. And Mario Praz, in *The Flaming Heart* (Garden City, 1958), suggests that this poem's ideas and love-images carry resemblances to those of Bruno, p. 197.

48. The general orientation which looks more to the heroic quality and inspiration of main characters, and less to moral judgments, has been indicated by Waith in *The Herculean Hero*, and by Edwin Muir in " 'Royal Man': Notes on the Tragedies of George Chapman," *Shakespeare's Contemporaries*, eds. Max Bluestone and Norman Rabkin (Englewood Cliffs, 1961), pp. 230-238. The more specifically Hermetic influence has been traced by Maurice Evans, particularly p. xxiv.

49. This set of observations can be expanded to include Edgar Wind's recognition that Renaissance art speaks on different levels to different members of an audience. To the initiate, the elite mind, philosophical ideas will be clear which to an unenlightened mind will not even seem present. Indeed, each image, for the enlightened, is thought to have "an inherent eloquence, that speaks the universal language of the imagination" (*Pagan Mysteries in the Renaissance*; New Haven, 1958; p. 187). Eugenio Garin observes in the same vein, relating magic to art, that "physical and astrological and religious things are rarely divulged; therefore in these things the older artists conceal the art of magic." ("Le cose fisiche e astrologiche e religiose, rarissime volte si divulgano; però in queste gli antichi ritirarono l'arte [magiam]"—*Medioevo*, p. 150.) In England, one of many obvious examples of this use of surface details in narrative to express deeper meaning is broadly, though playfully,

NOTES

hinted at in the anonymous editor's "Epistle to the Reader" prefatory to
Wilobie his Avisa (p. 6): the unknown author is said to be "desirous . . .
to imitate a far off, ether Plato in his Common wealth, or More in his Utopia."
Further, that in certain sections "he had, as I take it, out of Cornelius Agrippa,
drawen the several dispositions of the Italian. . . ." Given this aesthetic situation, it is certainly conceivable that Marlowe's use of ideas about man which
are similar to those implied by the concept of the magus might have been
meant mainly for the enlightened few who would be most willing to entertain
ideas at variance with the generally-held beliefs of the age.

50. Thomas B. Stroup, *Microcosmos: The Shape of the Elizabethan Play*
(Lexington: University of Kentucky Press, 1965), p. 179.

51. See Frances A. Yates, *The Art of Memory* (Chicago, 1966), Chapter
XVI.

52. Lily B. Campbell, *Scenes and Machines on the English Stage During
the Renaissance* (Cambridge, 1923), p. 119.

53. Joan Gadol, *Leon Battista Alberti: Universal Man of the Early Renaissance* (Chicago: University of Chicago Press, 1969), p. 99.

54. Yates, *Theatre*, p. 116.

55. The importance of this sense of universal analogues in the Renaissance
view of architecture may in part be suggested by seeing how closely Vitruvius
is followed by Leon Battista Alberti in his insistence that architecture is a
universal kind of art, requiring for its proper exercise an expertise in far-
flung fields of endeavor. A parallel with those views of the ideal Renaissance
man, which we have already associated with the idea of the magus, can be clearly
seen here. Thus M. Vitruvio Pollione, in *Dell'Architettura, Libri Dieci*, trans.
Marchese Berardo Galiani (Milano: Allessandre Dozio, 1832), p. 1, argues
that the architect must have studied grammar, design and drawing, geometry,
optics, arithmetic, history, philosophy, music, medicine, jurisprudence, astronomy, the motions of the sky and their causes. This view is echoed by Alberti
in his *Architetto*, ed. and intro. Corrado Ricci (Torino, 1917), p. 18.
In this regard we should not underestimate the importance of geometry,
and the sense of man as the measure of all things, whose geometric proportions must form the essential principle of harmony in buildings, as they
mirror that of the universe. Thus Vitruvio asserts, "In fact nature has composed the human form in such a way that the front of the face from the beard
to the roots of the hair is the tenth part of the body . . . and similarly all
the other members have also their correspondences of proportions, in obeying
which the celebrated painters and sculptors of older times acquire infinite
praise." ("In fatti la natura ha composto il corpo umano in guisa, che la
faccia dall barba fino a tutta la fronte, cioè all radice de'Capelli, è la decima
parte del corpo . . . e così tutte l'altre membra hanno ancora le loro corris-
pondenze di proporzione, delle quali servitisi i celebri pittori e scultori antichi,
n'acquistarono infinita lode"—pp. 44-45.) In the same vein the Renaissance
magus Agrippa argues that buildings, like the proportions and harmony of
the universe, are best built to human proportions, and he specifically mentions theatres as one of those types of buildings, along with temples and
others (*La Filosofia Occulta*, p. 89). Alberti, again, agrees (p. 18). And
Leonardo's sketch of a man inscribed simultaneously within a circle and a
square, illustrating Vitruvius' concept, is also well-known.

56. Yates, *Theatre*, p. 116.

191

57. D. P. Walker, in discussing Ficino's opinion of the spiritual efficacy of music (particularly in *De Triplici Vita*), observes this idea's history back to Plato's *Timaeus* and, earlier, to the Pythagoreans. He recounts "the persistent theory . . . that both the universe and man, the macrocosm and microcosm, are constructed on the same harmonic proportions; that there is a music of the spheres, . . . of man's body, spirit and soul, . . . of voices and instruments, ... Thus the use of anything having the same numerical proportions as a certain heavenly body or sphere will make your spirit similarly proportioned and provoke the required influx of celestial spirit, just as a vibrating string will make another, tuned to the same or a consonant note, vibrate in sympathy" (p. 14). See also Gretchen L. Finney, "Music: A Book of Knowledge in Renaissance England," *Studies in the Renaissance*, VI (1959), 36-63. And John Hollander, *The Untuning of the Sky* (N.Y.: Norton, 1970; c. 1961) for a full discussion of English poets' ideas about the spiritual and other values of music.

58. T. S. Eliot, "Christopher Marlowe," *Essays on Elizabethan Drama* (New York: Harcourt, Brace, 1960; c. 1932), p. 62.

59. See, for example, H. B. Charlton, *The Dark Comedies* (Manchester, 1937); also E. M. W. Tillyard, *Shakespeare's Problem Plays* (London: Chatto & Windus, 1951), pp. 89-117.

60. See, for example, Joseph G. Price, *The Unfortunate Comedy. A Study of "All's Well That Ends Well" and its Critics* (Toronto: Toronto University Press, 1968).

61. The play as black comedy was directed by Michael Kahn and starred Morris Carnovsky as Shylock at the Stratford, Conn., Festival in 1967.

62. See, for example, Hermann Sinsheimer, *Shylock: The History of a Character* (New York: B. Blom, 1963; c. 1947).

63. See, for instance, Peter Phialas, *Shakespeare's Romantic Comedies* (Chapel Hill: University of North Carolina Press, 1966), p. 170; and John R. Brown, *Shakespeare and his Comedies* (London: Methuen, 1957), pp. 61-62. Both argue that the main issue of the play is internal virtue and how to achieve it, but do not consider the issue in the context of Hermetic or neo-Platonic ideas. Perhaps the closest approach to that suggested in the text is John Vyvyan's in *Shakespeare and Platonic Beauty* (N.Y.: Barnes & Noble, 1961): *All's Well* is seen as a Platonic allegory about the pilgrimage toward ideal love, pp. 151-152. See the next two paragraphs for an application of this view.

64. D. P. Walker argues that the kind of magic a Christian neo-Platonist like Marsilio Ficino could espouse "had many sources. Perhaps the most important, though Ficino does not avow it and may not even have been conscious of it, is the mass, with its music, words of consecration, incense, lights, wine and supreme magical effect—transubstantiation" (p. 36). Marriage, of course, often includes a mass in its ritual, and is certainly approached by the religious with the same sense of awe and humility which accompanies their participation in the mass.

65. Not only was the famous "Contre-Machiavelli" of Gentillet available in English, translated by Simon Patericke in 1577. *The Prince* had been available in its entirety, in a more honest representation, since 1553. And although the Machiavel in the play's Prologue clearly is evil, Barabas is also

the only character in the play for whom we have any sympathy (with the probable, but very brief, exception of Abigail). Irving Ribner has most recently argued that Marlowe in fact knew and understood the real Machiavelli very well, in *The English History Play in the Age of Shakespeare* (London, 1965), p. 18, and therefore that he also knew the difference between him and the false "Machiavel" who is well represented as a stage villain and is often joined with the Senecan villain-type.

66. See Franklin M. Dickey, *Not Wisely But Too Well: Shakespeare's Love Tragedies* (San Marino, 1966), who argues that there are no finally happy illicit lovers in Shakespeare, and that he adheres strongly to the moral tradition of his age.

67. Bonamy Dobrée, *Restoration Tragedy, 1660-1720* (Oxford, 1929), gives a cogent summary of Dryden's aesthetic views and of their partial derivation from Hobbes and the epic poem.

68. Many writers have commented on the essentially intellectual and experimental nature of his mind. J. R. Mulryne and Stephen Fender in "Marlowe and the 'Comic Distance'," *Christopher Marlowe*, ed. Brian Morris (London: Ernest Benn, 1968), discuss his aesthetic distance from the events of *Tamburlaine*, his ambivalence, his "uncertainty between opposing attitudes" (p. 64). Robert Knoll feels that Marlowe "was, in fact, haunted by what are essentially philosophical questions: for what purpose were we created and for what end do we live" (*Christopher Marlowe*, p. 139)? John Bakeless, in *Christopher Marlowe* (New York, 1937), agrees that he had a "fiery, passionate mind" (p. 4), open to the inspirations of his age (p. 3). Harry Levin sees in him an antireligious fascination with ceremonial (*The Overreacher*, p. 20).

More of the same could easily be collected. The portrait of a restless, unsettled, curious mind accumulates even when reading scholars with whom one totally disagrees about the plays themselves.

69. Francis R. Johnson, "Marlowe's Astronomy and Renaissance Skepticism," *ELH*, XIII (1946), 252. See also note 38 to chapter I.

70. Bradbrook, *School of Night*, p. 8. See also G. B. Harrison's "An Essay on *Willobie His Avisa*" in his edition of the work, pp. 210-211.

71. Bradbrook, *School of Night*, p. 70.

72. Yates, *Florio*, p. 109. See also notes 39-42 to chapter I.

73. Bakeless, *Marlowe*, p. 39.

74. Eleanor Grace Clark, *Ralegh and Marlowe* (New York: Russell and Russell, 1965; c. 1941), pp. 320-321.

75. Yates, *Giordano Bruno*, p. 288; see also pp. 289-290.

76. Giordano Bruno, *Five Dialogues on Cause, Principle, and Unity*, trans. Jack Lindsay (New York: International Publishers, 1962), p. 75.

77. Dorothea Singer, *Giordano Bruno*, pp. 35-44. Philip Henderson, in *Christopher Marlowe* (London, 1952), encourages our belief in this influence: "He was clearly influenced by both Bruno and Machiavelli. Whether he read these authors himself (and there is no reason why he should not have done so, with this widespread Elizabethan enthusiasm for everything Italian)," is uncertain (p. 11). However, he argues, "The heroic frenzy of *Tamburlaine* would seem to derive straight from Bruno's *De gli eroici furori*" (p. 12).

193

Henderson believes that Marlowe "caught the Nolan's [Bruno's] sense of infinity . . ." (p. 149).

Benvenuto Cellini similarly believes, "Moreover, by this time he must have come to a knowledge of the neo-Platonic philosophy with its cabbalistic and magical elements. Various works of Giordano Bruno were published in London between 1584 and 1585, and it does not seem probable to me that they would remain unknown, especially *The Expulsion of the Triumphant Beast*, and the *Cabala of the Pegassean Steed*, traces of which we find in the accusation of Baines, and above all *The Heroic Frenzies*." ("Inoltre egli dovera essere venuto fin d'allora a conoscenza della filosofia neoplatonica con i suoi elementi cabbalistici e magici. Verie opere di Giordano Bruno s'erano stampato a Londra fra il 1584 e il 1585, e a me no sembra probabile che gli siano rimaste sconosciute, specialmente *Lo spaccio della bestia trionfante*, e la *Cabala del cavallo pegaseo*, di cui retroveremo traccie nelle accuse del Baines, e sopra tutto *Gli eroici furori*"—*Marlowe*, I, p. 19.)

Harry Levin, too, observes that in *Tamburlaine* "the upward reach of the verse, along with the dynamic force of the diction, is . . . likely to remind us that . . . Giordano Bruno was in England during his lifetime" (*Over-reacher*, p. 38).

78.   Robert Knoll, *Marlowe*, p. 19.

79.   Muriel Rukeyser notes that "It was Mauvissière who acted as the drop for letters for Mary Queen of Scots. There were only two embassies in London, the Spanish and the French, and it was through Walsingham's skill in planting a returned Catholic exile that he finally was able to read the correspondence that uncovered the Babington Plot to kill Elizabeth and put Mary on the throne" (*The Traces of Thomas Hariot*; New York: Random House, 1970; p. 82).

80.   Yates, *Florio*, p. 108.

81.   Yates, *Florio*, pp. 112-123.

82.   Yates, *Florio*, p. 109.

83.   Henderson, *Marlowe*, pp. 66-67.

84.   One clear exposition of this state of affairs is P. M. Handover's *The Second Cecil. The Rise to Power. 1563-1604* (London, 1959).

Chapter II

1.   Giordano Bruno, *On the Infinite Universe*, p. 303. For a full discussion of the infinity of the universe, see particularly the complex geometrical and mathematical arguments in the third dialogue.

2.   Giordano Bruno, *The Expulsion of the Triumphant Beast*, trans. Arthur D. Imerti (New Brunswick: Rutgers University Press, 1964), p. 89.

3.   Giordano Bruno, *Five Dialogues on Cause, Principle and Unity*, trans. Jack Lindsay (New York: International Publishers, 1962), p. 25.

4.   Bruno, *Cause*, p. 26.

5.   Bruno, *Cause*, p. 87.

6.   Bruno, *Cause*, p. 89.

7.   See the description of Jove in Bruno's *Expulsion*, pp. 75-78.

8. Bruno, introductory epistle to *The Infinite Universe*, p. 229.

9. Bruno, *Cause*, p. 57.

10. Bruno, *Cause*, p. 26.

11. Bruno, *Cause*, p. 83.

12. Bruno, *Expulsion*, p. 89.

13. Bruno, *Cause*, p. 57.

14. Bruno, *Expulsion*, p. 115.

15. Giordano Bruno, *The Heroic Frenzies*, trans. P. E. Memmo (Chapel Hill: University of North Carolina Press, 1966), p. 107.

16. Bruno, *Heroic Frenzies*, p. 108.

17. Bruno, *Expulsion*, p. 78.

18. *Hermetica*, ed., trans., notes Walter Scott, 4 vols. (London, 1968; c. 1924), I, 221.

19. *Hermetica*, I, 295.

20. *Hermetica*, I, 153.

21. Sypher, "Magical Mystery Tour," p. 25.

22. Bruno, *Cause*, p. 66.

23. Bruno, *Cause*, p. 67.

24. Levin, *Overreacher*, p. 24.

25. Bruno, *Heroic Frenzies*, p. 107.

26. Bruno, *Cause*, pp. 65-66.

27. Bruno, "To his Own [Bruno's] Spirit," poem dedicatory to *Cause*, pp. 54-55.

28. Bruno, *Cause*, p. 131.

29. Bruno, *Expulsion*, pp. 89, 90.

30. Bruno, *Heroic Frenzies*, pp. 184-185.

31. Bruno, *Heroic Frenzies*, p. 117.

32. Memmo, introduction to *Heroic Frenzies*, p. 33.

33. Memmo, introduction to *Heroic Frenzies*, p. 45.

34. Memmo, introduction to *Heroic Frenzies*, p. 45.

35. Bruno, *Heroic Frenzies*, pp. 96, 216.

36. Bruno, *Cause*, p. 87.

37. Bruno, *Cause*, p. 35.

38. Bruno, *Cause*, p. 31.

39. See the middle paragraph, p. 42. This dual vision, in which ones sees the physical figure as real, tangible; and sees the same figure as the physical embodiment of a spiritual form of equally "real" existence; and both perceptions occurring at the same time: this dual vision has obvious aesthetic implications. A dramatist who confronts an audience, at least the more educated of whom habitually exercise this double vision, can tell an entertaining story—of a shepherd turned world-conqueror, say—which implies to the initiate (in the way Edgar Wind suggests of Renaissance art) a deeper level of meaning. The sword of man implies the power of the soul. This view

of art, not uncommon in medieval art, nor generally in considering Renaissance visual art, is championed on a universal scale by Bruno's conception
of man and his universe. We should not think it strange if Marlowe were
found to follow this view—a view of art which, by making both metaphor and
its interpretation equally "real," enriches our sense of the meaning and
experience of reading, and which may help to account for that excitement
and heightened perception which are peculiar to Renaissance literature.

40. See particularly Petrus Perondinus. This and other sources are
available in appendices to Una M. Ellis-Fermor's edition of *Tamburlaine*.

41. Two fairly recent unpublished doctoral dissertations have seen this
combination of seemingly opposed qualities as typical of Marlowe. Barry
Phillips sees conflicting aims and currents in the plays, like those in the age
generally, in "Marlowe: A Revaluation," *DA* (University of Connecticut,
1968), 2681-A. LeRoy E. Annis finds that "Marlowe's dramatic technique
[is] consistently a dialectic of condemnation and approval" in "Christopher
Marlowe's Multiple Perspective: The Source of Dramatic Ambivalence," *DAI*,
30 (University of Washington, 1969), 1975-A.

42. Samuel Shellabarger, *The Chevalier Bayard* (New York: Biblo and
Tannen, 1971; c. 1928), p. 91.

43. Shellabarger, p. 152.

44. Vergil, *The Aeneid*, trans. Patric Dickinson (New York: Mentor, 1961),
pp. 233-234.

45. Bruno, *Cause*, p. 57.

46. Bruno, *Expulsion*, pp. 151-152.

47. Bruno, *Expulsion*, pp. 172-173.

48. Bruno, *Heroic Frenzies*, pp. 108-109.

49. Bruno, *Cause*, p. 54.

50. Bruno, *Cause*, p. 63.

51. Bruno, *Cause*, p. 57.

52. Bruno has Prudenzio say of him, Giordano Bruno, at the end of *La
Cena de le Ceneri*, a cura di Giovanni Aquilecchia (Messina, 1955), "I
implore you, Nolan, for the hope I have in the Most High, the infinite Unity
which breathed life into you, and which you adore. Through the eminent
gods who protect you and whom you honor; through the divine Genius who
defends you, and in whom you trust. . . ." ("Io ti scongiuro Nolano per la
speranza ch'hai nell'altissima, et infinita unità che t'avviva, et adori. Per
gli eminenti numi, che ti protegeno, che onori; per il divino Genio che ti
defende, et in cui ti fidi. . ."—p. 230.)

53. Pachter, P. 191.

54. Don Cameron Allen, "Renaissance Remedies for Fortune: Marlowe
and the *Fortunati*," *SP*, XXXVIII (1941), 192.

55. Allen, p. 192.

56. This use of the word "virtue" to suggest a connection between inner
and outer qualities—to combine Christian "virtue" with Roman "virtú"—is
not unusual in the Renaissance in England. The *Oxford English Dictionary*
records the word's use in 1579 by Fenton in his translation of Guicciardini
to mean "manly qualities": "he fought with great virtue." Also in *Tamburlaine*,
Part One itself, this time to mean "by the power or efficacy of": "With

vertue of a gentle victory, / Conclude a league of honor to my hope." Another sixteenth-century English meaning to this word, related primarily to precious stones, is "occult efficacy or power."

Professor Masinton agrees, observing that to Tamburlaine, vertue and virtú are the same (p. 33), although for him this fact morally condemns the hero. Professor Waith, in *Ideas of Greatness*, reaches a similar conclusion about "vertue," p. 58.

57. It is interesting to compare this view of Tamburlaine with the opinion of one of the Florentine neo-Platonists who also believed in magic, Marsilio Ficino. In his *Sopra Lo Amore*, a cura di Giuseppe Rensi (Lanciano: R. Carabba, 1914), he makes clear the distinction between spiritual and carnal affections: ". . . the appetites of lust and of love are not only not the same urges, but show themselves to be contradictory." (". . . lo appetito del coite e lo Amore, non solamente non sono i medesimi moti, ma essere contrarii si mostrano"—p. 23.) He also makes clear the nature of this higher kind of love, and its relation to ideal beauty: "Thus we confess to all men that love is God, great and miraculous: both noble and useful: and in such a way do we say that love works, that of its objective, that is Beauty itself, we remain content." ("Adunque confessiamo al tutto che Amore sia Iddio grande e mirabile: ancora nobile e utilissimo: e in tal modo allo Amore opera diamo, che del suo fine, che è essa Belleza, remangliamo contenti"—p. 24.)

58. It is at this point that Mr. A. D. Hope's interpretation of the play begins to fall short of what was, in my view, Marlowe's original inspiration.

59. *Hermetica*, I, 295.

60. *Hermetica*, I, 153.

61. Pachter, p. 327.

62. Bruno, *Cause*, p. 144.

63. *Hermetica*, I, 221.

64. See notes 29 and 30 to chapter II.

65. The connection in the informed Elizabethan mind between geography and magical speculations is very clear. Ethel Seaton, "Marlowe's Map," *Marlowe, A Collection of Critical Essays*, ed. Clifford Leech, Twentieth Century Views Series (Englewood Cliffs, 1965), demonstrates that Marlowe was well versed in contemporary geographical studies, and used Ortelius' *Theatrum Orbis Terrarum* "with the accuracy of a scholar and the common sense of a merchant-venturer" (p. 54). What this implies for Marlowe's sense of the meaning of geography may be inferred from E. G. R. Taylor, *Tudor Geography, 1485-1583* (London: Methuen, 1930), who observes that "geography . . . has its roots in astronomy, in a knowledge of the shape and size of the earth, of the apparent motion relative to the earth of the heavenly bodies, knowledge which allows accurate fixing of position" (p. 2). Other basic knowledge included mathematics, history, natural history, geometry, and cosmography (p. 2). And the greatest Elizabethan in these matters, as his library was the greatest in the nation (see Peter French, pp. 40-61; also Francis Yates, *Theatre of the World*, pp. 10-13), John Dee, was "the man behind the scenes of overseas enterprise" for Elizabethan England (Taylor, p. v). Indeed, Peter French argues that compared to the preface to Dee's edition of Euclid in 1570, "no other single work was so influential in encouraging the development in England of . . . navigation" (p. 177). Both Taylor and French assert that this magus, whose universal scholarship makes him the great geographer of his

age in England, often consulted with Raleigh and his circle, very possibly including, more likely still influencing the geographical thinking of, Marlowe (See French, p. 171; Taylor, p. 76).

Joan Gadol, in her *Leon Battista Alberti*, argues impressively that Alberti knew Ptolemy's *Geography* and the principles of cartography which it implies. Indeed, she asserts that "the scaled survey map of ancient cartography was . . . the intellectual ancestor of the scaled checkerboard pavement" which Alberti used for his perspective pictures (p. 74). Thus the geometrical symbolism which is near the root of Alberti's aesthetic theory—itself becoming the basis for most other Renaissance aesthetic theorists—is as clearly embodied in maps as in paintings and other art forms. Again we see forcefully the connection between geography and intellectual insight into the hidden forms of things.

This suggestion about the intellectual seriousness which Marlowe may have held for geographical studies is shown to be likely in still another way by Nicholas of Cusa, who indicates the widespread nature of these beliefs in the early Renaissance in Europe. Cusa speaks of the mind of man as being like a living compass (an instrument, of course, used much in mapmaking and other diagrammatic functions) which possesses a sidepiece for measuring the degree of the angle it draws. Thus this compass, while drawing circles (its normal function), measures itself: "Libro III, La Mente" in "Idiota," *Scritti Filosofici*, ed. Giovanni Santinello (Bologna, 1965), I, 166. It is a measurer which is also that which is measured. So Tamburlaine. By external action, he comes to realize his inner potential.

It is interesting, then, that Bruno too saw a related kind of significance in compasses at precisely this time, as is shown by his dialogue titled *Idiota Triumphans*. It is almost as if he were picking up Cusa's treatment of the inspired but non-understanding person, the "idiota," and transforming it for his own uses. In this dialogue, Bruno puts forth the mystic significance of the new compass of Mordente. For a full discussion, see Yates' *Giordano Bruno*, pp. 294 ff.

66. John P. Cutts, in "The Ultimate Source of Tamburlaine's White, Red, Black and Death," *N & Q*, V (April, 1958), 146-147, backs this view by noticing that the same colors, followed by death, are revealed in precisely the same order in the *Book of Revelation*. This similarity is seen as emphasizing Tamburlaine's role as scourge of God.

67. This unusual metaphoric use of literal dramatic action is paralleled by Marlowe's literal treatment of the normally metaphoric figure of the pastoral shepherd. Normally, as has been argued on p. 51 above, the shepherd is a metaphor for ideal human qualities. Tamburlaine, as the play opens, is not only ideal, but literally a shepherd. To enlarge his dimensions, he must therefore cast off his shepherd's "weeds" and take on the clothing of a soldier. So here in Act IV, characters who are spiritually dead have this inner quality represented metaphorically by the literal act of death, which if seen *only* as a literal act may seem cruel. It should not be seen in this way. Marlowe's techniques at critical junctures are similar throughout.

68. Castiglione asserts: "There are also many men concerned solely with physical activities, and these differ from men versed in the things of the mind as much as the soul differs from the body. As rational creatures, however, they share in reason to the extent of being able to recognize it; but they do not possess it themselves or profit from it. These, then, are essentially

slaves, and it is more advantageous for them to obey than to command" (p. 298). Marlowe has simply chosen to express this common Renaissance view literally.

It is not surprising, in this context, to find Ariosto describing victims in the seige of Paris as "that common rabble, folk fit to die even before their birth" in *Orlando Furioso*, trans. Guido Waldman (London: Oxford U. Press, 1974), pp. 168-169.

69. See I, ii, 154-157; also II, i, 3-4; and the argument on my pp. 57-58, above.

70. Once more Castiglione speaks to the poet: "outward beauty is a true sign of inner goodness" (p. 330). How much closer must inner beauty and virtue be? Thus it is not surprising for one of his speakers also to assert that "it is more fitting for a warrior to be educated than for anyone else; and I would have those two accomplishments [letters—the pursuit of intellectual beauty—and skill at war], the one helping the other, as is most fitting, joined together in our courtier" (p. 93).

71. See note 56, above.

72. Fieler emphasizes that this speech is a *Mirror for Magistrates*-style "lament over the fall of princes," a clear parallel to the "strongest literary convention of the day" which would be taken literally, straightforwardly, seriously by Marlowe's audience (p. 77). But Waith argues that this speech "both presents the conventional view of hubris more convincingly than any other character, and shows the inadequacy of this view in judging Tamburlaine" (p. 75). Obviously, literary conventions can be played against, even used as straw men, as well as taken seriously, and in a given dramatic context, may be used in several ways at once.

73. Ficino, in *Sopra Lo Amore*, equates love with divinity—with God—and Beauty is seen as love's (virtue's, divinity's) working in this world: see note 57 above, to this chapter. Zenocrate seems to conform to the ideal vision of this well-known fount of Renaissance neo-Platonism. But to find this ideal in this physical world took more than neo-Platonism, and it is perhaps well to remember here that Ficino had translated the Hermetic Books as well as Plato into Latin.

74. Eugenio Garin discusses, in *Medioevo e Rinascimento*, this concept of the perfect human being: "The infinite power of man is concentrated in the unity of the act. And here is the sage who rules the stars, the magician who shapes the elements; here is the unity of being and of thought, and the full span of reality. This, and no other, is the defense of magic which the Renaissance meant to include in its celebration of man." ("L'infinta potenza dell'uomo si raccoglie nell'unità dell'Atto. Ed ecco il sapiente che domina le stelle, il mago che plasma gli elementi; ecco l'unità dell'essere e del pensare, e l'apertura totale della realtà. Questo, e non altro, intendera la difesa della magia, che il Rinascimento inseri nella sua celebrazione dell'uomo"—p. 169.) It is the magical-Hermetic view of man which not only conceives of human ideality, but believes in its physical perfection in this world.

75. D. P. Walker argues that "perhaps the most important" source of magic was indeed not the Hermetic influence, but "the mass, with its music, words of consecration, incense, lights, wine and supreme magical effect—transubstantiation" (p. 36).

76. This parallel was briefly noticed earlier, on p. 63.

77. Masinton, in *Marlowe's Tragic Vision*, sees this irony among the over-ambitious, but includes Tamburlaine in their number, p. 7.

78. Francis R. Johnson argues, in "Marlowe's 'Imperiall Heaven'," that this "imperial heaven" was "the immovable heaven lying just beyond the outermost moving sphere (the *primum mobile*) and enclosing within its concavity all the movable celestial spheres. The throne of God and the abode of the angels lay in this steadfast empyreal heaven, a region which shone perpetually with the purest light" (p. 35).

79. For example, Pico della Mirandola writes, in his "Oration on the Dignity of Man," that the "true interpretation of the Law" as "divinely handed down to Moses . . . was called the Cabala" (p. 251). Further, he writes that "I saw in [this law] . . . not so much the Mosaic as the Christian religion" (p. 252). Pico, one of the most famous spokesmen for the Platonic-Hermetic strain of Renaissance thought, sees not only Hebraism and Christianity as the same, but also magic—the Cabala, and Christianity.

80. See note 38 to Chapter One above, on Agrippa's *De incertitudine et vanitate scientarum et artium*.

81. A. D. Hope, pp. 117-128.

82. O. B. Hardison, Jr. *Christian Rite and Christian Drama in the Middle Ages* (Baltimore: Johns Hopkins Press, 1965), pp. 226 ff. Jocelyn Powell refers to the play's characters as "living emblems" in "Marlowe's Spectacle," *Tulane Drama Review*, VIII (1964), 197.

83. Thus Cellini argues of *Tamburlaine*'s title character, "Probably one deals with a symbol—and any other would be unfit, considering that it is Tamburlaine who speaks,—with a symbol of the greatest conquest of the spirit, the attainment of divinity, toward which the Middle Ages, from the Vittorini to Bonaventura, from Bagnoregio and to Dante, inclined by means of a mystical enthusiasm, and toward which the Renaissance, from Ficino to Pico della Mirandola, from Bruno to Campanella, tended more naturalistically by means of an intellectual process." ("Probabilmente si tratta di un simbolo—e tutt'altro che inaddatto, considerando che è Tamerlano che parla,—del simbolo cioè della più grande conquista dello spirito, il raggiungimento della divinità, a cui il medio evo, dai vittorini a Bonaventura da Bagnoregio e a Dante, tendeva per mezzo di uno slancio mistico, e il Rinascimento dal Ficino a Pico della Mirandola, dal Bruno al Campanella, più naturalisticamento mediante un processo intelletualistico"—p. 115.)

84. Perhaps it is appropriate at this point to record Muriel Rukeyser's impression of Bruno's depth and power. She sees him as a "Pioneer of certitude that is based on something other than rock." He is a "swimmer of infinity." Many have followed him, "not knowing whom they followed, yet swimming ever in those shoreless floods" (*Traces of Thomas Hariot*, p. 161).

Chapter III

1. See notes 1-16 to the Introduction above. Only Eugene Waith, in *The Herculean Hero*, believes that the noble hero of Part One maintains his stature in Part Two. As we have seen, however, this stature is below the divinity which Tamburlaine seems to demonstrate.

2. Hope believes that his "Argument of Arms" is either carried so far as to prove its invalidity, or shows the tragedy of the hero in spite of the thesis' validity (pp. 125 and ff.).

3. Battenhouse, p. 252.

4. Jan Kott, *Shakespeare, Our Contemporary* (Garden City: Doubleday, 1964), pp. 74, 92.

5. Bruno, *Infinite Universe and Worlds*, p. 377.

6. "Asclepius," *Hermetica*, I, 295.

7. "Asclepius," *Hermetica*, I, 339.

8. Bruno, *Cause, Principle, and Unity*, p. 68.

9. Even Marsilio Ficino distinguishes between the masculine and feminine, the proper and the degenerate, man: "But some are more inclined, either by nature or custom, to the side of the soul than of the body, to that of the Spirit. The first follow celestial love; the second follow the vulgar kind. The first love the masculine more than the feminine, the adolescent more than the childish, because in them reigns much more vigorously the keen intellect. This quality is most actively suggested by one's excellent beauty in receiving that discipline which, quite naturally, is able to generate its own special tastes and desires. The second, on the contrary, is moved by the voluptuousness of the sexual act to the result whose purpose is corporeal generation. But because the power to generate, which is in the soul, lacks cognition, therefore there is no difference between sexes in this lower form of love." ("Ma alcuni o per natura o per uso sono più atti al parto dell'animo che del corpo, che dell'Animo. I primi seguitano il celeste Amore: i secondi seguitano il vulgare. I primi amano i maschi piuttosto che le femmine, e adolescenti piuttosto che puerili: perchè in essi, molto più vigoreggia lo acume dello intelletto: il quale è suggetto attissimo, per la sua eccellente Bellezza a ricevere la disciplina, la quale per natura generare coloro appetiscono. I secondi per il contrario mossi dalle voluttà dello atto venereo, a lo effetto della generazione corporale intendono: ma perchè la potenzia di generare, che è nella Anima, manca di cognizione, pero non fa differenzia tra sesso e sesso"—*Sopra Lo Amore*, p. 117.)

10. One is again reminded of the parallel in these lines to Bruno's image of asininity in his *Cabala*. See pp. 89-90, above.

11. The hero's sarcasm and mockery should perhaps remind us of Bruno's "Candelaio," whose motto states the sad-humorous quality of life from an exalted perspective like Tamburlaine's: "In tristitia hilaris, in hilaritate tristis." It is a comedy about the usual failure of men to live up to their great possibilities.

12. I think that we should not necessarily read "Christian God" into this statement, although Christians might if they liked, and such an interpretation would not lose Marlowe any admirers. But "heaven" probably means the Imperial Heaven, and "God" the divinity within that Heaven, rather than a specifically Christian conception. Indeed, the God who is full of thunder and lightning sounds more like Him of the Old Testament than of the New.

13. I do not believe that this scene represents the fascination which an anti-religious man holds for religious ceremony, a view which Harry Levin suggests for other religious scenes in Marlowe, in *The Overreacher*, p. 120.

14. To appreciate the magical-mystical significance of this knowledge of

both architecture and geography, see note 55 to Chapter One, and note 65 to Chapter Two, above. See also Peter French, *John Dee*, and Francis Yates, *The Theatre of the World*, for the significance of Dee's ideas in their intellectual and their national contexts.

It is also well known that "the new principles of fortification were based on geometrical calculations" (John R. Hale, *The Art of War and Renaissance England*, Folger Booklets on Tudor and Stuart Civilization; Charlottesville: The University Press of Virginia, 1961; p. 28).

15. See note 70 to Chapter Two above for a reference to Castiglione's high regard for the intellectual qualities of the ideal warrior.

16. The astrological argument advanced by Johnstone Parr in *Tamerlane's Malady and Other Essays* (Tuscaloosa: University of Alabama Press, 1953) that a flaw in his character, excess of passion, as well as his astral destiny, caused the hero's death, does not seem inconsistent with this final view of him (pp. 19, 23). His passion is so noble that in him it is no defect, but an inevitable aspect of such greatness. One is reminded of Achilleus, who was given the choice of a short, noble life, or a long but peaceful one with less dignity. No hero really has a choice; nobility, achievement, aspiration are his elements. As with Achilleus, so with Tamburlaine. If it were otherwise with them, they would not have been who they were.

17. Zenocrate too was perfect. The union between her and Tamburlaine wed two equal spirits and two magnificent bodies into one entity. It is her death, therefore, which is the initial test of Tamburlaine's conviction that the earth is perfectible, that eternity can be transient.

18. Bruno, *Heroic Frenzies*, pp. 110, 112.

19. *Hermetica*, I, 227.

20. "Asclepius," *Hermetica*, I, 339.

21. "Asclepius," *Hermetica*, I, 363.

22. Viewed in this way, metamorphosis is the physical embodiment, as well as continuation, of the aspiration and achievement of the magus. Agrippa writes, "All things were created to be used by us; thus, not without foundation, the magicians believe that we are easily able to ascend these same steps again, to penetrate successively into each of these same worlds and to go as far as to the animating archetype of the world, the first cause on which all things depend and from which they proceed. . . ." (". . . cose tutte create per essere da noi usate; così, non senza fondamento, i Magi credono che noi possiamo agevolmente risalire gli stessi gradini, penetrare successivemente in ciascuno di tali mondi e giungere sino al mondo archetipo animatore, causa prima da cui dipendono e procedono tutte le cose. . ."—p. 12.)

23. Bruno, *Expulsion*, pp. 75-78.

24. See also Bruno's "Cabala del Cavallo Pegaseo," *Le opere italiane di Giordano Bruno* (Gottinga: Paolo de Lagarde, 1888), vol. 2, 585. Perhaps even more clearly Bruno later writes: "Nabuchodonosor . . . [and] Saduchin del Battista [exemplify transformation] not only in the same body, but by the same spirit in another body. In such a method of resuscitation do some promise themselves the execution of divine justice according to the affections and acts which they have exercised in another body." ("Nabuchodonosor . . . [e] Saduchin del Battista non già per medesimo corpo, ma per medesimo spirito in un'altro corpo. In cotal modo di resuscitatione alchuni si promettono

l'exequtione della giustitia divina secondo gl'affetti et atti ch'hanno exercitati in un'altro corpo"—p. 589.)

25. Muriel C. Bradbrook and M. G. Lloyd Thomas, *Marvel* (Cambridge, 1940), p. 61.

26. Bruno, *Cause*, p. 89.

27. A comparison of any extended passages in Bruno's works published while he was in London, with passages from Pietro Bembo's *Gli Asolani* (p. 154 illustrates the point well), will clearly show the essential difference in viewpoints. Bembo denies the possibility that earth and heavens could in any way touch, yet asserts their correspondence on different planes of being. Statements of correspondence and of common spiritual inspiration likewise abound in Bruno, despite his very different orientation.

28. Cellini, *Marlowe*, I, 19: "Ecco dunque gli elementi necessari per risolvere la sua crisi spirituale, e ceo certamente la genesi di *Tamburlaine*." (My English translation in the text.)

29. Cellini, *Marlowe*, I, 155: " . . . il contrasto tra le iperboliche aspirazioni dell'eroe, che spesso assumono un valore trascendentale, e l'inadeguatezza delle realizzazioni, che non altrepassano per lo più il piano materiale." (My translation into English in the text.)

30. Similarly, Pico della Mirandola, in his oration "On the Dignity of Man," asserts that "the *magus* wed[s] earth to heaven, that is, he weds lower things to the endowments and powers of higher things" (p. 249).

31. Bruno, "To his Own Spirit," *Cause*, pp. 54-55.

32. Parr, pp. 19, 23.

33. Kott, pp. 91-100, 107.

34. Amaresh Datta, *Shakespeare's Tragic Vision and Art* (Delhi, 1963), pp. 18 ff.

35. See pp. 108 and ff. above.

36. Robb, p. 245.

37. Cellini's view. See note 28 above.

38. Bruno, *Expulsion*, p. 91. It is taken from *Orlando Furioso*, XLV, 2.

39. In isolation, of course, this sun-imagery is widespread during the Renaissance. Its application to the ideal man of this world, however, may find its fullest expression in Bruno's fellow magus and somewhat later contemporary, Tommaso Campanella. In *The City of the Sun*, the prince of this ideal city is called "Sole"—the Sun. He is a metaphysician with ascendance over three collateral princes: Power, Wisdom, and Love (pp. 5-6)—the three basic qualities of Tamburlaine. However, that others in this age were working, at roughly the same time, in the same current of inspiration, which seems to stem largely from Bruno's influence, may lend an air of plausibility to the present thesis about Marlowe's plays.

40. Bruno, *Heroic Frenzies*, p. 155.

41. See pp. 170-172 below.

42. Bruno, *Heroic Frenzies*, p. 159.

43. Bruno, *Heroic Frenzies*, pp. 159-161.

44. See again V, iii, 224-227.

45. *The Notebooks of Leonardo da Vinci*, ed. Jean Paul Richter (New

York: Dover, 1970; *c.* 1883), I, 15-16: Leonardo writes that "among all the studies of natural causes and reasons Light chiefly delights the beholder; . . . Thus if the Lord—who is the light of all things—vouchsafe to enlighten me, I will treat of Light."

Leonardo continues later, "Here [in the eye] forms, colours, here the character of every part of the universe are concentrated to a point" (p. 19). Perspective, which forms so large a part of Leonardo's—and of Renaissance—aesthetics, is defined as "a thorough knowledge of the function of the eye" (p. 29). Most clearly, perhaps, he states that "the eye, which is called the window of the soul, is the principal means by which the central sense can most completely and abundantly appreciate the infinite works of nature" (p. 327). It may not, therefore, be surprising that at least on one occasion Leonardo sounds a bit like Tamburlaine:

> Obstacles cannot crush me
> Every obstacle yields to stern resolve
> He who is fixed to a star does not change his mind. (p. 356)

See also D. P. Walker's explanation of the importance of the eyes both in inspiring the emotions, and in receiving divine illumination, p. 33.

46. See Eugenio Garin, *Medioevo*, p. 334, quoted fully on pp. 135-136 below.

47. This was also true in Part One. See pp. 166, 170-172 below.

48. See again pp. 170-172 below.

49. Bradbrook, *School of Night*, pp. 115-116.

50. *Michelangelo: Artista, Pensatore, Scrittore*, Comitato Nazionale Per Le Onoranze A Michelangelo (Novara: Istituto Geografico de Agostini, 1965), II, 531. Quoted from his *Rime*, a cura di Enzo Girardi (Bari, 1960), p. 20: "un concetto di bellezza immaginata o vista dentro al core amico di virtute e gentilezza. . . ." (My English translation in the text.)

51. See also note 45 to Chapter Three above. And Garin, *Medioevo*, pp. 334-335.

52. Garin, *Medioevo*, p. 334: "Il magico punto d'unione fra la scienze del pittore e la scienza della natura, per entrambe le quali la mente dell'uomo 《 si trasmuta in similitudine di mente divina》; quel nesso ideale—che è l'anima stressa del pensiero di Leonardo—trova la radice proprio nella filosofia platonico-ficiniana." (My English translation in the text.)

53. Cellini, *Marlowe*, I, 115: ". . . probabilmento si tratta di un simbolo —e tutt'altro che inadatto, considerando che è Tamerlano che parla,—del simbolo cioè della più grande conquista dello spirito, il raggiungimento della divinità, a cui il medio evo, dai vittorini a Bonaventura da Bagnoregio e a Dante, tendeva per mezzo di uno slancio mistico, e il Rinascimento, dal Ficino a Pico della Mirandola, dal Bruno al Campanella, più naturalisticamente medianto un processo intelletualistico." (My English translation in the text.)

54. See the quotation from Garin, *Medioevo*, p. 150, on my p. 137 below.

55. See particularly the "Epistle to the Reader" of *Willobie his Avisa*, and Professor Harrison's speculations in his accompanying essay.

56. Campanella, as quoted in Garin, *Medioevo*, p. 150: "Tutto quello che si fa dalli scienziati imitando la natura, o aiutandola con l'arte ignota, non solo all plebe bassa, ma alla communità degli uomini, [appare] opera magica." (My English translation in the text.)

204

57.   See Maurice Evans' introductory essay to *Bussy D'Ambois* (New York: Hill and Wang, 1966).

CHAPTER IV, PART ONE

1.   It is not my intention here to argue fully a new interpretation for each of the remaining plays written by Marlowe. Rather, I wish briefly to sketch the implications of the argument just completed on the Tamburlaine plays for an interpretation of the others. It is a direction on interpretation in these other plays which I wish to indicate. The case for specific points in specific plays necessary to demonstrate this direction have pretty much been argued already by other writers. My method here, then, is to indicate ideas, and to rely for supporting evidence on the references to other scholars in these notes.

2.   Ejner J. Jensen expresses this view of the play, as well as showing its parallels with modern world-views, in "Marlowe Our contemporary? Some Questions of Relevance," *CE*, XXX (1969), 627-632.

3.   Fredson Bowers, *Elizaethan Revenge Tragedy: 1587-1942* (Princeton: Princeton University Press, 1957), pp. 104-109.

4.   T. S. Eliot, "Christopher Marlowe," p. 62.

5.   J. B. Steane, p. 203.

6.   Harry Levin, *The Overreacher*, p. 73.

7.   F. P. Wilson, *Marlowe and the Early Shakespeare*, pp. 57-59.

8.   Hiram Haydn, *The Counter-Renaissance*, p. 150.

9.   J. P. Brockbank, *Marlowe: Dr. Faustus* (Woodbury, N.Y.: Barron's, 1962), pp. 59-60.

10.   C. L. Barber, "The Form of Faustus' Fortune, Good or Bad," *Tulane Drama Review*, VIII (1963-1964), 101.

11.   Steane, pp. 156-157. Also Masinton, pp. 114, 138, 141.

12.   Levin, p. 116.

13.   Eliot, "Marlowe," p. 6.

14.   Masinton makes a closely related observation: "Faustus epitomizes the man of the Renaissance and modern periods" whose "optimistic dream . . . turns into a hell of dread, because instead of creating his utopia he has become the slave of forces that he either fears to use or cannot control" (p. 141).

15.   Barber, "The Form," p. 118.

16.   Michel Poirier asserts that, with the probable exception of *Tamburlaine*, Part One, "Marlowe starts his dramas in a revolutionary spirit; he concludes them in full conformity with the opinions commonly accepted" (p. 71).

17.   George Chapman, *Bussy D'Ambois*, ed. Robert J. Lordi (Lincoln: University of Nebraska Press, 1964), V, iv, 78.

CHAPTER IV, PART TWO

18.   R. E. Knoll, p. 109.

19.   Irving Ribner, "Introduction" to *The Complete Plays of Christopher Marlowe*, p. xxxiv.

20. W. Sanders, pp. 121-142.

21. Thomas M. Parrott & Robert H. Ball, *A Short View of Elizabethan Drama* (New York: Scribner's, 1958; c. 1943), p. 89. See also Bakeless, pp. 190-191.

22. Steane, p. 208.

23. Charles G. Masinton, "Marlowe's Artists: the Failure of Imagination," *Ohio University Review*, XI (1969), 23.

24. Masinton does suggest a kinship between Tamburlaine and Edward, but I think he goes too far by over-generalizing the term "artist," and by not adequately distinguishing the different ways in which these different characters use their "creative imaginations." Obviously, characters and people are artists, and are imaginative, in very different ways and for very different reasons. Such differences seem to be epitomized by the dissimilarities between Tamburlaine and Edward, and their parallels almost to be incidental.

25. Steane, pp. 216-220.

26. R. E. Knoll believes that in *Edward II* "all the dramatis personae are essentially petty" (*Christopher Marlowe*, p. 124). Steane has essentially the same view; see pp. 206, 222-226, 233-234.

27. This may be the inevitable price for what Masinton calls Marlowe's stress "on the psychological pain of his protagonists" (*Marlowe's Tragic Vision*, p. 5), for even he recognizes that Marlowe's characters are steadily diminished in stature as the career goes on (p. 6).

CHAPTER V

1. Irving Ribner,"Introduction" to *The Complete Plays of Christopher Marlowe*, p. xxx.

2. Parrott and Ball, for example, observe that "he was a born poet who only by degrees made himself a master playwright" (p. 91).

3. Fieler, *Tamburlaine, Part I and its Audience*. See note 1 to the Introduction.

4. Indeed, Paul H. Kocher believes Tamburlaine to be "separated both from God and man" (p. 301), a character for whom "the moral code dissolves under the primacy of the will to power" (p. 78). To Kocher, Tamburlaine is morally worse than Machiavelli (p. 72).

5. Ribner, "Introduction," p. xxx.

6. M. M. Mahood, pp. 54-86.

7. Levin, p. 82.

8. For fuller treatment of this subject see pp. 26 & ff. above.

9. See, for example, Parrott and Ball, pp. 40-41.

10. Frances Yates, *Giordano Bruno*, pp. 155-156.

11. Johan Huizinga, *The Waning of the Middle Ages* (Garden City: Doubleday, 1954; c. 1949), p. 218.

12. Huizinga, p. 274.

13. T. S. Eliot, "Ben Jonson," *Essays on Elizabethan Drama*, p. 75.

14. Eliot argues that "what holds the play together is a unity of inspiration that radiates into plot and personages alike" ("Ben Jonson," p. 76).

15. William Archer, in his 1919 review of a production of the play, may make the most extreme condemnation: he says of the scene generally that "any morbid-minded schoolboy could have conceived it, and that the humblest melodramatist of today would not dare to affront his transpontine audiences by asking them to applaud such a grisly absurdity." *John Webster*, ed. G. K. and S. K. Hunter (Baltimore: Penguin, 1969), p. 96.

16. Karl L. Holzknecht,"The Dramatic Structure of *The Changeling*," *Shakespeare's Contemporaries*, eds. Max Bluestone and Norman Rabkin, 2nd ed. (Englewood Cliffs, 1970), pp. 367-377. See also my article, "Ford's *The Lady's Trial*: A Play of Metaphysical Wit," *Genre*, VII (December, 1974), 342-361.

17. Pico della Mirandola, "Oration," p. 223.

Appendix A

1. M. C. Bradbrook, *School of Night*, p. 68.

2. R. Adamson, *Greek Philosophy Before Plato*, p. 44. Quoted from Bradbrook, *School of Night*, p. 68.

3. By contrast, Masinton sees Marlowe's fire and its associated imagery as reflecting the objective Christian Hell, and also the inward hell of the sinner, p. 6.

4. Bradbrook, *School of Night*, pp. 68, 69.

5. Bruno, *Heroic Frenzies*, pp. 108, 33.

6. Bruno, *Heroic Frenzies*, pp. 211-213.

7. Bruno, *Heroic Frenzies*, p. 145. His explanation of the emblem's meaning continues onto pp. 146-147.

8. Bruno, *Heroic Frenzies*, p. 96.

9. Paul E. Memmo's "Introduction" to Bruno's *Heroic Frenzies*, p. 45.

10. Bruno, *Heroic Frenzies*, p. 198.

11. Bruno, *Heroic Frenzies*, pp. 199-200.

12. Bruno, *Heroic Frenzies*, p. 156.

13. Bruno, *Heroic Frenzies*, p. 157.

14. Bruno, *Heroic Frenzies*, p. 158.

15. *Hermetica*, I, 159.

16. Bruno, *Heroic Frenzies*, pp. 108-109. Campanella too shows the strong inclination of the magus to glorify the sun as a kind of god: "They [the citizens] honor the sun and the stars like living things, and as statues of God and celestial temples; but they do not worship them, and they honor the sun more. They worship no created thing, but only God, and therefore they serve him only under the sign of *the sun, which is the emblem and face of God*, from which come light and heat and every other thing. Therefore the altar is made like a sun, and the priests pray to God in the sun and in the stars, as in altars, and in the sky, as in a temple; and they call the good angels as intercessors who are in the stars, in their living houses, and who show the beauties of their God the more in the sky and *in the sun, as his trophy and statue*." ("Onorano il sole e le stelle come cose viventi e statue di Dio e tempii celesti; ma non l'adorano, e più onorano il sole. Nulla creatura *adorano di latria*, altro che Dio, e però a lui serveno solo sotto l'insegna *del sole, ch'e insegna e volto di Dio*, da cui viene la luce e 'l calore e ogni altra

cosa. Però l'altare è come un sole fatto, e li sacerdoti pregano Dio nel sole e nelle stelle, com'in altari, e nel cielo, come tempio; e chiamano gli angeli buoni per intercessori, che stanno nelle stelle, vive case loro, e che le bellezze sue Dio più le mostrò in cielo e *nel sole, come suo trofeo e statua"—La Città del Sole*, p. 52.)

17.   Pachter, p. 337.

18.   Bruno, *Heroic Frenzies*, pp. 147-148.

19.   Edgar Wind, *Pagan Mysteries in the Renaissance*, p. 187.

20.   Bruno, *Expulsion*, p. 90. This book is, of course, one of those written in London, though ostensibly published in Paris in 1584.

Appendix B

1.   Bruno, *Heroic Frenzies*, p. 96.

2.   Bruno, *Heroic Frenzies*, p. 208.

3.   Dorothy L. Sayers' and Barbara Reynolds' notes to *The Comedy of Dante Alighieri the Florentine, Cantica III, Paradise* (Baltimore: Penguin, 1962), pp. 218, 228.

4.   Bruno, *Heroic Frenzies*, pp. 154-155.

LIST OF WORKS CITED

Agrippa, Enrico Cornelio. *La Filosofia Occulta*, trans. Alberto Fidi. Vol. I. Milano, 1926.

Alberti, Leon Battista. *Architetto*, ed. and intro. Corrado Ricci. Torino, 1917.

Allen, Don Cameron. "Renaissance Remedies for Fortune: Marlowe and The *Fortunati*," *SP*, 38 (1941).

Archer, William. A review of a 1919 production of *The Duchess of Malfi*. Cited from G. K. and S. K. Hunter, eds., *John Webster*. Baltimore: Penguin, 1969.

Ariosto, Lodovico. *Orlando Furioso*, trans. Guido Waldman. London: Oxford U. Press, 1974.

Bakeless, John. *Christopher Marlowe*. New York, 1937.

Barber, C. L. "The Form of Faustus' Fortune, Good or Bad," *Tulane Drama Review*, 8 (1963-1964).

Battenhouse, Roy W. *Marlowe's Tamburlaine: A Study in Renaissance Moral Philosophy*. Nashville, 1941.

Baumgardt, Carola. *Johannes Kepler: Life and Letters*. New York, 1951.

Bembo, Pietro. *Gli Asolani e le Rime*. Torino, 1932.

Benaquist, Lawrence M. "The Ethical Structure of *Tamburlaine*, Part I," *Toth*, X, 2 (spring 1969).

Bluestone, Max, and Norman Rabkin, eds. *Shakespeare's Contemporaries*. Englewood Cliffs, 1961.

Bowers, Fredson. *Elizabethan Revenge Tragedy: 1587-1642*. Princeton: Princeton U. Press, 1957.

Bradbrook, Muriel C. and M. G. Lloyd Thomas. *Marvel*. Cambridge, 1940.

Bradbrook, Muriel C. *The School of Night*. New York: Russell and Russell, 1965; c. 1936.

Brockbank, J. P. *Marlowe: Dr. Faustus*. Woodbury, N.Y.: Barron's, 1962.

Brown, John R. *Shakespeare and his Comedies*. London: Methuen, 1957.

Bruno, Giordano. "Cabala del Cavallo Pegaseo," *Le opere italiane di Giordano Bruno*, II. Gottinga: Paolo de Lagarde, 1888.

———. "Candelaio," *Opere Italiane*, ed. V. Spampanato, 2nd rev. ed., III. Bari, 1923.

———. *Five Dialogues on Cause, Principle and Unity*, trans. Jack Lindsay. New York: International Publishers, 1962.

———. *La Cena de le Ceneri*, a cura di Giovanni Aquilecchia. Messina, 1955.

———. *On the Infinite Universe and Worlds*, trans. Dorothea W. Singer. New York, 1950.

———. *The Expulsion of the Triumphant Beast*, trans. Arthur D. Imerti. New Brunswick: Rutgers U. Press, 1964.

————. *The Heroic Frenzies*, trans. P. E. Memmo. Chapel Hill: U. of North Carolina Press, 1966.

Burckhardt, Jacob. *The Civilization of the Renaissance in Italy*, trans. Ludwig Geiger and Walther Gotz, 2 vols. New York: Harper and Row, 1958.

Campanella, Tomasso. *La Città del Sole*, a cura di Alberto Agazzi. Siracusa, 1958.

————. "Magia e Grazia," inediti *Theologicorum Liber XIV*, ed. Romano Amerio. Edizione Nazionale dei Classici del Pensièro Italiano, Series II, No. 5. Roma, 1957.

Campbell, Lily B. *Scenes and Machines on the English Stage During the Renaissance*. Cambridge, 1923.

Cassirer, Ernst. *The Platonic Renaissance in England*, trans. J. P. Pettegrove. Austin: U. of Texas Press, 1953.

————, et al, eds. *The Renaissance Philosophy of Man*. Chicago, 1948.

Castiglione, Baldesar. *The Book of the Courtier*, trans. George Bull. Baltimore: Penguin, 1967.

Cellini, Benvenuto. *Marlowe*, I. Roma: A. Signorilli, 1937.

Chapman, George. *Bussy D'Ambois*, ed. Robert J. Lordi. Lincoln: U. of Nebraska Press, 1964.

Charlton, H. B. *The Dark Comedies*. Manchester, 1937.

Clark, Eleanor Grace. *Ralegh and Marlowe*. New York: Russell and Russell, 1965; c. 1941.

Cole, Douglas. *Suffering and Evil in the Plays of Christopher Marlowe*. Princeton, 1962.

Craig, Hardin. *The Enchanted Glass*. New York: Oxford, 1936.

Cruttwell, Patrick. *The Shakespearean Moment*. New York: Random House, 1969.

Cusa, Nicholas of. "Idiota," *Scritti Filosofici*, I, ed. Giovanni Santinello. Bologna, 1965.

Cutts, John P. "The Ultimate Source of Tamburlaine's White, Red, Black and Death," *Notes and Queries*, 5 (April 1958).

D'Agostino, Nemi. *Shakespeare e il Rinascimento*. Trieste: Università degli Studi di Trieste, 1959.

Datta, Amaresh. *Shakespeare's Tragic Vision and Art*. Delhi, 1963.

Dickey, Franklin N. *Not Wisely But Too Well: Shakespeare's Love Tragedies*. San Marino, 1966.

Dobrée, Bonamy. *Restoration Tragedy, 1660-1720*. Oxford, 1929.

Duthie, G. I. "The Dramatic Structure of Marlowe's *Tamburlaine the Great, Part I*," *Shakespeare's Contemporaries*, eds. Max Bluestone and Norman Rabkin. Englewood Cliffs, 1961.

Eliot, Thomas Stearns. *Essays on Elizabethan Drama*. New York: Harcourt, Brace, 1960; c. 1932.

Ellis-Fermor, Una M., ed. "Introduction" to *Tamburlaine*, by Christopher Marlowe. New York, 1966; c. 1930.

Evans, Maurice, ed. "Introduction" to *Bussy D'Ambois*, by George Chapman. New York: Hill and Wang, 1966.

Ferguson, Wallace K. *The Renaissance in Historical Thought*. Cambridge, Mass., 1948.

Ficino, Marsilio. *Sopra Lo Amore*, a cura di Giuseppe Rensi. Lanciano: R. Carabba, 1914.

———. *Théologie Platonicienne*, trans. Raymond Marcel, I. Paris, 1964.

Fieler, Frank B. *Tamburlaine, Part I and its Audience*. U. of Fla. Monographs in the Humanities, No. 8. Gainesville: U. of Fla. Press, 1961.

Finney, Gretchen L. "Music: A Book of Knowledge in Renaissance England," *Studies in the Renaissance*, VI (1959).

French, Peter. *John Dee, The World of an Elizabethan Magus*. London: Routledge and Kegan Paul, 1972.

Gadol, Joan. *Leon Battista Alberti: Universal Man of the Early Renaissance*. Chicago: U. of Chicago Press, 1969.

Garin, Eugenio. *Medioevo e Rinascimento*. Bari: G. Laterza & F., 1954.

Greene, Robert. "Perimedes the Blacke-Smith," *The Life and Complete Works in Prose and Verse of Robert Greene*, ed. A. B. Grossart, VII. New York: Russell and Russell, 1964; c. 1881-1886.

Hale, John R. *The Art of War and Renaissance England*. Folger Booklets on Tudor and Stuart Civilization. Charlottesville: The University Press of Virginia, 1961.

Hamilton, A. C. "Sidney and Agrippa," *Review of English Studies*, New Series, 7 (April 1956).

Handover, P. M. *The Second Cecil. The Rise to Power. 1563-1604*. London, 1959.

Hardison, O. B., Jr. *Christian Rite and Christian Drama in the Middle Ages*. Baltimore: Johns Hopkins Press, 1965.

Haydn, Hiram. *The Counter-Renaissance*. New York, 1950.

Henderson, Philip. *Christopher Marlowe*. London, 1952.

Hollander, John. *The Untuning of the Sky*. New York: Norton, 1970; c. 1961.

Holzknecht, Karl L. "The Dramatic Structure of *The Changeling*," *Shakespeare's Contemporaries*, eds. Max Bluestone and Norman Rabkin, 2nd ed. Englewood Cliffs, 1970.

Hope, A. D. *The Cave and the Spring: Essays on Poetry*. Chicago: U. of Chicago Press, 1965.

Howe, James. "Ford's *The Lady's Trial*: A Play of Metaphysical Wit," *Genre*, VII (December 1974).

Hughes, Merritt Y. "The Lineage of 'The Extasie'," *Modern Language Review*, 27 (January 1932).

Huizinga, Johan. *The Waning of the Middle Ages*. Garden City: Doubleday, 1954; c. 1949.

Jensen, Ejner J. "Marlowe Our Contemporary? Some Questions of Relevance," *CE*, 30 (1969).

Johnson, Francis R. "Marlowe's Astronomy and Renaissance Skepticism," *ELH*, XIII (1946).

Jump, John D. "Introduction" to his edition of *Tamburlaine the Great, Parts I and II*, by Christopher Marlowe. Lincoln, Neb.: U. of Neb. Press, 1967.

211

LIST OF WORKS CITED

Knoll, Robert E. *Christopher Marlowe*. New York: Twayne, 1969.

Kocher, Paul. *Christopher Marlowe: A Study of his Thought, Learning, and Character*. New York: Russell and Russell, 1962; c. 1946.

Kott, Jan. *Shakespeare, Our Contemporary*. Garden City: Doubleday, 1964.

Koyré, Alexandre. *From the Closed World to the Infinite Universe*. Baltimore, 1957.

Kristeller, Paul Oskar. *Renaissance Thought*, 2 vols. New York: Harper and Row, 1961.

Lerner, Lawrence S. and Edward A. Gosselin. "Giordano Bruno," *Scientific American*, 228 (April 1973).

Levin, Harry. *The Overreacher: A Study of Christopher Marlowe*. Cambridge, Mass., 1952.

Mahood, M. M. *Poetry and Humanism*. New Haven, 1950.

Marlowe, Christopher. *The Complete Plays of Christopher Marlowe*, ed. Irving Ribner. New York: Odyssey, 1963.

Masinton, Charles G. *Christopher Marlowe's Tragic Vision*. Athens, Ohio: Ohio U. Press, 1972.

———. "Marlowe's Artists: the Failure of Imagination," *Ohio University Review*, XI (1969).

Michelangelo. *The Complete Poems of Michelangelo*, trans. Joseph Tusiani. New York: Noonday, 1960.

Michelangelo: Artista, Pensatore, Scrittore. Comitato Nazionale Per Le Onoranze A Michelangelo. Novara, 1965.

Muir, Edwin. " 'Royal Man': Notes on the Tragedies of George Chapman," *Shakespeare's Contemporaries*, eds. Max Bluestone and Norman Rabkin. Englewood Cliffs, 1961.

Mulryne, J. R. and Stephen Fender. "Marlowe and the 'Comic Distance'," *Christopher Marlowe*, ed. Brian Morris. London: Ernest Benn, 1968.

Pachter, Henry M. *Magic Into Science: The Story of Paracelsus*. New York, 1951.

Pagel, Walter. *Paracelsus: An Introduction to Philosophical Medicine in the Era of the Renaissance*. Basel, 1958.

Parr, Johnstone. *Tamerlane's Malady and Other Essays*. Tuscaloosa: U. of Alabama Press, 1953.

Parrott, Thomas M. and Robert H. Ball. *A Short View of Elizabethan Drama*. New York: Scribner's, 1958; c. 1943.

Pauli, Wolfgang. *The Influence of Archetypal Ideals on the Scientific Theories of Kepler*. New York, 1955.

Phialas, Peter. *Shakespeare's Romantic Comedies*. Chapel Hill: U. of North Carolina Press, 1966.

Pico della Mirandola, Giovanni. "Oration on the Dignity of Man," trans. Paul O. Kristeller, *The Renaissance Philosophy of Man*, eds. Ernst Cassirer, et al. Chicago, 1948.

Poirier, Michel. *Christopher Marlowe*. London: Archon, 1968; c. 1951.

Pomponazzi, Pietro. "On Immortality," trans. William H. Hay, *The Renaissance Philosophy of Man*, eds. Ernst Cassirer, et al. Chicago, 1948.

212

Powell, Jocelyn. "Marlowe's Spectacle," *Tulane Drama Review*, VIII (1964).

Praz, Mario. *The Flaming Heart*. Garden City, 1958.

Price, Joseph G. *The Unfortunate Comedy. A Study of "All's Well That Ends Well" and its Critics*. Toronto: Toronto U. Press, 1968.

Ralegh, Sir Walter. "History of the World," *The Works*, II. Oxford: Oxford U. Press, 1829.

Ribner, Irving. "Introduction" to *The Complete Plays of Christopher Marlowe*. New York: Odyssey, 1963.

———. *The English History Play in the Age of Shakespeare*. London, 1965.

Riggs, David. *Shakespeare's Heroical Histories*. Cambridge, Mass.: Harvard U. Press, 1971.

Robb, Nesca A. *Neoplatonism of the Italian Renaissance*. London: Allen and Unwin, 1935.

Rossi, Paolo. *Francis Bacon, From Magic to Science*, trans. Sacha Rabinovitch. London, 1968.

Rukeyser, Muriel. *The Traces of Thomas Hariot*. New York: Random House, 1970.

Saitta, Giuseppe. *La Filosofia di Marsilio Ficino*. Messina: G. Principato, 1923.

Salvestrini, Virgilio. *Bibliografia delle Opere di Giordano Bruno*. Pisa, 1926.

Sanders, Wilbur. *The Dramatist and the Received Idea: Studies in the Plays of Marlowe and Shakespeare*. Cambridge, 1968.

Sayers, Dorothy L. and Barbara Reynolds. Notes to *The Comedy of Dante Alighieri the Florentine, Cantica III, Paradise*. Baltimore: Penguin, 1962.

Scott, Walter, ed. and trans. *Hermetica*, I. London, 1968; c. 1924.

Seaton, Ethel. "Marlowe's Map," *Marlowe, A Collection of Critical Essays*, ed. Clifford Leech. Twentieth Century Views Series. Englewood Cliffs, 1965.

Shellabarger, Samuel. *The Chevalier Bayard*. New York: Biblo and Tannen, 1971; c. 1928.

Siciliano, Italo. *Medio Evo e Rinascimento*. Milano: Albrighi, Segati, & C., 1936.

Singer, Dorothea. *Giordano Bruno, his Life and Thought, with Annotated Translation of his Work "On the Infinite Universe and Worlds."* New York, 1950.

Sinsheimer, Hermann. *Shylock: The History of a Character*. New York: B. Blom, 1963; c. 1947.

Smith, Warren D. "The Substance of Meaning in *Tamburlaine Part I*," SP, LXVII, 2 (April 1970).

Spampanato, V. *Vita di Giordano Bruno*, 2 vols. Messina, 1921.

Steane, J. B. *Marlowe: A Critical Study*. Cambridge, 1964.

Stroup, Thomas B. *Microcosmos: The Shape of the Elizabethan Play*. Lexington: U. of Kentucky Press, 1965.

Sypher, Wylie. *Four Stages of Renaissance Style*. Garden City: Doubleday, 1955.

———. "Magical Mystery Tour," *New York Review of Books* (January 29, 1970).

Taylor, E. G. R. *Tudor Geography, 1485-1583*. London: Methuen, 1930.

LIST OF WORKS CITED

Thomas, Keith. *Religion and the Decline of Magic*. New York: Scribner's, 1971.

Tillyard, E. M. W. *Elizabethan World Picture*. New York: MacMillan, 1944.

———. *Shakespeare's Problem Plays*. London: Chatto and Windus, 1951.

Vergil. *The Aeneid*, trans. Patric Dickinson. New York: Mentor, 1961.

Vinci, Leonardo da. *The Notebooks of Leonardo da Vinci*, ed. Jean Paul Richter, I. New York: Dover, 1970; c. 1883.

Vitruvio (M. Vitruvio Pollione). *Dell'Architettura, Libri Dieci*, trans. Marchese Bernardo Galiani. Milano: Allessandre Dozio, 1832.

Vyvyan, John. *Shakespeare and Platonic Beauty*. New York: Barnes and Noble, 1961.

Waith, Eugene M. *Ideas of Greatness*. New York: Barnes and Noble, 1971.

———. *The Herculean Hero*. New York: Columbia U. Press, 1962.

Walker, Daniel P. *Spiritual and Demonic Magic from Ficino to Campanella*. London: The Warburg Institute, U. of London, 1958.

Willobie his Avisa, ed. G. B. Harrison. The Bodley Head Quartos. London: The Bodley Head Ltd., 1926.

Wilson, Frank P. *Marlowe and the Early Shakespeare*. Oxford, 1953.

Wind, Edgar. *Pagan Mysteries in the Renaissance*. New Haven, 1958.

Yates, Frances A. *Giordano Bruno and the Hermetic Tradition*. Chicago: U. of Chicago Press, 1964.

———. *John Florio, The Life of an Italian in Shakespeare's England*. New York, 1968; c. 1934.

———. *The Art of Memory*. Chicago, 1966.

———. "The Hermetic Tradition in Renaissance Science," *Art, Science, and History in the Renaissance*, ed. Charles S. Singleton. Baltimore: Johns Hopkins Press, 1967.

———. *The Rosicrucian Enlightenment*. London, 1972.

———. *Theatre of the World*. Chicago: U. of Chicago Press, 1969.